Postfeminism and Organization

This edited book inserts postfeminism as a critical concept into understandings of work and organization. While the notion of postfeminism has been extensively investigated in cultural and media studies, it has yet to emerge within organization studies—remaining marginal to understandings of work-based experiences and subjectivities. Understanding postfeminism as a discursive cultural context not only draws on an established epistemological orientation to organizations as discursively constructed and reproduced, but also allows us to highlight how postfeminism may underpin and be underpinned by other discursive regimes.

This book, as the first in the field, draws on key international authors to explore: the contextual 'backdrop' of PF and its links with neoliberalism, transnational feminism and other hegemonic discourses; the different ways in which this backdrop has infiltrated organizational values and practice through the primacy attached to choice, merit and individual agency; the widespread perception that gender disadvantage has been 'solved'; and the implications for organizational subjectivity and for how inequality is experienced and perceived.

This book introduces postfeminism as a critical concept with contemporary importance for the study of organizations, arguing for its explanatory potential when

- exploring women's and men's experiences of managing and organizing;
- investigating the gendered aspects of organizational life;
- analyzing the contemporary validation of the feminine and the associated feminization of management/leadership and organizations;
- tracing the emergence of new femininities and masculinities within organizational contexts.

The book is ideal reading for researchers working in the area of gender and organization studies, but it is also of interest to researchers in the areas of cultural studies, media studies, women's studies and sociology.

Patricia Lewis is a Reader in Management at the Kent Business School at University of Kent, United Kingdom.

Yvonne Benschop is a Professor of Organizational Behavior at the Institute for Management Research at Radboud University Nijmegen, the Netherlands.

Ruth Simpson is a Professor of Management at the Brunel Business School at Brunel University, United Kingdom.

Routledge Studies in Gender and Organizations

Series Editor: Elisabeth K. Kelan

Although still a fairly young field, the study of gender and organizations is increasingly popular and relevant. There are few areas of academic research that are as vibrant and dynamic as the study of gender and organizations. While much earlier research has focused on documenting the imbalances of women and men in organizations, more recently, research on gender and organizations has departed from counting men and women. Instead research in this area sees gender as a process: something that is done rather than something that people are. This perspective is important and meaningful as it takes researchers away from essentialist notions of gender and opens the possibility of analysing the process of how individuals become women and men. This is called 'gendering', 'practising gender', 'doing gender' or 'performing gender' and draws on rich philosophical traditions.

Whilst Routledge Studies in Gender and Organizations has a broad remit, it will be thematically and theoretically committed to exploring gender and organizations from a constructivist perspective. Rather than focusing on specific areas of organizations, the series is to be kept deliberately broad to showcase the most innovative research in this field. It is anticipated that the books in this series will make a theoretical contribution to the field of gender and organization based on rigorous empirical explorations.

Postfeminism and
Organization

Edited by Patricia Lewis,
Yvonne Benschop, and Ruth Simpson

Routledge
Taylor & Francis Group

LONDON AND NEW YORK

First published 2018
by Routledge

2 Park Square, Milton Park, Abingdon, Oxfordshire OX14 4RN
52 Vanderbilt Avenue, New York, NY 10017

Routledge is an imprint of the Taylor & Francis Group, an informa business

First issued in paperback 2019

Library of Congress Cataloging-in-Publication Data
A catalog record for this book has been requested

ISBN: 978-1-138-21221-3 (hbk)
ISBN: 978-0-367-88958-6 (pbk)

Typeset in Sabon
by Apex CoVantage, LLC

For Paul and Adam with love
Patricia Lewis

For Frederique and Kjell and a bright future for feminisms
Yvonne Benschop

For Rachel, Matthew, Alexander, Joshua and Molly
Ruth Simpson

Contents

About the Contributors

Helene Ahl is Professor in Business Administration at the School of Education and Communication, Jönköping University, Sweden. Her research interests include women and entrepreneurship, motivation and adult learning, empowerment, gender in higher education and feminist analyses of government policy for women's entrepreneurship. She has published widely in international journals including in the *Scandinavian Journal of Management, Entrepreneurship Theory and Practice, Organization, The International Small Business Journal* and the *Journal of Business Venturing*.

Yvonne Benschop is Professor of Organizational Behaviour at the Institute for Management Research, Radboud University, the Netherlands. Her main inspirations are feminist organization studies and critical management studies. Current research interests include gender practices in informal organization processes such as networking, gender and precarious work in academia and the role of power and resistance in the organizational changes brought about by gender mainstreaming and diversity management. She is Co-editor-in-chief of *Organization*; Associate Editor of *Gender, Work and Organization*; and serves on the editorial boards of several other journals. Publications in English include articles in *Organization Studies, Journal of Management Studies, Human Relations, Organization, Accounting, Organization and Society, The International Journal of HRM, Sex Roles and Gender, Work and Organization*.

Marta B. Calás is Professor of Organization Studies and International Management at the Isenberg School of Management, University of Massachusetts, United States. Since the late 1980s, she and Professor Linda Smircich have collaborated to explore the epistemological roots and gendered features of contemporary issues in management and organization. Together with Linda, she is a recent recipient of the Pasmore-Woodman Award from the Organization Development and Change (ODC) Division of the US Academy of Management, an award made to two or more colleagues who, for a sustained period of time, have maintained a significant working relationship resulting in work that is original and innovative, and that has informed ODC research and practice.

Seray Ergene is a PhD Candidate in management organization studies at the Isenberg School of Management, University of Massachusetts, United States. She also completed a graduate certificate in advanced feminist studies in the Women, Gender, Sexuality Studies Department at the same university. Her research focus is on sustainability, and she is informed by feminist materialist frameworks and feminist ecological theories.

Gina Grandy is Professor of Strategy and Leadership, RBC Women in Leadership Scholar and Associate Dean of Graduate Programs and Research with the Hill-Levene Schools of Business at the University of Regina, Canada. Her research interests include leadership, gender and women's experiences at work, stigmatized work, identity, qualitative research methods and case writing. She is the Associate Editor for *Case Research Journal* and serves on the international advisory board for *Management Learning* and *Gender in Management: An International Journal*. Her research has been published widely in such journals as *Human Relations*; *Journal of Business Ethics*; *Journal of Management Studies, Gender, Work and Organization*; *Organization, Management Learning*; *Gender in Management, Qualitative Research in Organizations and Management*; and *Case Research Journal*.

Philip Hancock is Professor of Work and Organization at Essex Business School, United Kingdom. His research interests include the aesthetic management of work and society, critical approaches to workplace recognition and Christmas as a global medium of sociomaterial organization. His work has been published in a range of journals including *Organization Studies, Human Relations, Organization, Gender Work and Organization* and *Work Employment and Society*, as well as authored and co-authored books and edited volumes.

Elisabeth K. Kelan is a Professor of Leadership at Cranfield School of Management, Cranfield University, United Kingdom. Her research focuses on gender and leadership, gender in organizations, inclusion and diversity. She has written extensively on these issues in a range of journals including *British Journal of Management, Gender, Work and Organization, Human Relations, Journal of Business Ethics and Management Learning*. She has also authored two books—*Rising Stars: Developing Millennial Women as Leaders* and *Performing Gender at Work* both published by Palgrave. She is an Associate Editor of *Gender, Work and Organization* and the series editor of the book series Routledge Studies in Gender and Organization. She sits on the editorial boards of the *British Journal of Management, Management Learning* and *Gender in Management*.

Savita Kumra (BA (Hons.), MSc (Econ.), PhD (CIPD)) is an Associate Professor at Middlesex University Dubai, United Arab Emirates. Savita completed her master's at the London School of Economics and her doctorate at Cranfield School of Management where she is a Visiting Fellow in the School of Management. Savita is also an International Research Fellow at the Said Business School, University of Oxford, Centre for Professional Services. Savita has held a number of academic posts including Brunel University and Oxford Brookes University, both in the United Kingdom. Savita is an Associate Editor for *Gender, Work and Organization*. She is a member of the Chartered Institute of Personnel and Development. Savita's key research interests focus on leadership, diversity, the career development process and the importance of developing and deploying key career enhancement strategies—e.g., impression management, and building and leveraging social capital. She co-wrote *Managing Equality and Diversity* with her colleague Professor Simonetta Manfredi and edited the *Oxford Handbook of Gender in Organizations* with Professor Ruth Simpson and Professor Ronald Burke. She has published articles in *British Journal of Management, Gender, Work and Organization, Journal of Business Ethics* and *Fordham Law Review*. She has also contributed chapters to several volumes on women in organizations and leadership.

Patricia Lewis is a Reader in Management at the University of Kent, United Kingdom. In her research, she mainly draws on a poststructuralist feminist perspective manifest in her work on female entrepreneurial identity, which has explored issues including the masculine norm, authenticity and identity, and she has written about the emergence of postfeminist entrepreneurial femininities. In addition, she enjoys re-reading influential texts through the lens of poststructuralist feminism including Kanter's *Men and Women of the Corporation* published in the *International Journal of Management Reviews* (with Ruth Simpson) and Hakim's much criticized text *Work-Lifestyle Choices in the 21st Century: Preference Theory* published in *Gender, Work and Organization* (with Ruth Simpson). She has also published in a range of journals including *Organization Studies, Human Relations, Work, Employment and Society, British Journal of Management* and *Journal of Business Ethics* She is the incoming Joint-Editor-in-Chief of the journal *Gender, Work and Organization* and will be taking up this post in January 2018.

Susan Marlow is Professor of Entrepreneurship at the Haydn Green Institution of Enterprise and Innovation at the University of Nottingham, United Kingdom. She is a holder of the Queens Award for Enterprise Promotion, Editor and Consulting Editor of the *International Small Business Journal* and Fellow of the Institute for Small Business and Entrepreneurship. Her research interests lie in the broad area of entrepreneurship with a particular focus on the influence of gender on women's entrepreneurial behavior.

Sharon Mavin is Professor and Director of Newcastle University Business School, United Kingdom, a Fellow of the British Academy of Management, Co-editor of *Gender in Management: An International Journal* and an Associate Editor of *International Journal of Management Reviews.* Her research interests include women leaders' experiences and relationships with other women, female misogyny, doing gender, dirty work, identity, vulnerability and leadership. She has published in journals such as *Human Relations, Gender, Work and Organization, British Journal of Management, Organization* and the *International Journal of Management Reviews.*

Nick Rumens is a Professor in Human Resource Management at the University of Portsmouth, United Kingdom. His research interests include lesbian, gay, bisexual, transgender and queer workplace issues, critical perspectives on men and masculinities, workplace friendships and queer theory. He has published on these topics in journals including *Human Relations, Organization Studies, British Journal of Management, Organization, Human Resource Management Journal, Critical Perspectives in Accounting* and *Gender, Work and Organization.* He has also sole authored and co-edited a number of books including *Contemporary Perspectives on Ecofeminism* (2016 Routledge), *Sexual Orientation at Work: International Issues and Perspectives* (2016 Routledge), *American Pragmatism and Organization* (2013 Gower) and *Queer Company: Friendship in the Work Lives of Gay Men* (2011 Ashgate). His next research monograph is on queer theory and forthcoming from Routledge titled *Queer Business: Queering Organization Sexualities and Genders.*

Ruth Simpson is Professor of Management and Director of Research at Brunel Business School, Brunel University, United Kingdom. Her research interests include gender and management education, gender and emotions and the careers of men in non-traditional occupations. She is an Associate Editor of *Gender, Work and Organization* as well as a regular reviewer for a broad range of management and organization journals. She has published widely in a variety of journals including *Human Relations, Academy of Management (Learning and Education), Gender, Work and Organization, Work, Employment and Society, British Journal of Management* and *International Journal of Management Reviews.*

Linda Smircich is Professor of Organization Studies in the Department of Management at the Isenberg School of Management, University of Massachusetts, United States. Since the late 1980s, she and Professor Marta B. Calás have collaborated to explore the epistemological roots and gendered features of contemporary issues in management and organization. Together with Marta, she is a recent recipient of the Pasmore-Woodman Award from the ODC Division of the US Academy of Management, an award made to two or more colleagues who, for a sustained period of time, have maintained a significant working relationship resulting in work that is original and innovative and that has informed ODC research and practice.

Elaine Swan is a Senior Lecturer based in the Future of Work Hub at the University of Sussex, United Kingdom. Her research interests are in studies of race, gender and food work, and the sociology of workplace psychology. Recent publications include chapters on digital food cultures and ethnic food tourism. She has established an international network on feminist and critical race studies of food, work and organizing with Rick Flowers and Maud Perrier, and recently published an edited book on *Food Pedagogies* with Rick Flowers.

Itari Turner received her doctorate at Brunel Business School, Brunel University, United Kingdom in 2017. Her thesis explored experiences of work-life-balance among medical doctors in the context of Nigeria. Her research interests include gender and careers and the work-life interface in Western and non-Western contexts.

Melissa Tyler is Professor of Work and Organization Studies at Essex Business School, United Kingdom. Her research interests include gender, sexuality and embodiment at work; organizational space, place and setting; and emotional, aesthetic and sexualized forms of labor. Her work has been published in a range of international journals, including *Organization Studies, Human Relations, Work Employment and Society* and *Gender Work and Organization*; she has also authored and co-authored books and edited volumes.

Part I
Introduction

Postfeminism
Negotiating Equality With Tradition in Contemporary Organisations

Patricia Lewis, Yvonne Benschop and Ruth Simpson

Feminist Traditions and Postfeminism

These are certainly interesting times for feminism and feminists. For many years, negative stories dominated the public discourse about feminism; self-identifying as a feminist was inconceivable for many women, and authors recurrently claimed that feminism was obsolete, especially in the popular press. This latter phenomenon has been analysed as the specific genre of 'false feminist death syndrome' (Smith, 2003, in Tyler, 2005), and it has proven false indeed. The tide is turning, and feminism has been rehabilitated but in a moderate form (Dean, 2010). Feminism is now embraced by celebrity feminists (from Beyoncé and Emma Watson to Sheryl Sandberg and former Euro commissioner Neelie Kroes) and is nurtured by social media discussions and activist blogs that reclaim the importance of gender equality. As observed by Sarah Banet-Weiser (cited by Pruchniewska 2017: 1), 'Feminism is on the cultural radar . . . we are moving beyond a wide cultural resistance to the "F" word, especially among younger women'. However, we argue that this new discourse and representation of feminism has a strong affinity with postfeminism, challenging core feminist traditions of collective and political action against gender inequality. Postfeminism has supported the *selective* take-up and *restrained* implementation of the feminist values of choice, empowerment and agency. As Banet-Weiser and Arzumanova (2012, cited in Pruchniewska, 2017: 5) argue the feminist principle of empowerment now manifests as entrepreneurship and 'in this context, the empowered feminist voice shifts to the confessional postfeminist voice, seeking out visibility through consumption and a continually normalized feminine subjectivity'. This book considers the effect of this transformation within the field of management and organisation studies. It explores how postfeminism and its associated valorisation of a feminism which promotes the empowerment of individual women while eschewing a broader critique of gendered inequalities impacts on organisations and those who work within them.

Concerning the tradition of collective action, there is an influential representation of feminism as a social women's movement that comes and goes in waves. Several waves of feminism are usually distinguished (Wrye, 2009), even though the very notion of waves is in itself contested as confusing, excluding and overly oppositional (Evans and Chamberlain, 2015; Springer, 2002). In the first wave at the turn of the twentieth century, the suffragette movement called for political change and women's right to vote. In the second wave around the 1960s and 1970s, the women's movement put women's liberation, violence against women, the body, reproductive rights and labour market inequalities on the agenda. The third wave was dominated by a younger generation of feminists, who, in the media-saturated culture of the 1990s, emphasised sex-positive girl power, inclusion, intersectionality and the queer multiplicity of identities (Snyder, 2008). Some authors even see the contours of a fourth wave emerging from the technological opportunities provided by social media, encompassing grassroots activism, an engagement with global politics and ecology, a focus on intersectionality and an emphasis on redistribution (Bell et al., 2015; Wrye, 2009).

The wave metaphor suggests a temporality with one distinct wave after the other, but it is more helpful to see the feminist waves as particular approaches then to pin them to distinct periods in time. Evans and Chamberlain (2015: 399) note, 'The fact that the second, third and fourth waves exist simultaneously, but have been defined through their dissimilarities, exacerbates arguments between the three, and creates confusion surrounding what constitutes each wave'. This means that there is not only a tradition in feminism of multiple issues and concerns, but also one of debate and controversy between different feminists over the importance of those issues and who they may concern. For instance, one of the key debates between the second and third waves is around inclusivity and the intersectionality of gender with race, class, sexuality and age. The second wave with its attention to the detrimental effects of the public-private divide and women's access to the workplace is accused of a profound white, middle class bias. This inspired the earliest calls for a third wave by women of colour interrogating racialised positions of privilege and marginality within the workplace and the family (Holvino, 2010). Nevertheless, the third wave became equated with the 'girl power' of young, white, well-educated women and so again with the more privileged positions (Snyder, 2008; Evans and Chamberlain, 2015).

The multiplicity in feminism is not only restricted to representations of the women's movement but also pertains to the different academic strands of feminism. There are of course connections between the waves and the strands of feminist theory. For instance, the time period of the second wave coincides with the development of liberal, radical, psychoanalytical and socialist feminist thought, but it is beyond the scope of this introduction to provide a detailed analysis of these connections. Within management and organisation studies, there tends to be more attention to different strands of feminist thought than to different waves of feminism. The different positions of women and men, constructions of masculinity and femininity in the labour market and gender inequalities connected to work and organisation are typically cast as second-wave issues, but it is clear that the persistent inequalities in this major domain of life continue to influence feminist thinking. In an influential book chapter written in the 1990s and revised ten years later, Calás and Smircich (1996, 2006) analyse how liberal, radical, psychoanalytical, socialist, poststructuralist/postmodern and transnational/ postcolonial strands of feminism have influenced thinking about gender in organisations in organisation studies. Another decade after, Benschop and Verloo (2016) discuss the contributions of four strands of feminist thought, (neo)liberal feminism, socialist feminism, social construction feminism and poststructuralist feminism, to contemporary management and organisation theories. We situate postfeminism, the focus of this book, as deeply enmeshed with a neoliberal feminism that emphasises individualistic, entrepreneurial, empowered women who embrace the full responsibility for their own lives and careers (Rottenberg, 2014).

In this array of feminist thought, the tradition of the community and collectivity of women is both a common denominator and a battleground. As a common denominator, the 'category of women' foregrounds the idea that women have something in common as women, that women as a group differ from men as a group, and that women share experiences of identity with other women, giving rise to collective action to improve the situation of women as a group. Gender is presented as a fundamental organising principle in all spheres of social life (Jaggar, 1983; Ridgeway and Correll, 2004) meaning that all social relations in patriarchal society are structured by hierarchical differences between women and men. In some strands of feminist theory, notably in radical feminism and to an extent also socialist feminism, the emphasis on the collective is strong, with women uniting in their desire to change the gender order and to get to cultural, economic, psychological and social equality in the public and private spheres (Tyler, 2007). To accomplish this change, the consciousness-raising groups of radical feminism served as a place for women to collectively interrogate their experiences in light of systematic male domination (Calás and Smircich, 2006). In loosely organised women's groups, collectives or alternative women's organisations, women discussed their personal experiences with each other as a basis from which to develop political analysis and alternative feminist values such as equality and community. Interestingly, the *Lean In* circles connected to Sheryl Sandberg's book of the same name, which seek to support women in their individualist pursuit of career success, are described by McRobbie (2015: 133) as 'a ghostly version of its more overtly feminist predecessor the consciousness-raising group of the 1970s'. Socialist feminism developed a critique of the patriarchal capitalist system, with a pronounced focus on classed, gendered and racialised divisions of labour both in work organisations and in the family. As a feminist perspective, it emphasizes the systemic and structural dimensions of capitalist inequality regimes, showing how these work to marginalize and oppress particular groups of employees (in particular lower-class and migrant women). Recently, the increasing insecurity and instability of employment relations of the 'precariat' are said to lead to 'an emergent class in the making' (Standing, 2011). The collective empowerment of this emergent class is a socialist feminist ideal.

As a battleground, the ideal of female community forms the basis for strong disagreement among feminists regarding the ontological and epistemological assumptions which underpin the notion of collective. There are strands of feminist theory that reject the ideas of a collective identity or a community of women as a central characteristic of feminism. Poststructuralist feminism, for instance, questions the ontological basis of gender categories and challenges the identity politics based on these categories: What are the universal experiences that all women allegedly share? What constitutes this identity of 'woman' that makes it so fundamentally different from the identity of 'man?' The immense variety between women of different classes, races, ages, sexualities and all the possible intersections of such categories problematise the significance of the single category of women. Poststructuralist feminism aims to deconstruct the binary logic of gender, to disrupt the gender order and to call attention to the situatedness, fluidity and multiplicity of gender as a performative social practice (Butler, 1990; Poggio, 2006). For entirely different reasons and notwithstanding the phenomenon of *Lean In* circles, the idea of a community of women bears no relevance in neoliberal postfeminism either. In this strand, the individual takes centre stage; there is no role for the collective or the community. In the guise of corporate feminism, equal opportunities for (elite) women are propagated within a neoliberal capitalist system that emphasises the market value and the personal responsibility of individual enterprising women for their own success. The postfeminist emphasis on individualism, choice and empowerment has led some to ask 'Who put the "me" in feminism?' (Tyler, 2005). The collectivist feminist battle against patriarchal oppression and male dominance is traded in for the axiom of individual female power and freedom of choice. With postfeminism, we thus witness the surfacing of a restrained form of feminism which abandons the search for collective solutions to the shared problems of ongoing gendered inequalities and systemic male dominance (Lewis, Benschop, and Simpson, 2017). Thus, it is the individualisation of postfeminism which makes feminism more palatable than before, because it has traded in social criticism for self-criticism (Benschop, van den Brink, and Verloo, 2015).

A more in-depth analysis of the dichotomy between collectivist and individualist feminism shows a more complicated relationship between feminism and individualism, which is relevant for our understanding of the place of postfeminism in the feminist tradition. Calás and Smircich (2006: 286) argues that feminist theories are always *critical* of the status quo and therefore *always political* (italics in original), even when the scope and nature of the politics varies across different perspectives. This brings us to the second core tradition in feminism, the tradition of feminist political action. As we have argued earlier, one significant feature of postfeminism is its lack of social critique and thus its lack of a political agenda. Whereas its predecessor liberal feminism used the liberal ideals of individual freedom, choice, opportunity and equality to critique gender inequalities in wages and positions of authority, the feminism attached to postfeminism does nothing to critique the neoliberal capitalist system. This lack of critique leads Fraser (2009: 108) to speak of a 'disturbing convergence' of neoliberal capitalist and feminist ideas, when the cultural recognition of identity and difference in feminism prevails over the redistribution of economic resources. The cooptation of feminism in capitalism takes place through popular business case arguments for gender equality and empowerment projects for women, integrating feminism into the neoliberal ideology of market, free choice and, prominently, individualism. While the 'business case' is seen as creating urgency and legitimacy for gender equality in organisations, it comes at the high cost of making feminist ideals subsidiary to competitive advantage (Noon, 2007). Prügl (2015) argues that liberal feminism has always been the hegemonic strand of feminism, something that certainly resonates with the impact of liberal feminism in management and organisation studies. The liberal feminist emphasis on equal opportunities for women and men allows only a limited social critique of capitalism, accepting race- and class-based exploitations in the home and in the workplace. For Williams (2013: 627) it has become clear that a feminism that is divorced from a critique of capitalism will only make things worse for most women.

The ideology of individualism in (neo)liberal postfeminism may be devoid of a political agenda, but individualism in feminism is not always apolitical. Notably, the consciousness-raising groups of radical feminism organised around 'the personal is political', politicising women's private feelings, challenging traditional femininities of being-for-others and the unequal distribution of power in their everyday lives (Tyler, 2007). Radical feminism thus was redefining what counts as politics (Tyler, 2005). Yet, the identity politics in 'the personal is political' is often downplayed in order to highlight the personal part of feminism. This focus on the personal, the individual, made feminism vulnerable to being scorned for selfishness, narcissism and navel-gazing. One of the central arguments of the cultural narcissism of feminism is that the political project degenerates into individual quests for self-awareness and self-realisation (Tyler, 2007: 180).

Instead of raising the collective, of improving the situation of women as a group, the selfish feminist is only thinking of herself. This representation of the radical, selfish feminist provided fertile ground for a backlash towards and dis-identification with what is perceived as an 'excessive' feminism. The renewed popularity of feminism today is also based on an individualised approach, but selfishness has been embraced and encouraged by the capitalist consumer culture ('because you are worth it' as the L'Oréal advertisements

have it). It thus seems that key to the popularity of contemporary postfeminism and its subdued feminism is exactly its aversion to politics. In reaction
to radical 'excessive' feminism, modern feminists have patented free choice.
In choice feminism (Hirshman, 2006), the most important achievement of
feminism is that it provides the freedom for women to make any choice
they want. Staying at home, 100-hour working weeks—anything goes—and
importantly, no choice can be denounced as not properly feminist. Feminism
thus becomes inclusive, non-threatening and non-judgmental, but also void
of political power losing the potential for political change (Ferguson, 2010).

Postfeminism and Gender Identities

We have argued that the discursive phenomenon of postfeminism challenges
the two core traditions of feminism: the traditions of collective and political action. The history of individualism in radical feminism however gives
rise to some optimism, as it shows how individualism or narcissism can
be political (Tyler, 2005) when used to develop a feminist politics about
identity. Yet a recent consideration of how self-defined feminist online writers reconcile individualistic self-promotion with collectivist feminist values
indicates that such radical individualism is currently muted. While being
well-versed in the feminist language of 'patriarchy', 'micro-aggression' and
'standpoint', the self-identified feminist respondents redefined feminism in
general to align with the postfeminist values of choice, empowerment and
individualism, to secure the required reconciliation. The respondents' claim
to a feminist subjectivity co-exists with the traditional feminine norm of
non-confrontation as they sought to make feminism more 'palatable' such
that they 'could be said to be 'sneaking' feminism into their audience's lives'
(Pruchniewska, 2017: 11). This is indicative of one of the most notable features of a postfeminist gender regime which has reshaped feminism into a
moderate form—the rapprochement between feminism and femininity.

   Increasing attention (e.g. Kauppinen, 2013; Lewis, 2014; Sullivan and
Delaney, 2017) has been directed at this détente, showing how postfeminism
has contributed to the complex reshaping of female and male subjectivities which form the basis of women's and men's inclusion in contemporary
organisations. In the construction of postfeminist subjectivities, there is an
interdependence between postfeminist masculinities and postfeminist femininities, with the important caveat that the discursive processes for constituting each may vary and that it is not a single act of constitution which brings
a subject into being (Dow, 2006; Kolehmainen, 2012; Rumens, 2017). In
a postfeminist context, these subjectivities can be seen to undermine traditional gender relations—seemingly allowing greater agency, particularly
for women in the individualised pursuit of success—whilst at the same time
reinforcing conventional gender based norms (Adkins, 2001). Undoubtedly,
the cultural phenomenon of postfeminism has influenced the shaping of
contemporary male and female subjectivities but there are variations in how

the postfeminist reconfiguration of gender identities is interpreted, which can be summed up in one of three ways: negative (men lose and women gain leading to a reinvigoration of traditional masculinity), positive (both men and women gain through a de-traditionalisation of gender), or complicated (men gain and women lose through processes of re-traditionalisation and the reinstatement of masculine privilege).

In the first response to the reconfiguration of masculinities and femininities, the postfeminist notion that 'the future is female' is experienced as exclusion by men (Kelan, 2008; Rumens, 2017). Surrounding this negative perception is a sense of vulnerability, anxiety and crisis regarding men's sense of self. Embedded in this sense of victimhood are claims of gendered double standards which operate against men, the perceived demonisation of male sexuality, the sense that a 'war' is being waged against men and finally that the take-up of successful, agentic, postfeminist identities by women is rendering men obsolete in contemporary organisations (Garcia-Favaro and Gill, 2016; Rumens, 2017). The desire for a 'fundamentalist certitude' (Stevenson et al., 2003) in the face of these changes in gender relations has led to various responses. These have included, as Gill (2014) suggests, a retreat to traditional masculinity through a 'new lad' culture where young men in particular have mobilised traditionally masculine attitudes and pursuits based on a hedonistic celebration of manhood—cheerfully unreconstructed in terms of predatory attitudes towards women. This distinctly postfeminist phenomenon (Gill, 2014) is based on a 'laddish' culture and the sexual objectification of women. Consequently, men's response to women becoming more like them, by being constituted as triumphant postfeminist subjects of economic capacity, is to take-up traditional masculine identities.

In contrast, the second response to the emergence of new gender identities within a postfeminist context is positive with both men and women being seen to benefit. Men's response to the reconstitution of women as empowered subjects in postfeminist times is one which considers the benefits of reconstructing men and masculinities in terms of domesticity and care based on the 'de-traditionalisation' of gender norms. This 'de-traditionalisation' has been captured in the female identities of the 'phallic girl' and economic woman, both characterised by boldness, confidence and, at times, aggression (McRobbie, 2007) and the male identity of the 'new man'. The latter is seen in popular terms as someone who rejects sexist attitudes and the traditional male role, especially in the context of domestic responsibilities and childcare, and who is held to be caring, sensitive and non-aggressive. The adoption of (feminine) caring behaviours and characteristics which are averse to the dominance connected to traditional, hegemonic masculinity is perceived as beneficial for men *and* women, proffering the opportunity of sustained social change for all (Elliott, 2016; Rumens, 2017). The focus here is on how masculinities and femininities, drawing on postfeminist discourses, can be reconstituted as agentic and caring such that the take-up of a postfeminist subjectivity (characterised by the co-existence of masculine and feminine behaviours) will support gender equality. This facilitates a move away from the assumption that the only way to secure equality is by women becoming more like men; instead, men can become more like women (Elliott, 2016).

This positive response to changes in gender identities is based on the supposition that gender and gendered practices are characterised by fluidity. Men and women are *both* 'doing gender' in ways that mirror the postfeminist co-existence of masculinity and femininity, suggestive of a re-articulation and re-figuration of gender identities in contexts such as family or work (Alvesson, 1998; Huppatz, 2009). For example, Roberts (2012) in a study of young men working in retail, reveals a 'softened masculinity' which incorporates aspects of femininity such as pride and satisfaction from interaction and customer care. Pullen and Simpson (2009) show how male nurses and primary school teachers draw on masculinity and femininity in terms of how they practice care, managing difference through challenging traditional gender norms. As Roberts (2012) argues, this potentially signals a more 'inclusive' masculinity (Anderson, 2009), that is less hierarchical and more tolerant of others and where the masculine and feminine co-exist. Thus, the second response to understanding men's experience of postfeminism is characterised by processes of de-traditionalisation and a postfeminist positivity which allocates gender hierarchy and any attendant tensions between masculinity and femininity to the past (O'Neill, 2015).

The third response to the postfeminist transformation of gender identities reminds us that while postfeminism as a discursive formation 'mainstreams' feminist principles into everyday life, it has done so *without* a renunciation of traditional gender roles. Here, it is the valorisation of tradition (alongside equality) which complicates the 'doing' of masculinity and femininity. What this means is that while it is possible for men and women to successfully mobilise postfeminist discourses of femininity and masculinity in activities such as management and leadership; it is also the case that in a postfeminist context which valorises tradition, 'stereotypical or hegemonic gender dispositions (when managing) may be the most rewarded . . . and are more likely to be symbolically legitimated' (Huppatz and Goodwin, 2013: 297). From the perspective of this response, it may well be that the requirements of tradition appear to apply more strongly to women—illustrated powerfully across the chapters in this volume—while men can enact tradition or more easily avoid tradition contributing to gender differences in terms of work-based experiences. For example, recent research (e.g. Adkins, 2001; Huppatz and Goodwin, 2013) suggests that men can be rewarded for the performance of femininity at work in ways which can often elude women who are seen to embody, in essentialist terms, feminine attributes. In Pullen and Simpson's (2009) research on men in caring occupations, men's caring capacities were seen as a 'special contribution' and were rewarded as such while women's were overlooked as an essential part of femininity. Therefore, women's 'doing' of femininity is perceived as 'natural' while men's performance of feminine behaviours is rewarded as a learned skill, a useful resource which brings value to the workplace. However, the reverse—women "doing" masculinity when managing—is not accorded value in the same way and women get no special recognition or reward for this ability. Within a postfeminist terrain, men may have more gender mobility than women in terms of subject positions, based on the uptake and co-optation of a newly valued 'feminine', while women are tied in essentialist terms to postfeminist understandings of 'natural' sexual difference—exerting a re-traditionalising effect through the reassertion and reconstruction of male power.

This suggests a diversity of experience where, in the context of postfeminism, traditional gender based norms are both repudiated and reinforced (McRobbie, 2009), and where, rather than casting tradition to a past era, traditional understandings, practices and subjectivities re-emerge and take on new (non-traditional) forms. This blurring and incorporation may serve to privilege rather than displace tradition (Lee, 2013) which can then act as a 'break' on more radical change, both within and outside organisations, allowing new patterns of discrimination to emerge. At the same time, as Hancock and Tyler note in their chapter on vintage feminism, upholding tradition and mixing the 'old and the new' may support reflexive engagement with the present, bringing new subjectivities into being as well as different ways of thinking and organising.

Chapter Outlines

These themes around tradition, progression and change permeate in different ways the chapters that make up this volume. In our first chapter within the section Postfeminism and Organization, Patricia Lewis outlines five different interpretations of postfeminism—historical, theoretical, backlash, positive and governance—exposing the contested nature of this complex phenomenon, drawing out the connections between these various understandings and making visible the gender mobility attaching to each version. She argues that within the field of management and organisation studies, the governance version which treats postfeminism as a discursive formation based around a complex set of discourses around gender, feminism and femininity is the most critically useful. Treating postfeminism as an object of analysis such that the discursive practices of power of which it is composed can be untangled and/or as a critical concept which brings to light enduring discrimination and inequalities within organisational contexts, makes the lens of postfeminism an invaluable aid to our understanding of contemporary organisations. As she illustrates, postfeminism is of particular use in making visible the complex reshaping of female subjectivities which form the basis of women's current inclusion in organisations. Focusing on the figure of the 'working woman-with-children', she presents a range of organisational femininities which she calls 'postfeminist maternal femininities'. These include the corporate mother, the working mother, the professional mother and the unruly mother. These femininities inhabit both the masculine and feminine realms associated with postfemi-nism performing the feminine characteristics of nurture, care, emotion, self-sacrifice and beauty alongside the masculine traits of ambition, choice, reinvention, self-regulation and autonomy, to varying degrees. In mapping out these femininities, she provocatively argues that while they are differ-ent in practice they are all similar in intent, with these subjectivities bring-ing women back to femininity, thereby restraining the advantage they can gain from their access to masculinity and the present-day valorisation of the feminine.

Responding to calls for a transnational approach to the critical study of postfeminism, and drawing on a study of female doctors in Nigeria, Itari Turner and Ruth Simpson explore the implications of the postfeminist emphasis on choice, individualism and agency through the concept of work-life balance (WLB). In Chapter 2 entitled 'Doing-It-All: Exploring Work-Life Balance in Nigeria Through a Postfeminist Lens' they bring debates around the postfeminist emphasis on 'balance'—namely, the choices women face between the 'masculine' world of work and the 'feminine' context of home—into a new domain. In their compelling account, they critically assess the postfeminist concept of 'having it all' and point to the significance of *'weight'* rather than balance in capturing the traditional obligations and pressures women in this national context face. As they argue, the concept of 'weight' helps to surface and hence critically examine traditionally ori-ented burdens of responsibilities imposed on women as both caregivers and professional workers. Drawing on women doctors' accounts of WLB, they discuss how Western based understandings of postfeminism may translate differentially into a non-Western context.

In Chapter 3, 'Keep Calm and Carry on Being Slinky: Postfeminism, Resil-ience Coaching and Whiteness', Elaine Swan examines the entanglements of whiteness, coaching and postfeminism through a thematic analysis of 'resil-ience coaching' in US and UK-based websites and associated media. Here she highlights the imbrication of 'psy practices' (that claim to diagnose and solve a range of life 'problems') and resilience through the concept of 'psy-resilience' in this online context—underlining how resilience can be radi-cal and progressive. As she argues, with its promise of transformation for mainly white, middle class women through 'makeover' and the incitement to become 'resilient' subjects in the workplace, coaching is an important site for postfeminist analysis—comprising a context where white middle class women have taken up psy practices as part of work or leisure commit-ments. Drawing links between psy-resilience, postfeminism and whiteness, she shows in this imaginative chapter how whiteness is reproduced through ideas about the psychological namely, notions of emotional control, positiv-ity and enterprise. As she suggests, these are based on the suppression of 'structurally produced' feelings of, as example, injustice and stress as well as on racialised understandings of emotionality to produce a particular form of classed and raced workplace femininity.

Noting an absence of accounts in organisation studies that bring 'postfeminism and queer into dialogue', Nick Rumens examines in Chapter 4—'Postfeminism, Queer and Work'—how a postfeminist sensibility is connected to the discursive construction of queer in the workplace. The chapter engages critically with both postfeminism and queer theory to examine how queer is discursively mobilised by both gay men and their employers, illustrated empirically by drawing on the perspectives of gay men. The chapter demonstrates how, in a modern 'post-gay' culture and in parallel with postfeminism, LGBT inequality is repudiated and consigned to the past, individualism and choice are emphasised over collective action and queer is discursively framed in neoliberal terms as adding value—reformulated as an organisational resource through the construction and performance of a 'desirable' organisational subject. Nick's captivating analysis breaks new ground by exposing the collaboration of postfeminist, neoliberal and post-gay discourses and how, together, they overlook heteronormativity as an organising principle and militate against queer as a form of anti-normative critique and politics in the workplace.

In Chapter 5—'Contested Terrain: The Power to Define, Control and Benefit From Gender Equality Efforts'—Elisabeth K. Kelan focuses on change agents who implement gender equality so as to appear 'good citizens' and gain credit. Drawing on a particular example of how in/equality is perceived by the two main parties involved in shaping organisational policy (a work-based women's lobby and the equal opportunities officer), she shows how this 'postfeminist moment' is defined by contestation over the 'prized resource' of gender equality involvement. As she demonstrates, this contestation over who controls and defines gender equality is acted out through particular ideological struggles (e.g. around who receives credit and around the inclusion of men) as expressions of a postfeminist sensibility where gender equality is prized as an 'obvious objective'—even though gender equality has not necessarily been advanced. Locating these expressions within a type of (individualistic, neoliberal) corporate feminism, she convincingly demonstrates the complex and multifaceted nature of postfeminism which, in this organisational context, moves postfeminist understandings of gender equality as repudiated and 'overed' towards one which, detached from actually achieving equality, sees equality as so central that it is a source of competition and prestige.

In Chapter 6, 'Postfeminism and the Performance of Merit', Savita Kumra and Ruth Simpson examine the postfeminist logic that underpins practices and discourses of 'merit'—a market-based allocative system which seeks to reward individual effort, agency and achievement—in the context of an assumed equality in the workplace. Drawing on previous research as well as media accounts of and attitudes towards successful women to support their case, they present the argument that, while merit is assumed to be an objective, gender neutral attribute, the *recognition* of merit and worth—i.e., the extent to which it is seen as deserved relies in traditional terms on masculine embodied performances and displays. In other words, merit is conveyed through embodied performance (such as through dress, language and comportment) and, as they convincingly demonstrate, the extent to which it is seen as 'deserved' is profoundly gendered. Here they show how some embodiments of the new postfeminist subject ('sassy, sexy, feminine') fail to 'fit' with gendered notions of what is appropriate for a leadership and/or management role. As they suggest, this highlights some of the contradictions within postfeminism that signal gender neutral choice and agency against a backdrop of gendered norms relating to work-based ambition, merit and success.

Drawing links between meritocratic achievement and postfeminist understandings of individualism within entrepreneurial research, Helene Ahl and Susan Marlow, in Chapter 7, 'Analysing Entrepreneurial Activity Through a Postfeminist Perspective—A Brave New World or the Same Old Story?' explore the implications of the complementarity of entrepreneurship and postfeminist discourses for women entrepreneurs. As they suggest, a fictive gender neutral space is generated where women are paradoxically positioned as free agents able to fulfil their personal, social and economic potential whilst discriminatory assumptions and biases around their entrepreneurial activities persist—and where differences between men and women regarding entrepreneurial propensity and firm performance are attributed to feminine lack and deficit. Focusing on governmental policy initiatives oriented towards encouraging women's business ownership in the United Kingdom and Sweden, they question the capacity of entrepreneurship to fuel a postfeminist future whereby women can claim new pathways to personal emancipation. Instead, as they compellingly suggest, the 'false promise' of entrepreneurship in a postfeminist era not only deceives but also generates a blame narrative to disguise this deception.

In Chapter 8—'How Postfeminism Plays Out for Women Elite Leaders'— Sharon Mavin and Gina Grandy re-read their previous empirical work on the experiences of women leaders through a postfeminist lens. In so doing, they highlight the significance of three themes informed by postfeminism— namely, double entanglements where women struggle with understandings and experiences of privilege and disadvantage, choice and agency through which women interpret options open to them and where change is seen to occur through an entrepreneurial spirit and commitment, and body-care and surveillance whereby women prioritise their own appearance, seeking empowerment through bodily self-presentations whilst distancing themselves from critiques of gender disadvantage. This fascinating chapter highlights how, as confident and powerful women, elite leaders disengage from outmoded notions of female disadvantage while at the same time drawing upon both femininity and feminism to deflect potential feelings of alienation from men. The chapter gives insight into some of the complexities involved as female elite leaders seek to assimilate into the mainstream whilst making sense, in different 'feminist' terms, of some of the difficulties they face.

Under the section Future Directions in Postfeminism and Organization, our last two chapters engage with new ways of thinking about postfeminism as a cultural entity and sensibility in the context of work, whilst at the same time acknowledging the role of tradition and of the past. In Chapter 9, 'Make Do and Mend? Working Postfeminism and Vintage', Philip Hancock and Melissa Tyler address key debates concerning feminism's past, present and future through the increasingly popular cultural phenomenon of vintage—delineated as a 'constellation' of ideals and practices that relate to the re-introduction and re-organisation of ways of living, working and consuming. Drawing on two organisational sites ('new burlesque' and 'make do and mend'), they develop the innovative and compelling argument that while vintage captures many postfeminist principles including individuality, the pursuit of glamour and the valorisation of traditional feminine practices such as cooking and baking, it also constitutes an organisational phenomenon that points to a more collaborative ethos of connection with the struggles and achievements of feminism's past. In seeking to question what vintage, as a forward looking 'window of the past', might mean for feminism and organisation studies, they suggest that vintage and 'vintage feminism' offer an alternative to postfeminism with its links to neoliberalism, denial and disavowal. This alternative is founded, as they suggest, on the latent progressive content of vintage femininity and its professed organisational values of connection and continuity—including a connection to a past that recognises the value and significance of women's histories and everyday working lives.

In Chapter 10—'Postfeminism as New Materialisms: A Future Unlike the Present?'—Marta B. Calás, Linda Smircich and Seray Ergene develop a 'guide and invitation' to scholars to prefigure new theoretical possibilities for feminist analyses in organisation studies. Addressing the critical issue of human-caused (anthropogenic) ecological harms, this thought-provoking chapter analyses and discusses the role of historically informed and ever changing 'humanist postfeminisms' within the area of work and organisation in helping us to become posthuman. This they see as a way to open space for the possibility of a 'posthumanist postfeminist subject' based on the ontological premises of critical new materialisms. In examining the co-production of the neoliberal and the humanist postfeminist subject, they draw attention to gender-related aspects of work and organisation, to the possibility of discontent as the workings of neoliberalism become transparent to more people leading to new forms of agency that hitherto have been overlooked and consider the kind of contemporary humanist postfeminisms that might emerge when and if neoliberalism is no longer viable. Here, they call for a re-think of the conditions of possibility for a posthumanist postfeminist sensibility based, as example, on hopeful forms of engagement, new models of 'making' and a politics of sustained materialism that promote

potential transformations in knowledge-production practices while fostering a 'more-than-human' and a 'more-than-capitalist' world which posthuman postfeminist figurations may help to bring about.

This book is motivated primarily by a scholarly fascination with the persistence of gendered inequalities. We present the concept of postfeminism
as a means of shedding new light on the tenacity of gendered disparities
between men and women in contemporary organisations and how the dominant masculine maintains the gendered status quo. Not only has the privileged position of masculinity held off the challenge of the valorised feminine,
it has done so at a time when it is claimed that gender discrimination is no
longer an issue, inequality is a thing of the past and women are told they
have 'never had it so good'. While some women have secured access to masculine power through the take-up of senior organisational positions, this is
only a minority, and this small group tends to be made up of white, middle
class women. Thus, the advantages that may be available to women within
a postfeminist gender regime are not easily secured by everyone, with access
to the benefits of the common sense acceptance of equality being heavily
'influenced by the structural position of individual women in terms of class,
ethnicity, race, age, sexuality and other forms of social difference' (Lewis,
2014: 1860). Through the chapters in this book, we hope to shed light
on the usefulness of postfeminism as a critical tool for exploring ongoing
inequality while also drawing out the complex and at times contradictory
experiences of living and working within a postfeminist gender regime.

References

Adkins, L. (2001). Cultural feminization: "Money, sex and power" for women. *Signs: Journal of Women in Culture and Society*, 26(3): 669–695.
Alvesson, M. (1998). Gender relations and identity work: A case study of masculini-
ties and femininities in an advertising agency. *Human Relations*, 51(8): 113–126.
Anderson, E. (2009). *Inclusive Masculinities: The Changing Nature of Masculinities*. London: Routledge.
Bell, E., Merilainen, S., Taylor, S. and Tienari, J. 2015 Fourth wave feminism? Bodies, practices, politics and ethics. *9th International Conference in Critical Management Studies*, Leicester, 8–10 July.
Benschop, Y., van den Brink, M., and Verloo, M. (2015). De mythe van het feminis-
tische paradijs. In Dudink, S.P. and Liedeke, P. (Eds.), *Mythen van gender. Essays
voor Willy Jansen* (pp. 35–46). Nijmegen: Vantilt.
Benschop, Y., and Verloo, M. (2016). Feminist organization theories: Islands of trea-
sue? In R. Mir, H. Wilmott, and M. Greenwood (Eds.), *The Routledge Compan-
ion to Philosophy in Organization Studies* (pp. 100–112). London and New York:
Routledge.
Butler, J. (1990). *Gender Trouble: Feminism and the Subversion of Identity*. New
York: Routledge.
Calás, M., and Smircich, L. (1996). From "the woman's" point of view: Feminist
approaches to organization studies. In S. Clegg, C. Hardy, and W. Nord (Eds.),
Handbook of Organization Studies (pp. 218–257). London: Sage.

Calás, M., and Smircich, L. (2006). From the "woman's point of view" ten years later: Towards a feminist organization studies. In S. Clegg, C. Hardy, T. Lawrence, and W. Nord (Eds.), *The Sage Handbook of Organization Studies* (pp. 284–346). London: Sage.

Dean, J. (2010). Feminism in the papers: Contested feminisms in the British quality press. *Feminist Media Studies*, 10(4): 391–407.

Dow, B.J. (2006). The traffic in men and the fatal attraction of postfeminist masculinity. *Women's Studies in Communication*, 29(1): 113–131.

Elliott, K. (2016). Caring masculinities: Theorizing an emerging concept. *Men and Masculinities*, 19(3): 240–259.

Evans, E., and Chamberlain, P. (2015). Critical waves: Exploring feminist identity, discourse and praxis in western feminism. *Social Movement Studies*, 14(4): 396–409.

Ferguson, M.L. (2010). Choice feminism and the fear of politics. *Perspectives on Politics*, 8(1): 247–253.

Fraser, N. (2009). Feminism, capitalism and the cunning of history. *New Left Review*, 56: 97-117.

Garcia-Favaro, L., and Gill, R. (2016). "Emasculation nation has arrived": Sexism rearticulated in online responses to Lose the Lads' Mags campaign. *Feminist Media Studies*, 16(3): 379–397.

Gill, R. (2014). Powerful women, vulnerable men and postfeminist masculinity in men's popular fiction. *Gender & Language*, 8(2): 185–204.

Hirshman, L.R. (2006). *Get to Work: A Manifesto for Women of the World*. New York: Viking.

Holvino, E. (2010). Intersections: The simultaneity of race, gender and class in organization studies. *Gender Work and Organization*, 17(3): 248–277.

Huppatz, K. 2009: Reworking Bourdieu's "Capital": Feminine and female capitals in the field of paid caring work. *Sociology*, 43(1): 45–66.

Huppatz, K., and Goodwin, S. (2013). Masculinised jobs, feminised jobs and men's "gender capital" experiences: Understanding occupational segregation in Australia. *Journal of Sociology*, 49(2–3): 291–308.

Jaggar, A.M. (1983). *Feminist Politics and Human Nature*. Lanham, MD: Rowman and Littlefield.

Kauppinen, K. (2013). "Full power despite stress": A discourse analytical examination of the interconnectedness of postfeminism and neoliberalism in the domain of work in an international women's magazine. *Discourse & Communication*, 7(2): 133–151.

Kelan, E. (2008). The discursive construction of gender in contemporary management literature. *Journal of Business Ethics*, 81(2): 427–445.

Kolehmainen, M. 2012: Managed makeovers? Gendered and sexualized subjectivities in postfeminist media culture. *Subjectivity*, 5(2): 180–199.

Lee, R. (2013). Modernity, modernities and modernization: Tradition reappraised. *Social Science Information*, 52(3): 409–424.

Lewis, P. (2014). Postfeminism, femininities and organization studies: Exploring a new agenda. *Organization studies*, 35(12): 1845-1866.

Lewis, P., Benschop, Y., and Simpson, R. (2017). Postfeminism, gender and organization. *Gender, Work & Organization*, 24(3): 213–225.

McRobbie, A. (2007). Top girls? *Cultural Studies*, 21(4–5): 718–737.

McRobbie, A. (2009). *The Aftermath of Feminism*. London: Sage.

McRobbie, A. (2015). Notes on the perfect. *Australian Feminist Studies*, 30(83): 3–20.

Noon, M. (2007). The fatal flaws of diversity and the business case for ethnic minorities. *Work, Employment & Society*, 21(4): 773.

O'Neill, R. (2015). Whither critical masculinity studies? Notes on inclusive masculinity theory, postfeminism and sexual politics. *Men and Masculinities*, 18(1): 100–120.

Poggio, B. (2006). Outline of a theory of gender practices. *Gender Work and Organization*, 13(3): 225–233.

Pruchniewska, U.M. (2017). Branding the self as an "authentic feminist": Negotiating feminist values in post-feminist digital cultural production. *Feminist Media Studies*. DOI: 10.1080/ 14680777.2017.1355339

Prügl, E. (2015). Neoliberalising feminism. *New Political Economy*, 20(4): 614–631.

Pullen, A., and Simpson, R. (2009). Managing difference in feminized work: Men, otherness and social practice. *Human Relations*, 62(4): 561–587.

Ridgeway, C.L., and Correll, S.J. (2004). Unpacking the gender system: A theoretical perspective on gender beliefs and social relations. *Gender & Society*, 18(4): 510–531.

Roberts, S. (2012). Boys will be boys . . . won't they? Change and continuities in contemporary young working-class masculinities. *Sociology*, 47(4): 671–686.

Rottenberg, C. (2014). The rise of neoliberal feminism. *Cultural Studies*, 28(3): 418–437.

Rumens, N. (2017). Postfeminism, men, masculinities and work: A research agenda for gender and organization studies scholars. *Gender, Work and Organization*, 23(4): 245–259.

Snyder, R.C. (2008). What is third-wave feminism? A new directions essay. *Signs: Journal of Women in Culture and Society*, 34(1): 175–196.

Springer, K. (2002). Third wave black feminism? *Signs: Journal of Women in Culture and Society*, 27(4): 1059–1082.

Standing, G. (2011). *The Precariat: The New Dangerous Class*. London: Bloomsbury Publishing.

Stevenson, N., Jackson, P., Brooks, K. (2003). Reading men's lifestyle magazines: cultural power and the information society. *The Sociological Review, supplement*: 112–131.

Sullivan, K.R., and Delaney, H. (2017). A femininity that "giveth and taketh away": The prosperity gospel and postfeminism in the neoliberal economy. *Human Relations*. 70(7): 836–859.

Tyler, I. (2005). "Who put the 'me' in feminism?" The sexual politics of narcissism. *Feminist Theory*, 6(1): 25–44.

Tyler, I. (2007). The selfish feminist: Public images of women's liberation. *Australian Feminist Studies*, 22(53): 173–190.

Williams, C.L. (2013). The glass escalator, revisited: Gender inequality in neoliberal times, SWS feminist lecture. *Gender & Society*, 27(5): 609–629.

Wrye, H.K. (2009). The fourth wave of feminism: Psychoanalytic perspectives introductory remarks. *Studies in Gender and Sexuality*, 10(4): 185–189.

Part II

Postfeminism and Organization

1 Postfeminism and Gendered (Im)Mobilities

Patricia Lewis

Philip Hammond was caught up in a sexism row after telling the cabinet that driving trains was so easy that even women could do it. The (British) chancellor asked other ministers on Tuesday why there were so few female train drivers, adding that the job was so simple in modern locomotives that 'even they can do it' . . . . Pauline Cawood, 53, a train driver, (said) 'It's an old-fashioned, sexist comment. He ought to be ashamed of himself. Women are just as capable as men at driving trains'. About 5.5 per cent of the 19,000 train drivers in Britain are women, up from 4.2 per cent in 2012.

(Zeffman & Worley, *The Times*, 15 July 2017)

Introduction

Postfeminism is a highly contested, malleable concept and the multiple interpretations of this cultural phenomenon are indicative of its pervasiveness, power and versatility (Koivunen, 2009; Lewis, Benschop, and Simpson, 2017; Negra, 2004; Projansky, 2001). Yet, despite being drawn on in many contradictory ways, central to various versions of postfeminism is a sense of transformation and mobility. This is particularly the case for girls and women whereby female individuals are encouraged to aspire to a new form of living—whatever that is—and to work on themselves as a means of moving towards it. In considering the movement characteristic of today's world, four types of mobility can be identified (Urry, 2007) and these can be distinguished from each other in terms of whether they are perceived positively or negatively, unrestrained or constrained. These include (i) 'positive' mobility which relates to an object or a person that is capable of physical movement and such mobility is increasingly perceived as unrestrained for all types of people and objects, (ii) 'negative' mobility connected to moving groups (e.g. travellers) which is believed to require some kind of regulation and is therefore seen as constrained, (iii) 'positive' and 'negative' mobility connected to migration where individuals move between countries in search of a better life or to escape persecution and is unrestrained or constrained depending on the origins of an individual; finally 'positive' social mobility which is connected to movement up or down a vertical hierarchy (e.g.

class). Whether this type of mobility is unrestrained or constrained is much debated, and according to Urry (2007: 8), 'There are complex relations between elements of physical movement and social mobility ' of any kind.

It is social mobility in relation to postfeminism which is the concern of this chapter with a specific focus on movement along the continuum of gender. In particular, attention is directed at the way in which postfeminism restricts the gender mobility of women within the public world of work. This notion of social mobility is connected to an understanding of gender as a self-conscious, fluid, strategic performance as opposed to an internal, fixed essence. The latter ascribes a type of permanency and stability to gender which unfolds over time based on 'naturalised' distinctions between male and female—gender as internalised biological property. In contrast, a focus on fluidity and performance understands gender as something which is discursively constructed and performed in line with cultural norms—gender as cultural work—an approach which signals the possibility of movement along the gender spectrum by both women and men (Adkins, 2001, 2002). Yet, the ability of women in work contexts to mobilise masculinity is restricted by the postfeminist expectation that they will only "do" masculinity in combination with feminine behaviours and practices. The chapter will consider how the subjectivities available to women require a carefully calibrated simultaneous embrace of masculinity and femininity and how this calibration acts to restrict women both physically and symbolically within organisations (Lewis et al., 2017). The chapter proceeds by outlining various interpretations of postfeminism, highlighting the contested nature of this complex phenomenon, while also explicating the notion of gender mobility connected to each version. Following this, the figure of the 'working woman-with-children' as a particular manifestation of the calibration of masculinity and femininity required by postfeminism is considered. This will include identification of the various subjectivities—referred to as postfeminist maternal femininities—open to her and the gender mobility attached to them.

Postfeminism and Gendered (Im)mobilities

Historical and Theoretical Interpretations of Postfeminism

One thing that all commentators can agree on is the contested nature and lack of consensus surrounding the meanings attached to and the interpretations of the term postfeminism. Nevertheless, central to all interpretations—historical, theoretical, backlash, positive or governance—is a sense of movement and mobility. For historical and theoretical accounts of postfeminism, the focus is on breaks, changes and movement within feminism. Looked at historically, what is notable about this interpretation of postfeminism is the slippage between it and (popular) third-wave feminism. Both (historical) postfeminism and the third-wave emphasise movement away from second-wave feminism with popular third-wave feminism offering a sexier brand of feminism and (historical) postfeminism, signalling the emergence of a different kind of feminism suitable for a new moment in time (Gill, Kelan, and Scharff, 2017; Lewis, 2014a). Similarly, the interpretation of postfeminism which understands it as a theoretical perspective also focuses on movement away from the second wave but this is an epistemological shift which connects feminism to other anti-foundational 'posts' such as postmodernism, poststructuralism and postcolonialism (Brooks, 1997). Such a move repositions feminism so that it is no longer solely concerned with equality but instead turns its attention to multiplicity and heterogeneity. The universal category of 'woman' is rejected, multiple subjectivities are highlighted and feminism's position in relation to other political and philosophical movements with a concern for transformation is explored (Genz and Brabon, 2009; Gill et al., 2017; Lewis, 2014a; Lewis et al., 2017).

What is notable about historical and theoretical accounts is that those who articulate these positions are unlikely to refer to themselves as 'postfeminists' (Blue, 2013; Gill, 2016; Gill et al., 2017; Lewis et al., 2017). Rather, they identify as a 'third-waver' or as one of the 'posts'—postmodernist, poststructuralist or postcolonialist—but never as a postfeminist. Indeed, take-up of the identity position of postfeminist would probably be met with criticism because it appears to suggest a *rejection* of feminism as opposed to *movement within* feminism. While rejection of the label of 'postfeminist' is understandable given the negative connotations that attach to it, this non-identification can mean that the complexities of the postfeminist phenomenon are lost within historical and theoretical accounts, as other aspects of these positions are highlighted.

Backlash and Positive Interpretations of Postfeminism

Despite their differences, backlash postfeminism and positive postfeminism (contemporary versions emerged in the 1990s) can both be understood as reactions to feminism. Both consider the way in which feminist thinking and feminist politics shifted women from immobile confinement within the home to a position of mobility away from family responsibilities and into the world of work. Where these two versions differ is in their interpretation of the consequences of this movement. For those who articulate a backlash version of postfeminism, the breaking of women's traditional 'moorings' within the home is presented negatively as something threatening to the family and constructive of an unrealistic expectation of 'having it all'. The exaggerated criticism of feminism which emanates from a backlash position, contributes to the surfacing of a traditionalist discourse which explicitly rejects feminism as damaging to women, promotes a return to conventional 'homespun' values and sets up an opposition between the 'professionally powerful feminist subject' and the traditional, family focused woman (Projansky, 2001: 72). Additionally, not only does the backlash version construct feminism as damaging to women it also fashions feminism as harmful to men. One central contemporary site for this backlash rejection of feminism is social media where the term 'feminazi' defined as a 'sexist person who believes in female domination . . . usually frustrated delusional ugly women" (Google Images accessed 14 July 2017) is applied to any woman who expresses any kind of feminist viewpoint, no matter how mild (Gill et al., 2017). Through social media, men are presented as the victims of and under constant attack from a tyrannical feminism which seeks to establish a new gender order where women dominate and men lose out. Here, feminism is presented as causing a crisis of masculinity connected to confident women, the collapse of traditional manufacturing jobs held by men and the increasing objectification of the male body (Garcia-Favaro and Gill, 2016).

In contrast, the positive interpretation of postfeminism highlights the success of feminism in securing gender equality and unparalleled opportunities for girls and women. Feminism is celebrated for providing equality through choice and this upbeat version of postfeminism suggests that all women irrespective of their origins and current circumstances are able to decide how they want to live (Lewis and Simpson, 2017). Movement between home and work is seen as unproblematic manifest in the ability to opt to work and succeed in historically masculine occupations or decide to stay home and engage full time in family work. The only caveat here is that successful mobility is dependent on choices and behaviours, responsibility for which lies with the individual. As Projansky (2001: 75) states,

> This version of postfeminism depends on essentialist definitions of women and of feminism, suggesting that as long as women are succeeding in typically male arenas, regardless of their political affiliations, feminism has worked, feminists are happy and thus there is no longer a need for feminist activism.

Consequently, the success of feminism means the end of feminism. Women accept the feminist principle of equality, expecting to be treated equally within the context of the professional world of work while dis-identifying with feminism as an identity, a way of thinking or a political position. From the perspective of positive postfeminism experiences of unequal treatment are not understood in terms of the persistence of inequality that requires continued feminist attention, rather such experiences are understood as 'personal problems' which can be addressed through appropriate personal strategies.

This 'successful but obsolete' account of postfeminism appears to chime with women's increased participation in the labour force. Nevertheless, within this version, it is also suggested that to enter the male dominated, masculine world of work, the successful postfeminist woman is required to not only disconnect from feminism but to also lose her femininity so that she can have the same career path as her male colleagues (Projansky, 2001). Such a position connects with masculinised stereotyping of the working woman as 'improper' through use of names such as the iron maiden (Kanter, 1993) or the oyaji-graru in Japan translated as 'girl acting like a middle-aged man' (Molony, 1995). In the positive version of postfeminism, the masculinised New Woman is problematic for some commentators 'because her feminist desire for equality with men means she must repress her maternal feminine side—her desire to have children or even just to nurture in any context—in order to succeed' (Dow, 1996 cited in Projansky, 2001: 76). The take-up of masculinity and the forfeiture of femininity form the basis of the central decision which this interpretation of postfeminism highlights. Women can be work-centred and masculinised in a similar way to men or home-centred and feminised in a (new) traditional way where staying/going home is a choice not an obligation (Projansky, 2001). While positive postfeminism sets up an equivalency between the 'either/or' masculine choice of work and the feminine choice of family, it does not fully consider how this equivalency is increasingly likely to manifest as a 'both/and' choice where women are required to perform well simultaneously in the work and domestic domains. As Oksala (2013: 39 cited in Lewis and Simpson, 2017: 215) argues, women not only want a fulfilling family life with a partner and children but also 'they too want money, power and success (and as such) they are atomic, autonomous subjects of interest competing for the economic opportunities available'. To fully grasp the implications of this co-existence and how this impacts on women's gender mobility we need to turn to the final interpretation of postfeminism, which approaches this cultural phenomenon as a governmentality which seeks to construct women in terms of postfeminist subjectivities (Repo and Yrjola, 2015).

Postfeminism as a Discursive Formation and Mode of Governance

Despite the lack of consensus regarding how we should decipher the phenomenon of postfeminism, many commentators would agree that the most useful interpretation is one which approaches it as a discursive entity made up of interrelated themes connected to a complex set of discourses around gender, feminism and femininity (Dean, 2010; Projansky, 2001). Here, postfeminism is not linked to an 'actual' historical event or moment but rather is approached as a discursive formation which governs our everyday life, framing and shaping our thinking and behaviour towards feminism and women's changing position in society as subjects of educational and economic capacity (McRobbie, 2007; Projansky, 2001). Within the context of this interpretation, it is argued that postfeminism should be treated as an object of analysis such that those who engage with this formation are understood as analysts of postfeminist culture, concerned with deciphering the discursive practices of power that make up this cultural phenomenon. Over the past decade and a half, largely within the field of media and cultural studies, this work has mapped out the emergence and evolution of the characteristics and features of postfeminism. It has made visible the empirical regularities and material effects of this powerful discursive formation, depicting how it has impacted significantly on how girls, women (and men) live their lives in the twenty-first century and emphasising how as a means of governing everyday life it is dynamic and ever changing, taking on new forms and developing new dimensions (Gill, 2014, 2016). Similarly, within the field of gender and organisation studies, it is argued that characterising postfeminism as a discursive formation which is adaptable, multifaceted and governs the everyday lives of individuals in a range of organisational settings facilitates it use as a critical concept. Used critically, postfeminism makes visible enduring discrimination and inequalities within organisational contexts, how organisational subjects are produced through the active regulation of bodies and subjectivities and how there has been a complex reshaping of female subjectivities in particular, giving rise to a range of postfeminist femininities which form the basis of women's inclusion in contemporary organisations (Gill et al., 2017; Lewis, 2014a; Lewis et al., 2017).

Postfeminism, understood as an object of analysis which requires the critical scrutiny of scholars to make visible its constantly evolving practices of power and as a critical concept which can scrutinise contemporary organisational practices, is systematically elucidated through the notions of a postfeminist sensibility (Gill, 2007a, 2007b) and a postfeminist gender regime (McRobbie, 2009). In explicating the governance interpretation of postfeminism as a sensibility and as a gender regime, both Gill and McRobbie reveal how feminist egalitarianism forms part of the common sense of everyday (Western) life and is now unremarkable. However, acceptance of the principle of equality in education and work co-exists with the re-stabilisation of traditional gender norms and stereotypes around motherhood, heterosexuality, beauty, fitness and body culture. Furthermore, McRobbie (2004) originally argued that this concurrence is dependent on a repudiation of feminism and feminist action such that feminism has to be understood as obsolete to be taken into account. In later work, McRobbie (2015) acknowledges that feminism has made a comeback but that the cost of this rehabilitation is the insertion of a strong individualist, competitive ethic into feminist action based upon the incorporation of selectively defined (liberal) feminist values into the mainstream. The welfarist and collectivist feminism of the past is abandoned and feminism is instrumentalised and personalised, converted 'into an inner drive, a determination to meet self-directed goals' (p. 12). Consequently, moderate feminism holds sway over a rejected 1970s 'excessive' feminism characterised by critique, collectivism and shared rights for women (Dean, 2010; Lewis and Simpson, 2017). Indeed, the moderate restoration of feminism has led some commentators to suggest that postfeminism as a critical concept is no longer needed as we now live in a post-postfeminism era. In response, Gill (2016: 620) argues that we should be sceptical about such calls and comments and that just as increased anti-capitalist activism does not mean that capitalism is dead, 'increased feminist activism does not mean that pre-feminist, anti-feminist and postfeminist ideas are not still in circulation and with powerful force'.

A significant aspect of the affirmation of moderate feminism and the repudiation of 'excessive' feminism is the consequent reconciliation between feminism and femininity, which no longer exist separately from each other instead manifesting as a symbiotic co-existence. The interdependent relationship between feminism and femininity which is emblematic of postfeminism is characterised by the amalgamation of masculine and feminine behaviours and aspirations such that contemporary femininity unavoidably interlocks with norms as well as social realms marked by masculinity (Carlson, 2011; Lewis and Simpson, 2017). This simultaneous take-up of masculine and feminine norms is not something which requires the forfeiture or undermining of femininity as might be suggested by the positive interpretation of postfeminism discussed earlier. In other words women do not have to sublimate their femininity and go through a process of masculinisation, rather the integration of feminine ideals with masculine-marked practices is a co-existence of norms which is constitutive of postfeminist femininity (Carlson, 2011; Heywood and Dworkin, 2003; Lewis, 2014a). This concurrence has a range of features which together occur as a set of 'interrelated practices, processes, actions and meanings' (Acker, 2006: 443). These include the prominence given to endless transformation through the ascendancy of a makeover paradigm; the importance of self-invention through the emphasis placed on individualism, choice and empowerment; constant self-surveillance; the reappearance of 'natural' sexual difference; the re-sexualisation of women's bodies; a focus on femininity as a bodily property; a shift from objectification to subjectification; and, finally, the retreat to home as a matter of choice not obligation (Gill, 2007a, 2007b; Negra, 2009).

Postfeminist femininity derives from an understanding of gender as something which is denaturalised and detachable from the individual and as such is mobile, fluid and indeterminate (Adkins, 2005). This fits with the patterns, practices and bodily states which postfeminist culture pulls women into based on an 'imperative of transformation' with contemporary meanings around women emphasising (masculine) capacity, success, attainment, entitlement, mobility and participation (Coleman, 2012; McRobbie, 2007). There is now a heavy expectation that women and girls should *want to* participate in the world of work and aspire to have career success even if the likelihood of fully securing that success is not there—an absence which is rarely acknowledged. Fulfilment of career aspirations is believed to be achievable if enough effort is expended. Lack of success is interpreted as deficient resolve and personal failure on the part of the individual with little attention paid to how material conditions, structures of inequality or a sense of belonging and identity might hinder mobility (Kyrola and Harjunen, 2017). Women are interpellated by postfeminist discourses to enact masculine behaviours of ambition and self-actualisation and as such are increasingly defined by what they are economically able to do as opposed to the traditional concern with what they ought not to do (McRobbie, 2007). Through take-up and enactment of masculine practices and behaviours the female working body is perceived as 'a site of potential, possibility and promise' (Adkins, 2012: 626).

Yet, it must be remembered that in postfeminist times, women are required to "do" such masculinity interdependently with femininity, maintaining a balance between the two and avoiding being located at one or the other extremity of the gender continuum. Securing equilibrium between masculine and feminine behaviours should not be interpreted as a type of androgyny manifest in the careful presentation of the agentic (masculine) and communal (feminine) aspects of a person. Rather, the combining of the masculine elements of individualism and control with the feminine elements of care and tradition, as a means of performing acceptable postfeminist femininity particularly in organisations, requires careful regulation and appropriate adjustment on an ongoing basis (Lewis and Simpson, 2017). What must also be recognised is that the postfeminist call for women to draw on masculine discourses of individualism and choice in the same way as their male colleagues is somewhat problematic as it places women in a position to secure access to masculine power. As McRobbie (2009: 60–61) argues, 'The Symbolic is faced with the problem of how to retain the dominance of phallocentrism when the logic of global capitalism is to loosen women from their prescribed roles and grant them degrees of economic independence'. However, access to power secured through women's movement along the gender spectrum towards masculinity is diminished by the cultural requirement to also enact feminine behaviours such as those attached to motherhood and beauty. For women in postfeminist times, doing masculinity—despite being hailed to do so—is less tenable, less desirable and less economically liveable without also doing femininity (adapted from Carlson, 2011; Lewis, 2014a). Cultural validation for women in a postfeminist gender regime is dependent on the successful calibration of masculine and feminine behaviours but 'the impact of *having* to enact the required rituals of femininity 'tilts' the balance of power in favour of men and masculinity as the postfeminist woman cannot shed her gender' (Lewis and Simpson, 2017: 218).

McRobbie (2009) refers to this as the postfeminist masquerade arguing that this is a new form of gender power. The cultural insistence that women must be brought back to technologies of self that are constitutive of the *spectacularly feminine* restricts women's physical and symbolic movement within organisations and prevents unfettered mobility along the gender continuum thereby restricting their ability to respond to the 'imperative to transform' (Coleman, 2012). The postfeminist masquerade acts as a mode of restraint on women which prevents them confronting ongoing gender inequalities in the workplace. By responding to the postfeminist call to be demonstrably feminine, confrontation is avoided, the competition which women pose for men is reduced and they become culturally intelligible as the 'gentler sex'—attractive, amenable, pleasant—a civilising addition to the workplace. At the same time the enactment of spectacularly feminine behaviour is understood as deriving from women's own choices, originating from self-regulative action and the self-imposition of feminine cultural norms and not as the outcome of male demands (McRobbie, 2009). Consequently, the reconfiguration of femininity wrought by postfeminism prevents women from fully securing the advantages that might accrue to them from the valorisation of the feminine and access to masculinity. As McRobbie argues, the postfeminist masquerade is a containment strategy whereby the working woman is required to

> mask her rivalry with men in the world of work (i.e. her wish for masculinity), and to conceal the competition she now poses. . . . The masquerade functions to re-assure male structures of power by defusing the presence and the aggressive and competitive actions of women as they come to inhabit positions of authority. It re-stabilises gender relations. . . . by interpellating women repeatedly and ritualistically into the knowing and self-reflexive terms of highly stylised femininity (and motherhood).
>
> (2007: 726)

In considering how the restoration of traditional femininity as a means of regulating 'free' economically active women co-exists with an instrumentalised feminism, McRobbie (2015) argues that a more hard-edged version of the masquerade has emerged. The fusion of a feminism which interpellates women to enact individualist masculine practices with a spectacular femininity which requires women to engage in highly stylised feminine behaviours, is the manifestation of what she refers to as 'the perfect' and characterises the postfeminist femininity which the governance interpretation of postfeminism brings forth. Looking at postfeminism in these terms reveals the power relations and struggles that are at the heart of this cultural phenomenon. Within a postfeminist gender regime, women are mobile in gender terms and this mobilisation has transformed contemporary gender arrangements. Nevertheless, the major qualification here is that the existing dominant masculine regime is largely left in place, relatively untouched by the revolutionary changes which have affected women's lives (McRobbie, 2015). To demonstrate how postfeminism and the femininity it gives rise to manifests within the contemporary world of work, an illustration is provided next. While the discussion earlier largely referred to femininity in the singular, this illustration draws out femininities in the plural—highlighting variations in the form postfeminist femininity takes around the dialectic tension between the feminism and femininity.

Women-With-Children and Postfeminist Maternal Femininities

What is presented next is illustrative and suggestive as it is not based on a systematic review of the gender literature or on empirical data. Rather, it draws on the notion of entrepreneurial femininities (Lewis, 2014a, 2014b), a postfeminist reading of Hakim's preference theory (Lewis and Simpson, 2017) and reflections on the maternal feminine by McRobbie (2013), alongside some newspaper accounts of women's work experiences. As such, I am not claiming that what I refer to as postfeminist maternal femininities are incontrovertible empirical realities. However, they are presented to provoke reflection and to make some suggestions about how the discursive formation of postfeminism has contributed to the complex reshaping of female subjectivities in work contexts through the emergence of work compatible gender identities. Before presenting these postfeminist maternal femininities in Table 1.1 three caveats must be noted: first, specification of these gender identities is underpinned by poststructuralist principles whereby the agency embedded in these subjectivities is understood 'not as a sovereign or masterful self-authoring but as a constituted effect' (Dosekun, 2015: 442). Postfeminism and its related discourses are understood to have a socially constructed influence that critically shapes the identities taken up by women. As such, the postfeminist maternal femininities presented next are not introduced as types which are chosen by individuals nor are they roles imposed by men upon women in organisational contexts or bodily practices which convey the impression of subordination. Instead, the suggested postfeminist maternal femininities are better understood as 'a set of available bodily and relational performances that can be embodied by women and will vary by context (Schippers and Sapp, 2010 cited in Lewis, 2014a: 1853). Second, at first glance the postfeminist maternal femininities could be interpreted as presenting feminine practices as complementary to masculine behaviours highlighting variation but understood as 'different but equal'. However, the poststructuralist principles which underpin the delineation of these post-feminist maternal femininities seek to make clear the ongoing binary and associated gender power imbalance between the masculine and the feminine. This power imbalance has a particularly negative impact on gender mobility as women's 'doing' of the masculine practices of reinvention and risk-taking cannot be disengaged from the essentialised feminine practices of nurture and care, thereby restricting women's movement along the gender continuum. Third, as we will see these postfeminist maternal femininities—corporate mother, working mother, professional mother, unruly mother—inhabit both the masculine and feminine realms associated with the features of postfeminism, performing to different degrees the feminine characteristics of nurture, care, emotion, self-sacrifice and beauty, alongside the masculinised traits of ambition, choice, reinvention, self-regulation and autonomy.

Table 1.1 Postfeminist Maternal Femininities[1]

Masculinity-Femininity	Femininity-Masculinity
Corporate Mother	*Working Mother*
Valorises Career	*Valorises motherhood*
In or moving to senior position	*Strong emphasis on career*
Individualist	*Focus on 'right' balance in life*
Ambitious	*Adopts blended work practices*
Separation between home and work	*around home and career*
Childless women	*May turn to entrepreneurship*
concentrated here	*Attention to Appearance*
Attention to appearance	*Veers towards 'balancing'*
Veers towards 'doing' masculinity	*the 'doing' of femininity*
with less 'doing' of femininity	*with the 'doing' of masculinity*
Professional Mother	*Unruly Mother*
Valorises career of partner	*Valorises children*
(normally husband)	*Home focused but lacks discipline*
Frustrated career aspirations	*No career*
Draws on corporate practices	*No ambition*
to run her home	*No desire to transform themselves*
Children are a project	*If employed usually part time*
May turn to entrepreneurship	*and low skilled*
Attention to appearance	*May turn to self-employment*
Veers towards 'balancing'	*May not attend to fitness and*
the 'doing' of masculinity	*appearance*
with the 'doing' of femininity	*Veers towards 'doing' femininity*
	without 'doing' masculinity

Particular emphasis is placed on the postfeminist features of individualism, choice and empowerment, notions of 'natural' sexual difference and retreatism and as the naming of these femininities implies there is a significant focus on the femininity attached to motherhood. Together, these three elements of postfeminism encapsulate the tension embedded in the reconciliation between feminism (interpreted in terms of achievement in the public, masculine world of work) and femininity (understood in terms of feminised behaviour and domestic responsibilities in the private feminine world of home) (Lewis, 2014a).

Corporate Mother Femininity

The corporate mother is a femininity which is taken up by women who are either already in a leadership position or aspire to be. It normally applies to those who have benefitted from the opening up of economic opportunities for women such that they can replicate the conventional career of their male colleagues. Building a career is hugely important to the women who enact this femininity with the construction of their identity based on the performance of masculine behaviours such as being individualist, competitive, forceful, ambitious and action-oriented. The postfeminist subtext here is that a person's destiny is in their own hands with everyone now having the right and obligation to choose a career path removing any impediments through the development of personal strategies. Consequently, those who take up this identity have sought to move along the gender continuum by drawing on and enacting the practices and skills associated with masculinity. These are rational, highly focused women who make a lifetime commitment to work manifest through firm choices in their single-minded pursuit of career goals (Lewis and Simpson, 2017). The orientation of this postfeminist femininity is summed up by Harriet Green, former CEO of Thomas Cook and now a senior manager in IBM: 'In the week, I don't see my family. I work. I breakfast with people. I will lunch with people if they eat salad' (Mills and Rayment, 2014).

Nevertheless, despite the strong enactment of masculine behaviours, women who take up this postfeminist identity are always brought back to femininity, preventing them from fully moving towards the masculine end of the gender continuum. One very stark example of how this occurs is the way in which women in leadership positions, who do not have children are categorised and analysed as 'childless'. The front cover of an issue of the periodical *New Statesman* (July 2015) which carried an article (Lewis, 2015) entitled 'The motherhood trap: Why are so many successful women childless' depicted four senior female politicians—Nicola Sturgeon (first minister of Scotland), Angela Merkel (German chancellor), Liz Kendall (Labour MP) and Theresa May (then British home secretary) as standing around a cot containing a ballot box. While Nicola Sturgeon was complimentary of the article's analysis of why British female MPs have on average 1.2 children compared to an average of 1.9 children for male MPs, she stated that the front cover reinforced prejudice about women with no children (Mason, 2015). Such prejudice manifests in assumptions that the childfree (as opposed to the more negative term 'childless') woman has no children because of ruthless ambition and putting career first. In a later *Sunday Times* interview, Sturgeon (who endured constant speculation as to when she would start a family) stated this:

> can be hurtful, if I am brutally honest . . . because people make assumptions about why we don't have children. The assumption that people sometimes make is that I have made a cold calculated decision to put my career ahead of having a family and that's not true. Sometimes things happen in life, sometimes they don't.
>
> (Rhodes, 2016)

In the same article, a section was included with photographs of other female politicians. Under the heading 'Childless Politicians' Theresa May

(British Prime Minister), Angela Merkel (German Chancellor), Angela Eagle (Labour MP), Ruth Davidson (Leader of the Scottish Conservatives), Justine Greening (British Education Secretary) and Natalie Bennett (Former Leader of the British Green Party) were cited as 'not mothers'. *The Sunday Times* was criticised for this representation of female politicians and in response expressed the view that 'we could have presented the sidebar more sensitively', but did not question if they should have used this characterisation of senior women in the first place.

In the same 2016 newspaper interview, Sturgeon further revealed how she had what was described as a 'secret' miscarriage in January 2011 which 'dashed' her hopes of having a child. This occurred during a commemoration of a Scottish footballing tragedy when 66 football fans were crushed to death and was described (Rhodes, 2016) in bleak terms as follows:

> It was a grim occasion and looking back at photos from that day (one of which was presented alongside the article), Sturgeon appears pale and tired, some images show her with her eyes tightly shut and while the occasion was undoubtedly sombre, she looks to be in real pain. The cause of which was something beyond the commemoration. In fact as she sat on the terraces that day, Sturgeon was going through her own personal anguish. She was miscarrying a baby. She should have been at home in her bed being looked after by her husband Peter Murrell, Chief Executive of the SNP and not sharing in what was public grief. But it was her public duty to be there so there she was.

What stands out about this depiction of Sturgeon's trauma, is the way in which it seeks to present her miscarriage as a physical wounding such that the 'persuasive force of corporeal pain' (Robinson, 2000: 6) means that she can be 'forgiven' for not having children. One may surmise that such a graphic account of pain and sorrow 'relieves' a woman of the 'guilt' of being childless—it is OK not to have children as long as you are sorry, sad and stoical about the situation and more importantly that this sadness is visible. It would appear that women leaders who have no children and who enact the postfeminist identity of corporate mother are brought to motherhood by being categorised as 'not a mother'. Additionally, in holding this status they are required to make clear that being childless is not a conscious choice. Thus, within a postfeminist gender regime women can 'choose' to work but they cannot 'choose' to be childfree—a very clear example of how their mobility along the gender continuum towards masculinity is marked (Robinson, 2000) and constrained by being brought back to femininity.

Working Mother Femininity

Within a postfeminist gender regime, the working mother is increasingly the dominant femininity, giving expression to the postfeminist co-existence of egalitarianism and familialism (Lewis and Simpson, 2017). This manifests in women's willingness to be 'subjects of economic capacity while also undertaking to retain their traditionally marked out roles in the household' (McRobbie, 2009: 81). Originally, the working mother was largely understood in terms of irreconcilable tensions between work and home thereby necessitating compromise on the part of women with children. This need for concession sets limits on their levels of engagement in the workplace manifest in the moniker 'the mommy track'. Here, the working mother does not seek to duplicate the orthodox male career but adjusts how she works to adapt to the new situation of children, establishing a postfeminist self-imposed gender immobility (Lewis and Simpson, 2017). For women with children who *do not* adjust their ambition there is a need to explain the reasons for this choice as well as to express and display feelings of pain and suffering connected to this preference. When Jayne-Anne Gadhia, chief executive officer of Virgin Money, was asked how much maternity leave she took when she had her daughter in 2002, she replied:

Not enough, I was at Royal Bank of Scotland at the time Amy was born and I was back in the office about six weeks later. It was my doing but it came from perception rather than reality. I perceived that if I wasn't in work, it would get away from me. I suffered postnatal depression and I really wanted to be with my baby and didn't want to go back to work, but my husband had given up his job, so I had to. We had agreed I was going to be the breadwinner because I was in a job that paid more. When we got there, we realised he hadn't really wanted to be home, so it was a difficult time. I decided I had to go home at a reasonable time and not work ridiculous hours. . . (my boss) had given me a really good bonus—much more than I had expected given that I hadn't worked as hard. I said 'I don't understand it' and he said 'even though you have something in your life that's more important than work, it has made your judgement better'.

(Mikhailova, 2016)

The postfeminist emphasis on choice emerges through Gadhia's assertion that having a shortened maternity leave was her own personal decision and nothing to do with organisational expectations. We see reference to the post-feminist feature of 'natural' sexual difference where experience of a 'difficult time' was due to a decision which usurped the 'natural' order of mothers being at home with children while fathers go out to work, making both her and her husband unhappy. Additionally, we also see an emphasis on physical 'suffering' through her reference to postnatal depression because she desperately wanted to be at home with her baby—anguish which resulted from her making the 'wrong' choice to go back to work early. Thus, to secure 'forgiveness' and 'understanding' for this choice as opposed to being perceived as 'tough' and 'uncaring', Gadhia's reference to postnatal depression can be understood as the presentation of being a physically wounded and emotionally traumatised woman. Gadhia is brought back to femininity away from the masculine choice of work through expression of female angst about missing out on nurturing her daughter. I am not suggesting here that Gadhia consciously sought sympathy or that her feelings were unreal, rather drawing on Robinson (2000), I am proposing that regular accounts of sadness or 'missing out' from women who haven't stayed home presents 'evidence' of what is believed to be the *real, natural* condition of women/mothers in a postfeminist gender regime. In this context a woman who openly 'chooses' work over children without the expression of regret is open to significant criticism and descriptions of being 'selfish', 'sad' or 'unnatural'. Indeed, a senior woman who is perceived as tough can have this description softened by becoming a mother. For example, Laura Wade-Grey, a senior manager 'once tipped to run Marks & Spencer' had an acquaintance say of her, 'I could never decide whether she reminded me more of Boadicea or Joyce Grenfell', but this perception of her appeared to change and soften when she adopted a child at the age of 50 (Hosking, 2015).

Yet, despite the corporeal pain associated with working as opposed to retreating home to be with children, what is also interesting about Gadhia's account is her reference to an increase in her bonus and her boss's view that motherhood had improved her judgement in a way that helped the bank. This valorisation of the benefits for business of the 'maternal feminine' (McRobbie, 2015) connects to the intensification of the postfeminist gender regime. Increasingly, there is an emphasis on nurturing ambition as well as children, with women being encouraged to simultaneously excel at *both* work and motherhood (Lewis and Simpson, 2017). Illustrations of the postfeminist woman who does extremely well at both work and home are often drawn from the ranks of celebrities. For example, a profile of the supermodel Gisele Bundchen describes her as follows:

> As feminist role models go, Gisele Bundchen, arguably the world's most famous supermodel, might not be the obvious option. But why not? As the highest-earning model in the world last year (in 2013 an estimated £29 million), businesswoman and mum of three, Bundchen is certainly doing 'the juggle', that peculiarly female dance of work/kids/life that defines most women of a certain age. Of course, Bundchen's 'juggle' is slightly different from yours and mine. . . . Still while it may be glossy, her version of having it all remains valid. . . . (As Gisele says herself) I think that it's a very empowering thing for me to be able to be successful in my job and not feel like I need to sacrifice being a mother.
>
> (Atkinson, 2014)

While the work-family 'juggling' of this celebrity mum is far from the experience of most women, it is interesting that the term 'sacrifice' is used when Gisele expresses a sense of relief at not having to inhabit the wounded body of the childless woman in order to work. Additionally, what is also notable about celebrity accounts of 'juggling' work and family is that mothering is always presented as more important than work as Gisele's account illustrates:

> Being a mother is the most important job. Now there is this little being that needs you for everything . . . I do the schedule of my children so I get their school breaks and my husband's schedule because my family is my number one priority. And once I get that in my calendar, I can work my schedule around that.
>
> (Atkinson, 2014)

Successfully coping with home and work concurrently is put down to good management and co-ordination strategies as well as recognising what is important in life—i.e., motherhood and family, not earning £29 million. Developing an ability to be more productive in work on fewer hours and adopting blended work strategies where care work such as reading to your children, being home for dinner or around at bath time are integrated into the time and space of the working day, are presented as central to being successful at home and work (Lewis and Simpson, 2017; McRobbie, 2015). This success is dependent on individual behaviours and personal strategies such as correctly anticipating what is required on any given day or making the right life decisions such as choosing an appropriate person to marry. As Harriet Green said about her husband: 'I chose my husband in about seven seconds. . . . I just knew. I knew he was very strong, very balanced' (Mills and Rayment, 2014).

The Professional Mother Femininity

The professional mother femininity can overlap with both the corporate mother femininity and the working mother femininity but in outlining the multiple femininities which postfeminism can give rise to, I differentiate between them while being mindful of the blurred boundaries and constant movement between them. The professional mother persona applies to those women who have previously had a corporate/professional career but have opted out of the labour force. Those who adopt this femininity believe in the importance of active maternal nurturing of children by the mother, treat marriage as a career and interpret the family as a small business or enterprise which requires strong leadership from the mother/wife expressed through the professional management of the family's social life, the children's education and (usually) the husband's career (Lewis and Simpson, 2017; McRobbie, 2015). The professionalism which attaches to this femininity elevates being a stay-at-home mum above the traditional image of the housewife who rears children and keeps house. It also implies an implicit criticism of those women with children who take up the corporate mother femininity as they are perceived to have prioritised their own careers at the expense of their children (McRobbie, 2015). The difference between the professional mother and the traditional housewife is encapsulated in the notion of the 'wife bonus' as follows:

> Polly Phillips gave up a lucrative career in the London insurance business to become a stay-at-home wife, follow her husband across the world and then bring up their daughter. It's true that her career has certainly suffered because of the change. But her income has not. Her husband is said to keep her sweet with a five-figure 'wife bonus'. In doing so, Mrs Phillips, 32, has become part of an army of educated women who claim a defined cut of the income their husband receives, for providing outstanding services in household management and childrearing, in compensation for the careers they have lost. . . . A wife bonus (is dependent) not only on how well her husband's (job has gone but on) her own performance—how well she managed the home budget, whether the kids got into a 'good' school—the same way their husbands were rewarded at investment banks.
>
> (Spence, 2015)

The notion of the 'wife bonus' was coined by an American anthropologist Wednesday Martin in her book *Primates of Park Avenue* (Spence, 2015). I draw on it here because it is imbued with the postfeminist modalities of individualism, choice and empowerment, 'natural' sexual difference and retreatism. While take-up of the professional mother identity might appear to locate a woman at the femininity end of the gender continuum given its emphasis on motherhood and family, the clear commitment to the masculine work practices of performance management and the achievement of targets maintains its ability to also move into the domain of masculinity. In doing this it is a clear example of the postfeminist requirement that to be seen as contemporaneously feminine requires the visible doing of both masculinity and femininity. Nevertheless, the contours of this particular femininity indicate that it is only likely to apply to a minority of wealthy or at least middle class women and additionally there is always the possibility that these women may return to work. The maintenance of their business skills through management of their families can facilitate such a return. It should be recognised however that this only tends to happen in extreme circumstances such as divorce and it therefore might be argued that a formal return to the labour market under these circumstances is based on the 'wounding' and 'marking' of the professional mother in relation to marital breakdown.

The Unruly Mother Femininity

Finally, we turn to the unruly mother femininity which is the postfeminist Other of the identities outlined earlier. This femininity is gender immobile being located at the feminine end of the gender continuum with no visible attempt made to move towards masculinity. While the women who take-up this postfeminist maternal identity are less likely to be working, if they do, it is normally in feminised low paid occupations. Women who enact this femininity are not culturally validated mainly because they are perceived as excessively feminine in a way which has no apparent value for the world of work or for the nurturing of children. Not performing the counterweight of masculinity either through a disciplined management of home or aspirational participation in the public world of work leaves them 'in explicit danger of occupying a pariah position due to the enactment of traditional femininity characterised by dependence, vulnerability, passivity. . . (leaving out) the elements of contemporary feminine behaviour—assertiveness, confidence, self-determination—which are valued in a postfeminist gender regime' (Lewis, 2014a: 1858). Thus, in contrast to the other three postfeminist maternal identities where injury can result from or is the cause of movement into masculinity, women who are constituted in terms of the unruly mother femininity are subject to symbolic violence not because they are 'doing' masculinity but because they are not. This manifests in injurious names such as 'pram face' and chav (Tyler, 2008). Such women are blamed for their 'shortcomings', which are never linked to structural or cultural constraints that act on them but to personal carelessness and inadequate life planning (Lewis, 2014a; McRobbie, 2015). The unruly mother identity communicates the negative consequences attached to not doing masculinity at all while the other three postfeminist maternal identities signal the cultural validation that attaches to the 'independent' woman who can correctly calibrate masculinity and femininity without moving to the extremes of one or other end of the gender continuum.

Conclusion

In this chapter I have outlined five different interpretations of the complicated cultural phenomenon of postfeminism—historical, theoretical, backlash, positive, governance—and considered their connection to women's (im) mobility on the continuum of gender. In reviewing all five of these interpretations, I have suggested that an understanding of postfeminism as a mode of governance which is discursively produced through the intersections of a group of hegemonic discourses around gender, feminism and femininity, is the most critically valuable interpretation for use in the field of gender and organisation studies (Gill et al., 2017; Lewis, 2014a; Lewis et al., 2017). Working with this interpretation of postfeminism, we can explore how it has reshaped and reconfigured both feminism and femininity thereby influencing the work identities taken up by women within the contemporary workplace. To illustrate this argument, four postfeminist maternal identities were presented with attention directed at how the living of these femininities entails the 'strategic crossing of gender boundaries' (Carlson, 2011: 88) within a postfeminist gender regime. However, as we saw earlier, the location within and movement between the masculine and feminine marked realms, varied across the four femininities (Lewis, 2014a).

Two observations about the desire and ability to move between the masculine and feminine realms which make up each of these femininities can be made. First, the level of mobility characteristic of the different modes of maternal femininity establishes a hierarchy between them. This is connected to the extent to which a particular femininity is perceived to be too masculinised or too feminised. The most highly valued and cultural validated femininities are those which can successfully calibrate the simultaneous embrace of the masculine and feminine elements which make up these postfeminist subjectivities. One can surmise that the working mother femininity is likely to receive the most cultural validation within a postfeminist gender regime. Here, equivalent priory is given to both public work outside the home and private work within the home, promoting the integration of career work and care work and the need to do both excellently (Lewis and Simpson, 2017).

Second, in looking at all of the postfeminist maternal femininities it is clear that there is no real choice around motherhood and/or work. The mobility of all of these postfeminist maternal femininities along the gender continuum is variously curtailed by the valorisation of motherhood, home and family ensuring that when doing masculinity in the world of work, women are always pulled back (usually painfully) to the doing of femininity. Additionally, women who are positioned nearer the feminine end of the gender continuum are not always permitted to stay there permanently. They are also pulled towards masculinity through the need or demand to secure employment. Consequently, constituting themselves through one or other of these femininities, women who 'choose' to stay in or return to work, usually experience some kind of visible wounding and corporeal pain. These injuries occur when women are constantly reminded they are childless or selfish mothers if they appear to prioritise work over home when taking up the corporate mother identity. Enacting the working mother femininity means experiencing sustained physical exhaustion connected to blended work strategies as those women who take up this postfeminist identity seek to excel both at home and at work. Equally, the professional mother and the unruly mother identities entail an element of 'force' regarding their engagement in the world of work. For the professional mother a return to work is often due to the painful loss of a marital partner through divorce. While for the unruly mother—constructed through the popular press as an abject maternal figure—there is regular and constant incitement to secure employment through negative stereotyping of their entire lives (McRobbie, 2015). What is interesting about the postfeminist maternal femininities outlined here is that take-up of any one of these subjectivities can potentially lead to an injurious experience in the public world of work and/or the private world of home connected to gendered understandings of women relationship to employment and family. The level and nature of the injury suffered may be associated with the amount of gender mobility, the intensity of the shifting power relations and the assertions of new gender ideals which each one of these femininities manifests. Here, it might be argued that the injury to the sense of self which those who take up the corporate mother identity endure is of a different order and magnitude to the more physical injury which the working mother experiences. Future research should continue to focus on the postfeminist reconfiguration of contemporary femininity and the way this influences how women are incorporated into the work force. On the one hand, such investigations could explore the potentially deleterious effect on women of postfeminist identities which compel women to 'give their all' to both work and home in a way that is potentially ruinous to their physical health, emotional well-being and family relationships. On the other hand, research attention could be directed at the issue of access to the postfeminist identities on offer as the injurious impact of any particular femininity may be heavily influenced by the structural position of individual women in terms of class, ethnicity, race, age, sexuality and other forms of social difference.

Note

1 An earlier version of the Postfeminist Maternal Femininities—previously referred to as Corporate Femininities—was presented as part of a seminar entitled *Postfeminism and Intersectionality: Exploring the Complexities of Women's Inclusion in Contemporary Organizations* delivered to the Gender and Power Research Group, Institute for Management Research, Radboud University, Nijmegen, the Netherlands (November 2014). I thank the group for helpful comments on the identification of these femininities.

References

Acker, J. (2006). Inequality regimes: Gender, class and race in organizations. *Gender and Society*, 20(4): 441–464.
Adkins, L. (2001). Cultural feminization: Money, sex and power for women. *Signs: Journal of Women in Culture & Society*, 26(3): 669–695.
Adkins, L. (2002). *Revisions: Gender & Sexuality in Late Modernity*. Berkshire: Open University Press.
Adkins, L. (2005). The new economy, property and personhood. *Theory, Culture & Society*, 22(1): 111–130.
Adkins, L. (2012). Out of work or out of time? Rethinking labour after the financial crisis. *South Atlantic Quarterly*, 111(4): 621–641.
Atkinson, L. (2014). Wonder woman. *The Sunday Times*, Style Magazine, 19 October.
Blue, M.G. (2013). The best of both worlds? Youth, gender and a postfeminist sensibility in Disney's "Hannah Montana". *Feminist Media Studies*, 13(4): 660–675.
Brooks, A. (1997). *Postfeminisms: Feminism, Cultural Theory and Cultural Forms*. London, UK: Routledge.
Carlson, J. (2011). Subjects of a stalled revolution: A theoretical consideration of contemporary American femininity. *Feminist Theory*, 12(1): 75–91.

Coleman, R. (2012). *Transforming Images: Screens, Affect, Futures*. London and New York: Routledge.

Dean, J. (2010). Feminism in the papers: Contested feminism in the British quality press. *Feminist Media Studies*, 10(4): 391–407.

Dosekun, S. (2015). "Hey, you stylized woman there": An uncomfortable reflexive account of performative practices in the field. *Qualitative Inquiry*, 21(5): 436–444.

Dow, B.J. (1996). *Prime-time Feminism: Television, Media Culture and the Women's Movement Since 1970*. Philadelphia: University of Pennsylvania Press.

Garcia-Favaro, L., and Gill, R. (2016). "Emasculation nation has arrived": Sexism rearticulated in online responses to Lose the Lads' Mags campaign. *Feminist Media Studies*, 16(3): 379–397.

Genz, S., and Brabon, B.A. (2009). *Postfeminism: Cultural Texts and Theories*. Edinburgh, UK: Edinburgh University Press.

Gill, R. (2007a). Postfeminist media culture: Elements of a sensibility. *European Journal of Cultural Studies*, 10(2): 147–166.

Gill, R. (2007b). *Gender and the Media*. Cambridge: Polity Press.

Gill, R. (2014). Unspeakable inequalities: Postfeminism, entrepreneurial subjectivity and the repudiation of sexism among cultural workers. *Social Politics: International Studies in Gender, State and Society*, 21(3): 508–528.

Gill, R. (2016). Post-postfeminism? New feminist visibilities in postfeminist times. *Feminist Media Studies*, 16(4): 610–630.

Gill, R., Kelan, E.K., and Scharff, C.M. (2017). A postfeminist sensibility at work. *Gender, Work and Organization*, 23(4): 226–244.

Google Images. (2017). How to tell a feminist from a feminazi. Accessed 14 July. https://images.google.co.uk

Heywood, L., and Dworkin, S. (2003). *Built to Win*: The female athlete as cultural icon. Minneapolis, MN: University of Minnesota Press.

Hosking, P. (2015). M&S star to extend her maternity leave. *The Times*, 24 December.

Kanter, R.M. (1993). *Men and Women of the Corporation*. New York: Basic Books.

Koivunen, A. (2009). Confessions of a free woman: Telling feminist stories in postfeminist media culture. *Journal of Aesthetics & Culture*, 1(1): 1–7.

Kyrola, K., and Harjunen, H. (2017). Phantom/liminal fat and feminist theories of the body. *Feminist Theory*, 18(2): 99–117.

Lewis, H. (2015). The motherhood trap: Why are so many successful women childless? *New Statesman*, 17-23 July.

Lewis, P. (2014a). Postfeminism, femininities and organization studies: Exploring a new agenda. *Organization Studies*, 35(12): 1845–1866.

Lewis, P. (2014b). Feminism, post-feminism and emerging femininities in entrepreneurship. In S. Kumra, R. Simpson, and R. Burke (Eds.), *The Oxford Handbook of Gender in Organizations* (pp. 107–129). Oxford: Oxford University Press.

Lewis, P., Benschop, Y., and Simpson, R. (2017). Postfeminism, gender and organization. *Gender, Work and Organization*, 23(4): 1–13.

Lewis, P., and Simpson, R. (2017). Hakim revisited: Preference, choice and the postfeminist gender regime. *Gender, Work and Organization*, 23(3): 213–225.

Mason, R. (2015). New Statesman cover on being childless reinforces prejudice says Sturgeon. *The Guardian*, 16 July.

McRobbie, A. (2004). Postfeminism and popular culture: Bridget Jones and the "new gender regime". In Y. Tasker and D. Negra (Eds.), *Interrogating Postfeminism* (pp. 27–39). London: Duke University Press.

McRobbie, A. (2007). Top girls? *Cultural Studies*, 21(4–5): 718–737.

McRobbie, A. (2009). *The Aftermath of Feminism*. London: Sage.

McRobbie, A. (2013). Feminism, the family and the new "mediated" maternalism. *New Formations*, 80(80): 119–137.

McRobbie, A. (2015). Notes on the perfect. *Australian Feminist Studies*, 30(83): 3–20.

Mikhailova, A. (2016). I cut my hours for my baby, but my bonus went gaga. *The Sunday Times*, 16 October.

Mills, E., and Rayment, T. (2014). How to muscle your way to the top: A women's guide. *The Sunday Times*, 30 November.

Molony, B. (1995). Japan's (1986) equal employment opportunity law and the changing discourse on gender. *Signs: Journal of Women in Culture & Society*, 20(2): 268–302.

Negra, D. (2004). Quality postfeminism? Sex & the single girl on HBO. *Genders OnLine Journal*, 39. Available at: www.atria.nl/ezines/IAV_6606661/IAV_2010_52/g39_negra.html

Negra, D. (2009). *What a Girl Wants? Fantasizing the Reclamation of Self in Postfeminism*. London: Routledge.

Oksala, J. (2013). Feminism and neoliberal governmentality. *Foucault Studies*, 16(September): 32–53.

Projansky, S. (2001). *Watching Rape: Film and Television in Postfeminist Culture*. New York: New York University Press.

Repo, J., and Yrjola, R. (2015). "We are all princesses now": Sex, class and neoliberal governmentality in the rise of middle-class monarchy. *European Journal of Cultural Studies*, 18(6): 741–760.

Rhodes, M. (2016). Nicola Sturgeon: "If the miscarriage hadn't happened would I be first minister now? I'd like to think so". *The Sunday Times*, 4 September.

Robinson, S. (2000). *Marked Men: White Masculinity in Crisis*. New York: Columbia University Press.

Schippers, M., and Sapp, E.G. (2012). Reading "Pulp Fiction": Femininity and power in second and third wave feminist theory. *Feminist Theory*, 13(1): 27–42.

Spence, M. (2015). I deserve my wife bonus, says stay-at-home mother. *The Times*, 30 May.

Tyler, I. (2008). Chav mum, chav scum: Class disgust in contemporary Britain. *Feminist Media Studies*, 8(1): 17–34.

Urry, J. (2007). *Mobilities*. Cambridge: Polity Press.

Zeffman, H., and Worley, W. (2017). Even a woman could drive new trains, says Hammond. *The Times*, 15 July.

Doing-It-All
Exploring Work-Life Balance in Nigeria Through a Postfeminist Lens

Itari Turner and Ruth Simpson

roduction

e choices women face between work and home are often captured in the
ɔular and well-used concept of 'work-life balance' (WLB). This has been
ıceptualised as a self-determined state of well-being a person can reach
t allows effective management of multiple responsibilities of work, home
l community (Buddhapriya, 2005). Clark defines it simply as "satisfac-
n and good functioning at work and at home, with minimum role con-
t" (Clark, 2000: 751).

n this chapter, we explore the implications of the postfeminist empha-
on choice, individualism and agency through the concept of WLB.
 respond to a call for a transnational approach to the critical study of
;tfeminism—how it has become a transnationally circulating culture that
; implications not only for women in the West (Dosekun, 2015) but also
 women in non-Western contexts. Through a study of female doctors in
;eria, we investigate attitudes towards and experiences of WLB, thereby
nging debates around the postfeminist emphasis on 'balance' (in terms
:he choices women face between the 'masculine' world of work and the
ninine' domain of home) into a hitherto under-explored domain. Stud-
of WLB across various countries have revealed contradictions (Lewis,
mbles, and Rapoport, 2007) suggesting that WLB fails to take contextual
cial, cultural) perspectives into account (Kaiser et al., 2011). Examples
en from our Nigerian study point to the significance of *'weight'* rather
n balance in capturing the obligations and pressures women face. We
ɔw how 'weight' leads us to examine traditionally oriented burdens of
ɔonsibilities imposed on women as mothers and caregivers and how
ght is bound up with notions of sacrifice and reward within what is often
ceived to be a 'reified' caregiving role. Drawing on the concept of 'doing-
ll' to capture the burdens of responsibilities Nigerian women face, we
sent and discuss examples from the study in relation to Western based
lerstandings of postfeminism and how these may translate differentially
 a non-Western context.

WLB and Postfeminism

Described as capturing the 'antecedents, correlates and consequences of the balance, conflict and facilitation between . . . work and non-work domains' (Ozbilgin et al., 2011: 177), the WLB metaphor has become mainstream in capturing the relationship between two 'entangled spheres' (Lewis et al., 2007; Sorensen, 2017) of paid and non-paid activities. Balance is synonymous with a state of steady equilibrium where 'things are of equal weight or force'—i.e., where, in our context, demands of a persons' job and personal life 'are equal' (Crompton, Lewis, and Lyonette, 2007). However, as Singh (2013) observed, work life balance is not only about equally dividing the time spent on one's work and personal life but also establishing congruence that reflects an individual's priories. This is based on the premise that personal life and working life are essentially complementary to each other in bringing 'completeness' in the form of psychological well-being, harmony and satisfaction (Clarke et al., 2004; Clark, 2000), indicating that it is possible to achieve a harmonious balance between work and home.

This notion of balance draws on postfeminist discourses relating to women's freedom to perform a traditional femininity combined with a more 'masculine' orientation to autonomy, independence and ambition. Looking at how women 'do' femininity and masculinity at work, Adams (2017) draws on postfeminism to show how women are expected to achieve a 'successful' balance between the two. As she points out, postfeminism places emphasis on female empowerment and individualism through an active subject who is seen as free to shape his/her own destiny—embracing the feminine while seeking success in the (masculine) world of work. The postfeminist subject balances progressive career aspirations with maintaining 'feminine' conduct and desires (Gill and Scharff, 2011)—e.g., through family and marriage and the domestic sphere. Therefore, the 'progressive and valuable feminine subject' is called upon to engage in balancing often contradictory expectations through participation in the world of work—achieving a balance 'on her own terms' through individual compromise and adjustment (Adams, 2017). However, as Adams points out, the balance has to be achieved in a "calculated, market-oriented and efficient way" (Adams, 2017: 316), offering the promise of success and 'partial inclusion' while curtailing the disruptive potential of the feminine to imagine structural change.

In the context of WLB, a 'successful balance' is therefore one which manages the division between the masculine domain of work and the feminine domain of home. In this respect, it has been well documented in the WLB literature (e.g. Hochschild, 1989; Singh, 2013) that women face particular tensions and conflicts between the two domains, given their primary responsibilities within the domestic sphere and given the potential for tangible and intangible work intrusions into domestic life. While managerial support for WLB such as through flexible working may go some way to relieve these tensions and restore a 'harmonious' state of equilibrium, the rationale is often to meet business needs (Hyman and Summers, 2004) through a focus on women's efficient and productive participation in employment. The solving of work-life tensions through 'partial inclusion' (Adams, 2017) as referred to earlier therefore obviates the need for a systematic change to cultures, structures and practices (Caproni, 2004). This places emphasis on the 'business case' for work-based flexibility as well as on the role of choice in creating balance between work and home.

Choice and WLB

Here, 'choosing' postfeminist subjects are seen to have independence and autonomy, making sense of their lives through notions of individual agency and responsibility (Lewis and Simpson, 2015) and where 'gains' from feminism are seen as progressive and irreversible—i.e., as 'permanent fixtures' of the present-day environment. Personal responsibility rather than structural conditions are seen as the basis for gender-based disadvantage where freedom to choose and access to choice are seen as a 'substitute' (Gill and Scharff, 2011; Lewis, 2014; McRobbie, 2009) for feminism and where women must self-discipline and adjust their ambitions while presenting their actions as freely chosen. Thus, while 'staying at home' used to articulate anti-feminist sentiment, it is now seen as every woman's choice—and as long as women choose, the outcome is seen as 'feminist' (Lazar, 2006). Drawing on Hakim's (2000) celebrated preference groupings, women can now choose a lifestyle centred on work ('work centred' women), on the home ('home centred' women) or a combination of the two ('adaptive' women)—the latter exemplified within 'have-it-all' discourses and the WLB domain. In other words, discourses of choice actively represent women as careerist, as 'having-it-all' (combining work with domestic responsibilities) or as repositioned in the home based on the postfeminist idea that women are free to return to 'normatively feminine pursuits' (Dosekun, 2015: 960).

As Probyn (1990) has noted, the choice agenda sets up an 'equivalency' between work and family as an 'either/or' of equal value which not only erases the dialectic that liberal feminism has constructed between work and home (where the latter was seen as a source of subordination and disadvantage) but also reveals a class and race bias in terms of the ability to take up particular options on offer. In this respect, the choice agenda overlooks the fact that many women approach work as an economic necessity rather than as a choice to be weighed up. Here, it is arguable that only white, middle class mothers with non-work means of support have all the options open to them and can choose to stay at home. This is captured in the slang term 'yummy mummy' used in the United Kingdom to describe young, groomed and wealthy (generally white) stay-at-home mothers with rich, high powered husbands—who are able to lead carefree and affluent lifestyles. As Springer (2007) argues, looking at popular culture, this positioning is not however open to all with black women excluded from a lifestyle of 'leisure' within the home. In this respect, the normative postfeminist 'choosing' subject is seen as white and middle class 'by default' (Tasker and Negra, 2007) through the centralisation of a white affluent elite with sufficient resources to choose.

This not only neglects the gendered contexts in which individual and household choices are produced but also how the changing nature of work, workloads and employer/manager practices and strategies can constrain choice (Pocock, Skinner and Williams, 2012). Thus, in terms of the former, the seemingly gender-neutral nature of the work-life balance concept and the 'depoliticisation' of choices made disguise its role in the reproduction of gender inequalities. The political consequences of choosing to 'opt out', as a form of retreatism and return to traditional identities (Gill and Scharff, 2011) are accordingly overlooked. Further, the obscuring of wider ongoing gendered discourses and practices serve to conceal how choices are socially embedded. In this respect, Lewis et al. (2007) show how the control of time is far from gender neutral. Despite the growth of women in paid work over the past 50 years, their study reveals time pressures that fall mainly on women because of their role in family care.

These differences may well be exacerbated in non-Western contexts and here Ozbilgin et al. (2011) argue for the incorporation of 'excluded groups' and for consideration of different non-traditional or non-Western family structures in WLB research. As they argue, WLB literature has tended to focus on a single strand of diversity namely gender, to the exclusion of other forms of difference such as those around ethnicity or race. They accordingly suggest attention be given to non-work factors such as leisure activities, religious affiliation, volunteer commitments and the support of extended families and how their influences 'play out' in different national and non-Western contexts.

Here they point to research suggesting that ethnic minorities living in the United Kingdom face greater difficulties reconciling employment and family responsibilities due to cultural factors that place greater burdens on women within the domestic sphere. Thus, Asian households are more likely to be multi-generational with grandparents providing childcare—though household responsibilities of women are often extended considerably to include care for parents and parents-in-law. As they argue, we, therefore, have to take into account different historical trajectories of 'feminist, religious, conservative and progressive politics' (Ozbilgin et al., 2011: 183) in looking at how WLB is experienced and the choices made. On this basis, the WLB literature in general tends to have highly Westernised dimensions (Bardoel, De Cieri, and Santos, 2008; Mordi, Mmieh, and Ojo, 2013) that overlooks how WLB is shaped by the community fabric. Little is known, however, about how these cultural sensibilities in relation to WLB coincide with a postfeminist gender regime and the implications for individuals concerned. For example, as Springer (2007) suggests, the black postfeminist subject is positioned through a racialised 'having-it-all' discourse and practice. With clear implications for WLB, she is seen to have excessive obligations both at work and in the home which is expected to expertly manage. She must continue to be 'everything to everybody' whilst maintaining her sense of self—a theme we pick up next.

Postfeminism in Non-Western Contexts

The tendency to see postfeminism as a Western phenomena that has significance for the white middle class, arguably excludes both Western women of colour as well as women in non-Western contexts. As McRobbie (2009) contends, pointing to the exclusionary nature of postfeminist discourses, the racialised and classed characteristics of postfeminism reinforces notions of Western superiority which positions Western women as 'sexually free' and unconstrained and non-Western women as victimised and oppressed. This serves to reinstate Western whiteness as the dominant cultural norm and forcloses any sense of solidarity and shared experience.

However, as Dosekun (2015) and Jess Butler (2013) argue, it is an oversimplification to see women of colour as excluded from postfeminism. Here they show how black women enact postfeminism in popular US culture through TV and film (e.g. *The Real Housewives of Atlanta*, an American TV series based on the personal and professional lives of several black women and *Keeping up with the Kardashians*, which similarly focuses on four sisters in an ethnic-minority family). This enactment can also be seen in celebrity culture where women of colour embrace femininity and consumerism (e.g. Rihanna, Jennifer Lopez). As they suggest, while postfeminism promotes a limited form of femininity that reinstates whiteness as the standard, nonwhite women are not wholly excluded or unaffected by postfeminist discourses. In this respect, Dosekun (2015) refers to a need to challenge the ideal postfeminist subject as a white, Western heterosexual woman and argues for a transnational approach. This recognises postfeminism as a transnational culture—as a global cultural sensibility (Lazar, 2011) that travels—placing emphasis on how it can incorporate racial difference. As Jess Butler (2013) notes,

> As a versatile and pervasive cultural discourse, postfeminism can travel through complex social terrains, deftly adapting to cultural, economic, and political shifts while maintaining its core characteristics.
>
> Jess Butler (2013: 45)

In other words, as she argues, a useful focus is on how postfeminist discourses are taken up and challenged—what "claims and boundaries are constructed by different groups across a variety of contexts" (Butler, 2013: 49) and how the forms of participation are regulated and policed. For example, Dosekun (2015) points to neoliberalist inspired 'turn to girls' in policy and popular discourses whereby young women are called upon in non-Western contexts to become empowered postfeminist subjects through institutionalised development programmes (e.g. from multi-national corporations and the World Bank). These 'global girls' (McRobbie, 2009) are incorporated as earners (ambitious, hard working, motivated) into largely unequal employment relations based on long hours and low wages. The ideal 'third world subject' is accordingly placated by minimal wages and by access to consumer culture (McRobbie, 2009). As with white women, political activism is rejected as 'redundant' in favour of (albeit limited) individual rewards including potential incorporation into the postfeminist space of consumption and greater visibility through work.

This leads us to address how postfeminist culture emerges outside the West and how nonwhite women are included within its relations of power. As example, Lazar (2006) shows, in the context of Singapore, how 'power femininity' is enunciated by international advertising companies through co-opting a notion of 'global sisterhood' and 'consumer feminism' that both erase and acknowledge difference through the aestheticisation of women's physical appearance. As Springer (2007) notes, this difference forms part of postfeminist's 'racial agenda' which seeks to make race another commodity for consumption—where racialised postfeminism means a commodifcation of otherness that 'spices up' an otherwise 'dull' mainstream white culture. Such 'exoticism' forms, in part, the basis of Dosekun's (2015) study of 'spectacular femininities' among Nigerian women in Lagos. Here, women's sense of empowerment is partly manifest through a 'hyper-feminine' aesthetic style (excessive make-up, eyelash extensions, long nails), seen as freely chosen and where beauty as a form of 'stylised freedom' is represented as strength and power. This taps into what Springer (2007) refers to as a racialised, postfeminist subject—namely, a 'strongblackwoman' as both 'sassy' and tough—a subject position which at the same time, as Jess Butler (2103) contends, celebrates femininity as being actively chosen.

Taken together, this helps young women in particular to challenge traditional associations of femininity with weakness and subordination while placing emphasis, along with postfeminism, on sexual difference. This overrides patriarchal associations and serves to resignify strength and a stylized femininity as "resources consciously embraced by women in the 'project of the self'" (Lazar, 2006: 508). Meanings around self-transformation, empowerment and agency help to refute suggestions of patriarchal power and serve to position the struggle for equality as complete. As Dosekun (2015) suggests, young black women take for granted celebratory and 'common sense' rhetorics of 'choice' and 'empowerment'—yet they struggle to articulate their national or local feminist histories or manage to make sense of their personal experience of pervasive sexism in critical feminist terms.

WLB as Weight: Examples From Nigeria

In addressing how WLB may be experienced in a non-Western context, we draw on examples from a Nigerian study of 18 female doctors, most of whom were married with children. The study explored how women interpret and manage WLB issues in their working lives—more specifically, how and to what extent postfeminist culture, particularly in relation to issues of obligation and choice, were emergent in this context and the implications for women concerned.

The largest African economy, with a substantial growth rate (7% over the last ten years), Nigeria is characterised by a stark dichotomy between rich and poor. Over two-thirds of Nigerians are classified as living in poverty (CIA World Factbook, 2016) with the proportion of total income earned by the poorest fifth of the population standing at only 4.4% (Umukoro, 2012). These levels of poverty and of income inequality have profound implications for the health-care sector: most households in Nigeria have sole responsibility for financing their own health costs. In addition, there are severe provider problems including unreliable infrastructures, shortages of manpower and limited funds. With a ratio of about 1 doctor to 5,000 people, health services (particularly in rural areas) struggle to provide essential care (Ojo and Akinwumi, 2015). This puts immense pressure on those working in the health-care sector in terms of long hours, workloads and limited resources. These pressures are arguably exacerbated for women given the deeply patriarchal nature of Nigerian society which, despite an increased relevance of dual career households (Akanji, 2013) still positions men in the breadwinner role.

As a collectivist culture, family and community play an important role in the lives of men and women though it is women who take a larger share of responsibility. Women must therefore combine a full-time and challenging career with the potential pressures associated with domestic responsibilities that can include childcare as well as care for elders and extended family members who may be residing with and dependent upon the family (while no doctor in the sample had more than three children, in many cases, up to ten people lived within the home). These responsibilities were exacerbated by the demands of frequent visitors who are expected to be afforded a high level of hospitality.

Spirituality and religion play a crucial role in managing this tension—supporting women and offering a way of life that gives meaning, helping individuals concerned to transcend the material demands of day to day living. As one registrar commented, "(The) *God factor has been the backbone to my ability to be able to cope with the things of life*". On a more pragmatic level, and in the absence of work-based support or provision such as flexible working, WLB can be managed through outsourcing (live-in maid, driver, cook)—a common practice among high income earners where family members or teenage children of friends are recruited from rural areas as 'house help'. Together, this highlights, as Lewis et al. (2007) suggest, the importance of cultural factors in understanding WLB issues, often overlooked in Western accounts.

Gender Denial and Resilience

The women doctors in the study were all highly educated, ambitious and exhibited traits associated with achievement and responsibility—often talking in terms of 'personal goals' and aspirations, resonant with neoliberal discourses of progress and social mobility. Belief in gender equality, underpinned by the passing in 2014 of the Gender and Equal Opportunity Bill, was widespread with all women expressing faith in the existence of equality of opportunity (within the confines of the greater demands made on women, discussed next). Reference to 'injustice' or 'unfairness' was avoided. This is despite the patriarchal nature of Nigerian society and the strict adherence to gender specific roles as well as the belief in what is seen as a 'natural' gender order that positions women disadvantageously.

Following the aforementioned, and as has been found in Western contexts (Gill and Scharff, 2011; McRobbie, 2009), Nigerian doctors distanced themselves from gender and were reluctant to consider whether and how gender might be an issue in their working lives. In one typical comment, a young intern gave preference to a gender-neutral discourse around professionalism and 'doing a job', with gender conflated in unwelcome terms with preferential treatment:

> I am not sure I have anything to say about that (gender discrimination). As a female doctor, I am not facing any challenge. There's no stereotype, and I like to do my job without taking advantage of anything.

Rather, female doctors had a strong sense of self-belief, celebrating their strength as women in overcoming adversity and overturning popular stereotypes of women's 'weaknesses'. Here, commitment to work could be seen as the basis of strength and fortitude. A senior registrar summarised, with implicit reference to particular difficulties she had encountered:

> There are some situations I have gone through . . . I never believed that I was able to cope. I have come to realise that as a woman you have strength, even though they look at us as the weaker sex I am not sure we are that weak, because when your heart is set to do something. No matter what you go through you keep focus, and you can get results because your mind is made up.

As Baker (2008) found in the context of Australia, one way in which young women reconcile claims to near equality with experiences of disadvantage is by reframing their experience on the basis of individual strength and resilience—tapping into postfeminist discourses around female ambition, perseverance and success. As she points out, neoliberalism promotes the message that individual success (as well as the need to overcome problems that might compromise that success) is determined by personal skills and capacities. Coupled with the postfeminist understanding of equality as having been achieved, it is perhaps not surprising that women, in both national contexts, adhere to narratives of personal responsibility, strength and agency 'no matter what'. More specific to Nigeria, as Akanji (2013) notes, survival and personal hardiness are traits that women develop as coping resources. Drawing on Springer's (2007) work, this resonates with the 'strongblackwoman' discourse referred to earlier, which, as she argues, is one way in which postfeminism interpolates a racialised postfeminist subject. This goes some way to assimilate black women into the rhetoric of 'having it all'—of successfully managing the demands of both work and home—a rhetoric, implicit in women's accounts, which we problematise further below.

Obligation and Choice

As we have seen, this rhetoric underpins the prominence of a postfeminist subject as a woman of agency with capacities for choice—captured in particular in Hakim's (2000) 'adaptive' preference grouping where women choose to combine work in the public with work in the home. This preference may involve compromise and adjusted ambition (Benschop et al., 2013) as women reconcile the demands of both domains. In Nigeria, there has been a long history of dual-income families where women could potentially be positioned as 'having it all' in choosing to combine home and a career. As doctors, the women in the study would be seen to be highly successful with the majority also having extensive domestic responsibilities to fulfil. It was common practice for women to manage the tension between work and home by compromising on their ambitions—sacrificing preferred specialisms for those seen as less demanding (e.g. in terms of being on call and/or the timing of shifts). As one intern commented ruefully, "*If I were a man I probably wouldn't be thinking about working in* (general outpatients) *because surgery is my passion*". But, as she subsequently claimed, the priority given to her role as mother—common across the sample—meant that "*family comes first*" and her preference for surgery would have to be delayed. As another commented firmly in relation to her status as mother and caregiver to members of her immediate and her wider family, "*I cannot sacrifice that!*" suggestive, as with many of the women interviewed, of a high level of satisfaction drawn from and primacy given to her traditional role.

The postfeminist notion of 'having it all' is not only affected by adjusted ambition but overlooks some of the cultural pressures and cultural constraints that women in some contexts face. As we have seen, in the context of Nigeria, the burden of responsibility for the domestic sphere falls almost entirely on women despite the heavy demands made on them in the world of work. Doctors work long hours—universally identified as a source of overload and stress—that involve shift work and being on call (women in our sample routinely work 48 hours at a stretch). High patient numbers and inadequate resources (poor or missing equipment; power cuts) add to the burdens and unpredictability of the job. This notwithstanding, domestic demands of the home are accepted as an inevitable part of their gender role:

> Although I had help from my little cousin, it was not easy for me, because it is not like I am the guy. I'm a female, so I have to cook, clean, organise the home, plan, things come up like your baby can fall ill, and you have to try and settle that. And of course cater to your husband's needs.

In some cases, the concept of choice was drawn upon to rationalise the unequal share in the domestic sphere. As in the quote, choice frequently transposed into *obligation* (as in a duty or requirement) though such obligations were often positioned as being freely given. A young registrar commented:

> Well my husband likes taking care of our baby, but household chores no. I do not know why he has a problem with that we have to fight and struggle, and I have made up my mind not to quarrel over things like this anymore. He says, is it not the job of a woman? Sometimes he might even add to the burden, because of the arguments to do it.

Here, choice (*"I have made up my mind"*) is used to denote consent to an inequitable situation which may otherwise lead to conflict and stress as well as an extra load (*"he might even add to the burden"*). Choice is, however, drawn upon to signify a 'voluntary and informed decision' (Baker, 2008: 57). This decision, oriented towards acceptance and consent in a context of entrenched social demands regarding domestic work (*"is it not the job of a woman?"*) is nevertheless presented in voluntarist terms rather than in terms of an obligation that has been imposed. This suggests that while gratification may be gained from yielding to cultural expectations and while satisfaction may be drawn from what is presented as a 'reified' role of mother and caregiver, consent in situations of inequality can never, as Baker suggests, be seen in neutral terms.

Discussion: WLB as Weight and 'Doing-it-all'

In this chapter, we have critically engaged with the postfeminist emphasis on balance and choice through consideration of WLB in a non-Western context. In this respect, Nigerian women doctors, all of whom were working full time and with the majority having domestic and caring responsibilities in the private sphere, largely conform to Hakim's 'adaptive' preference grouping based on the notion that, in combining work and home, women can 'have-it-all'. However, rather than focussing on *balance* between the 'masculine' world of work and the 'feminine' domain of home as a harmonious state of equilibrium (Clarke et al., 2004) or well-being (Buddhapriya, 2005), we interpret women's experience through the concept of burden and *weight*. This captures the burdens of responsibility Nigerian women face as they seek to manage the excessive demands of both domains—seeking to 'do-it-all' in an exemplary manner. Cultural expectations concerning women's role within the home and the weight of responsibilities towards family and community combine with long hours, limited resources and heavy workloads.

As Dosekun (2015) points out, existing scholarship on postfeminism overwhelmingly concerns the Western world and here she call for attention towards how postfeminism translates in non-Western contexts. As she suggests, postfeminism is readily 'transnationalised' in that, as a set of discourses and material practices, it can be 'broadcast' across borders with implications for how women see their lives and how they see themselves. Here we can identify how the postfeminist focus on agency and empowerment finds purchase in Nigerian women's accounts: how women display attachment to postfeminist and neoliberal notions of progress, aspiration and personal capacity, how through 'gender denial' women resist acknowledgement of structural gender based constraints (despite the deeply patriarchal nature of Nigerian society) and how domestic obligations and consent to the status quo are often presented as freely given as women recapture agency and draw on religious doctrine and cultural norms to justify career choices and inequalities at home.

At the same time, a racialised postfeminist sensibility emerges which fails to accommodate the Western idea of 'having it all' that seemingly results from free choices made, reflective of individual privilege and preference through 'pleasing oneself'. In other words, the Western context presents 'having it all' as a freedom and privilege that women 'deserve'. As Springer (2007) insists, black women have never been fully included in the postfeminist 'having it all' discourse, positioned as something to be desired and achieved. This is because, resonant with our examples, black women are doing too much and are carrying too many burdens already. In our terms, they experience the work/life interface as excessive loads and responsibilities, 'doing-it-all' in work and in the home. This finds purchase in Springer's (2007) account of the racialised 'strongblackwoman' discourse in popular culture which assumes that black women already have too many obligations—where from our examples women draw on a rhetoric of inevitability, commitments and duties as well as personal fortitude and strength.

Supported by the examples from our study, and as Springer (2007) suggests, racialised postfeminism means being available and 'doing everything for everyone' through personal sacrifice and care, with the black woman supposedly accommodating the demands made upon her with equanimity and ease. In fact, looking at popular culture, she argues that being middle class *demands* that black women remain in the public sphere of work in order to gain respectability, in our terms 'doing-it-all' in both the public and the private domains. While postfeminist white, middle class women can choose, as 'yummy mummies', to retreat to the home this choice is not open to all. The option of retreatism sits uneasily with black women's experiences because it carries racialised connotations of indolence—as well as classed and racialised associations with the stay-at-home 'welfare queen', dependent on the state and with more children than she can afford. Black women are expected to conform, in racialised terms, to a resurrected and modernised 'loyal servant' to others, sacrificing personal preferences for other people's welfare and interests at work and in the home. A 'yummy mummy' lifestyle of leisure and indulgence is accordingly not seen as suitable for this group.

Rather than seeing postfeminism as a white, Western phenomenon, with little purchase beyond this context, we can see how race is always present in articulations of its sensibility if only as a 'counterpart' (Springer, 2007) against which white women's ways are defined. We have shown in this chapter how postfeminism interpolates women in Nigeria into an understanding of capacity and agency—though the postfeminist sense of entitlement to self-fulfilment and 'pleasing oneself' have little relevance in Nigerian women's lives. We identify aspects of a 'racialised postfeminism' based on the ability to 'do-it-all', as manifest in the heavy burdens experienced at the work/life interface, and how cultural pressures and expectations actively promote choice as obligation and consent, supporting some subject positions whilst others are foreclosed. Further, by drawing on understandings of WLB among Nigerian doctors and the 'free' choices they supposedly face, we show how middle class black women must tread a contextually contingent 'delicate balance' between subordination to male authority, domestic responsibilities and ambition/achievement in a professional career.

References

Adams, M. (2017). Postfeminism, neoliberalism and a "successfully" balanced femininity in celebrity CEO autobiographies. *Gender Work and Organization*, 24(3): 314–325.

Akanji, B.O. (2013). An exploratory study of work-life balance in Nigeria: Employees' perspectives of coping with the role conflicts. *International Journal of Research Studies in Management*, 2(2): 100–114.

Baker, J. (2008). The ideology of choice: Overstating progress and hiding injustice in the lives of young women: Findings from a study in North Queensland, Australia. *Women's Studies International Forum*, 31: 53–64.

Bardoel, E.A., De Cieri, H., and Santos, C. (2008). A review of work-life research in Australia and New Zealand. *Asia Pacific Journal of Human Resources*, 46(3): 316–333.

Benschop, Y., van den Brink, M., Doorewaard, H., and Leenders, J. (2013). Discourses of ambition, gender and part-time work. *Human Relations*, 66(5): 699–723.

Buddhapriya, S. (2005). Balancing work and life: Implications for business. *Indian Journal of Industrial Relations*, 41(2): 233–247.

Butler, J. (2013). For white girls only? Postfeminism and the politics of inclusion. *Feminist Formations*, 25(1): 35–58.

Caproni, P.J. (2004). Work/life balance you can't get there from here. *The Journal of Applied Behavioral Science*, 40(2): 208–218.

Central Intelligence Agency. (2016). *The World Factbook.* Available at: www.cia.gov/library/publications/the-world-factbook/geos/ni.html Accessed 11 August 2016.

Clark, S.C. (2000). Work/family border theory: A new theory of work/family balance. *Human Relations*, 53(6): 747–770.

Clarke, M.C., Koch, L.C. and Hill, E.J. (2004) The work-family interface: Differentiating balance and fit. *Family and Consumer Sciences Research Journal*, 33(2): 121–140.

Crompton, R., Lewis, S. and Lyonette, C. (2007) Introduction: the unravelling of the male breadwinner model and some of its consequences. In R. Crompton, S. Lewis, and C. Lyonette (Eds.), *Women, Men, Work and Family in Europe* (pp. 1–16). Basingstoke: Palgrave Macmillan.

Dosekun, S. (2015). For western girls only? Postfeminism as transnational culture. *Feminist Media Studies*, 15(6): 960–975.

Gill, R., and Scharff, C. (Eds.). (2011). *New Femininities: Postfeminism, Neoliberalism and Subjectivity.* Basingstoke: Palgrave Macmillan.

Hakim, C. (2000). *Work-Lifestyle Choices in the 21st Century.* Oxford: Oxford University Press.

Hochschild, A. (1989). *The Second Shift.* New York: Avon Books.

Hyman, J., and Summers, J. (2004). Lacking balance? Work-life employment practices in the modern economy. *Personnel Review*, 33(4): 418–429.

Kaiser, S., Ringlstetter, M.J., Eikhof, D.R., and e Cunha, P.M. (2011). *Creating Balance? International Perspectives on the Work Life Integration of Professionals.* Heidelberg, Dordrecht and London: Springer.

Lazar, M.M. (2006). "Discover the power of femininity!": Analyzing global "power femininity" in local advertising. *Feminist Media Studies*, 6(4): 505–517.

Lazar, M.M. (2011) The right to be beautiful: Postfeminist identity and consumer beauty advertising. In R. Gill and C. Scharff (Eds), *New Femininities: Postfeminism, Neoliberalism and Subjectivity* (pp. 37–51). Basingstoke: Palgrave Macmillan.

Lewis, P. (2014). Postfeminism, femininities and organization studies: Exploring a new agenda. *Organization Studies*, 35(12): 1845–1866.

Lewis, P., and Simpson, R. (2015). Understanding and researching choice in women's career trajectories. In A. Broadbridge and S. Fielden (Eds.), *Handbook of Gendered Careers in Management: Getting in, Getting on, Getting out* (pp. 44–60). Cheltenham: Edward Elgar.

Lewis, S., Gambles, R., and Rapoport, R. (2007). The constraints of a "work-life balance" approach: An international perspective. *The International Journal of Human Resource Management*, 18(3): 360–373.

McRobbie, A. (2009). *The Aftermath of Feminism: Gender, Culture and Social Change.* London: Sage.

Mordi, C., Mmieh, F., and Ojo, S.I. (2013). An exploratory study of managers' perspective of work-life balance in Nigeria: A case analysis of the Nigerian banking sector. *Thunderbird International Business Review*, 55(1): 55–75.

Negra, D. (2009). *What a Girl Wants? Fantasizing the Reclamation of Self in Postfeminism.* London: Routledge.

Ojo, T.O., and Akinwumi, A.F. (2015). Doctors as managers of healthcare resources in Nigeria: Evolving roles and current challenges. *Nigerian Medical Journal: Journal of the Nigeria Medical Association*, 56(6): 375.

Özbilgin, M.F., Beauregard, T.A., Tatli, A., and Bell, M.P. (2011). Work-life, diversity and intersectionality: A critical review and research agenda. *International Journal of Management Reviews*, 13(2): 177–198.

Pocock, B., Skinner, N., and Williams, P. (2012). *Time Bomb: Work, Rest and Play in Australia Today*. Sydney: UNSW Press.

Probyn, E. (1990). New traditionalism and post-feminism: TV does the home. *Screen*, 31(2): 147–159.

Singh, S. (2013). Work life balance: A literature review. *Global Journal of Commerce & Management Perspective*, 2(3): 84–91.

Sorensen, S. (2017). The "performativity of choice": Postfeminist perspectives on work-life balance focuses. *Gender Work and Organization*, 24(3): 297–313.

Springer, K. (2007). Divas, evil black bitches and bitter black women. In D. Negra and Y. Tasker (Eds.), *Interrogating Postfeminism: Gender, Politics and Popular Culture* (pp. 249–276). Durham, NC: Duke University Press.

Tasker, Y., and Negra, D. (Eds.). (2007). *Interrogating Postfeminism*. London: Duke University Press.

Umukoro, N. (2012). Governance and public healthcare in Nigeria. *Journal of Health Management*, 14(4): 381–395.

3 Keep Calm and Carry on Being Slinky

Postfeminism, Resilience Coaching and Whiteness

Elaine Swan

Racism has long depended on hierarchies of civility, on cultural distinctions of breeding, character, and psychological disposition, on the relationship between the hidden essence of race and what were claimed to be its visual markers.

(Stoler and Cooper, 1997: 34)

I start with this quote as the authors insist on the imbrication of the 'psychological' with the racialisation of people. We might not associate the psychological with race. But historians, Ann Stoler and Frederick Cooper foreground the historical and cultural construction of what we take to be psychological traits and stress how these culturally mark white middle-class people as psychologically and emotionally superior. Drawing inspiration from this view, I examine the entanglements of whiteness, coaching and postfeminism. In particular, I situate coaching within what Nikolas Rose (1989, 1996) after Michel Foucault calls the 'psy' complex. Briefly explained, the 'psy' denotes a body of professional discourses and psychological practices, techniques, judgments and ethics, which proliferate across a wide range of cultural and social domains. Psy practices claim to diagnose and solve workplace, romantic, bodily, parenting and other life 'problems'. Scholars deploy the term 'psy' to indicate they work outside of psychology and critically evaluate the effects and politics of psychological disciplines such as psychology, psychiatry and psychotherapy. Often, but not always, these critiques are Foucauldian.

My research to date examines how such practices in the workplace—which includes coaching, interpersonal skills training, self-help, team building, positive psychology, emotional intelligence—are gendering, racialising and classing (Swan, 2006, 2008, 2010, 2017). In this chapter, I focus on 'resilience coaching' aimed at women through a thematic analysis of websites and associated media. The concept of resilience traverses as a new ethical and political ideal across many fields from the military to self-help culture (James, 2013; Neocleous, 2012). Feminist and music cultural theorist, Robin James (2014, 2015a) examines the gendered and racialised effects of postfeminist neoliberal resilience discourse in music. Her main argument is that in inciting minoritised groups to overcome the injuries and inequalities caused by neoliberalism, capitalism and patriarchy, resilience discourse reconsolidates them (James, 2014, 2015a, 2015b). In essence, 'white supremacist capitalist patriarchy' encourages minoritised groups to recycle the injuries it causes for their own personal gain and for surplus value for hegemonic institutions. James distinguishes postfeminist and neoliberal 'resilience discourse' from the more political, radical coping strategies of oppressed groups. Accordingly, I coin the term 'psy-resilience' in this chapter to emphasise the imbrication of psy practices and resilience in coaching, and I illustrate elements of psy-resilience in coaching from coaching websites and texts.

To build my argument for the relevance of this chapter within debates about postfeminism, I start by explaining why we need to study coaching to understand postfeminism in organisations. I will then discuss the lack of attention paid to whiteness in organisation studies and coaching studies. My focus on coaching for women forms part of a wider project in organisational theory pioneered by Patricia Lewis, Elisabeth K. Kelan and Rosalind Gill and others in deploying postfeminism as an analytic trained on organisational practices and femininities. In particular, Lewis argues that such an approach helps us see how workplace femininity is being reconfigured. I argue that we can understand this reconfiguring through studies of the psy and postfeminism. As several theorists stress, core tenets of postfeminism—individualism, choice, self-invention, makeovers (Baker, 2010; Gill, 2007, 2008; Lewis, 2014; McRobbie, 2009)—are the staples of workplace psychology, including coaching aimed at women (Swan, 2006, 2008, 2017).

Coaching for women is an important site for analysis in postfeminist scholarship on organisations for a number of reasons. First, as Rosalind Gill (2016) puts it, postfeminism has a 'psychic life', remaking our subjectivities and relationships and recasting injustice in terms of individual deficits and solutions. The makeover, self-surveillance and self-transformation are defining features of postfeminist psy culture (Baker, 2010; Gill, 2016; Gill and Orgad, 2015; Kauppinen, 2013; Negra, 2009; Ringrose and Walkerdine, 2008; Salmenniemi and Adamson, 2015). Postfeminist makeover culture promulgates the idea that women's minds, emotions, careers, lives and bodies can all do with a makeover, reinforcing white middle-class feminised characteristics of malleability and flexibility (Gill, 2008; Swan, 2008, 2010, 2017). As a practice of self-work, psychic labour, and self-transformation, much coaching for women conforms to the makeover paradigm with its postfeminist ideals of self-transformation, choice and individualism.

A second reason why coaching is important for organisational studies of postfeminism is that women are seen as the ideal subject of self-transformation. Indeed, Rosalind Gill and colleagues argue, women workers, much more than men, are incited 'to remodel their interiority, their subjectivity, for example to make themselves into more confident or "resilient" subjects in the workplace' (2017: 231). But scholars of postfeminism emphasise that it is middle-class, white women who are constructed as the 'ur' self-transforming subject. Such self-work is the project of middle-class white women economically in that they have the income to be able to purchase self-improvement services and culturally because middle-class, white women are positioned through postfeminist ideas of individualism, potential, emotional control and self-disciplining interiority (Baker, 2010; Blackman, 2004, 2005, 2007; Pfister, 1997). Seen as having a 'proper subjectivity', middle-class white women are constructed in opposition to racially minoritised and working-class white women, who are culturally viewed as less willing, and less able, to reinvent themselves, possessing shallow, and 'defective psychologies' (Lawler, 2005; Skeggs, 2002, 2004; Steedman, 2002). Racially minoritised and white working-class people are often forced to narrate themselves psychologistically by state institutions; in contrast, the middle-classes take up psy practices voluntarily as part of work or leisure commitments (Lawler, 2005; Skeggs, 2004; Steedman, 2002, Walkerdine, 1996).

Thirdly, postfeminism recognises and repudiates feminism (Lewis, 2014; McRobbie, 2009; Negra, 2009). Lewis (2014) and Gill and colleagues show how sexism and gender inequalities in the workplace are acknowledged rather than denied but seen as something 'past' or 'over', or cast in racist/Islamophobic discourse as found elsewhere (2017: 227). Organisational, societal, structural or collective solutions are disavowed through an emphasis upon the need for women to change through 'individualising tendences' (Gill and Orgad, 2015). In this vein, Rosalind Gill and Christina Scharff stress that individualism in postfeminism has 'almost entirely replaced notions of the social or political, or any idea of individuals as subject to pressures, constraints or influence from outside themselves' (2011: 7). As feminists show, psychology and psy practices chime with this 'postfeminist common sense'. Thus, popular psychology de-socialises and de-politicises women's understanding of themselves, and their problems through ideas symbiotic with the hyper-individualising tendencies of postfeminism (Swan, 2017).

To date, postfeminist analyses of resilience in popular psychology are limited. But in a related example, Gill and Shani Orgad (2015) discuss the rise of confidence as a technology of the self. Most infamously, Sheryl Sandberg's book and programme *Lean In* appears to embrace feminism but ignores collective politics and structural solutions. What is important here is that confidence discourse work to 'name, diagnose and propose solutions to . . . archetypal feminist questions about labour, value and the body' (Gill and Orgad, 2015: 325). Thus, Gill and Orgad argue that feminism itself is 'made over' into confidence. Like psy-resilience, confidence is a 'psy' approach involving 'techniques, knowledges and affective apparatuses, experts, programmes' (2015: 326), which incites a new kind of female subject. In characteristic postfeminist ways, confidence discourse denies 'the injuries inflicted by structures of inequality' (2015: 324), reproduces a 'deficit model of women' (2015: 327) and displaces collective feminist interventions with 'heightened modes of self-regulation' (2015: 324). Confidence discourse genders by suggesting that it is women's lack, individualised and abstracted from socio-cultural structures, and not patriarchal capitalism or institutionalised sexism which blocks women's progress in the workplace. Importantly then for this chapter, Gill and Orgad only allude to the reconfiguring of femininity through the psychological and emotional nor do they reflect on confidence in relation to race and whiteness.

Whilst there is scholarly interest in postfeminism and popular psychology, postfeminist analyses of coaching are few and far between, with much analysis focused on self-help discourse in books and magazines. This matters to organisation studies because of the rise of self-work, growth in women coaches, proliferation of therapeutic cultures in the workplace and the cultural and economic feminisation of coaching. Thus, as coaching sociologist Molly George notes, contemporary postindustrial conditions mean that self-improvement and 'a turn inwards' are sold 'as an antidote to economic uncertainty' (2013: 179). Furthermore, postfeminist analyses of 'psy' culture need to attend to race because as critical race theorists insist 'psy' practices including those in workplaces are not race neutral and reproduce whiteness and racism.

It might be difficult to imagine that coaching reproduce whiteness, partly because many white people normalise and universalise whiteness. Moreover, mainstream organisational theorists overlook whiteness studies in organisational studies (for instance, Grimes, 2002; Hunter, Swan, and Grimes, 2010; Liu and Baker, 2016; Nkomo, 1992; Nkomo and Al Ariss, 2014; Samaluk, 2014; Swan, 2010). Broadly speaking these theorists understand whiteness as a congeries of historic, economic, cultural, social, bodily phenomenological and psychological processes which reproduce racism, privilege, power and oppression. As Helena Liu and Colin Baker (2016) argue, organisational theorists need to 'denaturalise whiteness' to challenge white power and white privilege in organisations. In line with this, I show how whiteness is reproduced, not just through visual representations of coaches and coaching as I have written elsewhere, but through ideas about the psychological and more specifically, notions of emotional control, positivity and enterprise (Swan, 2017). Given psychology has intensive cultural authority as a form of expert knowledge, its whiteness needs interrogating. Extending studies of postfeminism and organisations to discuss whiteness matters because its invisibility sustains power, reproduces racial inequality and racism, with people of colour having to negotiate white expectations and racism in the workplace (Boulton, 2015). A few cultural theorists link postfeminism and whiteness to illustrate how postfeminist culture idealises white middle-class femininity and pathologises racialised and working-class others (Wilkes, 2015), although this does not mean that all postfeminist culture is white or Western (Baker, 2010; Dosekun, 2015; Lazar, 2006).

Furthermore, white feminism itself reproduces racism, exclusion and racial inequalities. As Caroline McFadden (2011) argues, white feminists exhibit racism towards nonwhite women by theorising only about white women, even when they claim to be writing about all women. In doing this, white feminists create an exclusionary feminism which ignores people of colour's needs and racism as a form of oppression. Indeed, organisational theorists Liu and Baker (2016), as with other leading critical race theorists, stress that white women's desire for innocence means they ignore their historic and contemporary complicity with white supremacy (Moon, 1999; Moreton-Robinson, 2000; Srivastava, 2005; Sullivan, 2014).

Thus, this chapter contributes to feminist studies of postfeminism in organisations through exploring how resilience coaching produces whiteness connected to postfeminism, resulting in a configuration of a particular form of workplace femininity. Thus, I analyse coaching websites and texts that profile resilience coaching in order to show how whiteness and postfeminism are entangled through the vehicle of coaching. In the rest of the chapter, I briefly describe coaching as a practice, introduce the rise of resilience discourse and subjects, define whiteness, before analysing websites and coaching media from the United States and United Kingdom which focus on resilience coaching aimed at women.

Resilience Coaching

A relatively new industry, and occupational group, coaching has proliferated phenomenally in the last ten years with coaches and their accrediting bodies working in countries such as the United States, United Kingdom, Germany, Scandinavia, Australia and Asia (George, 2013; Swan, 2017). Coaching advertising and practitioner literature attempt to distinguish different forms of coaching in relation to their purpose and intent: lifestyle, executive, business, performance and career, to name but a few. Hence, broadly speaking, life coaching is presented as more individually focused and aimed at a change in life or career; executive coaching is understood as organisationally focused on strategic decision making; and performance coaching on improving productivity and effectiveness. Coaching aimed at women uses this terminology but profiles career coaching, focused on the specific needs of women's career management. Resilience coaching sits under career coaching and is a recent development in the past five years or so. Practitioners claim that coaching is a more 'facilitative' or 'non-directive' relationship than training or consulting, relying less on business expertise than on the interpersonal expertise of listening and questioning. Feminist research insists that these ways of performing coaching are gendered, racialised and classed (Swan, 2006, 2017; George, 2013; Graf and Pawelczyk, 2014; Pawelczyk and Graf, 2011). By drawing on cultural feminisation strategies, coaching represents part of the shift to 'gender as work' and therefore an important site for postfeminist organisational studies (Adkins, 2001; Lewis, 2014). At the same time, race and whiteness have been overlooked.

Resilience coaching echoes the extensive deployment of resilience discourse in the military, anti-terrorism, international relations, ecological and disaster management, community development, post-2011 city riots and school programmes (James, 2015b; Joseph, 2013; O'Malley, 2010; Reid, 2012; Welsh, 2014). Generally meaning 'preparedness and prevention', resilience in this more macro sense, represents a 'reimagining of welfare state policy through a focus on: personal resilience, community resilience and economic resilience' (Welsh, 2014: 19). But as Mark Neocleous writes, the concept of resilience now

> straddle[s] the private as well as the public, the personal as well as the political, the subjective as well as the objective, and so systemic, organizational, and political resilience is connected to personal resilience.
>
> (2012: 192)

Indeed, Foucauldian social theorists, such as Pat O'Malley (2010), argue that not only are we incited to be entrepreneurial and responsible, but we now have to 'be resilient'. As he writes, we are expected to withstand shocks, grasp opportunities and develop self-awareness in a risky world. Echoing critiques of postfeminism, scholars worry about its individualised, depoliticising tactics. For example, Katie Aubrecht (2012), in her excoriating critique of university advice on resilience for students with disabilities, shows how the concept of resilience recasts the social experience of oppression as individual traits.

Scholars foreground the deleterious political effects of such models of resilience. For Neocleous, training in resilience 'weds us to a deeply conservative mode of thinking . . . a means of cutting off political alternatives' (2012: 189). Julien Reid goes much further:

> The human here is conceived as resilient in so far as it adapts to rather than resists the conditions of its suffering in the world. To be resilient is to forego the very power of resistance.
>
> (2012: 76)

But in spite of these swingeing critiques, very few authors refer specifically to gendered, classed or racialised politics and the implications of resilience discourse at the level of policy, organisation or the subjective. Aubrecht and James are two exceptions who focus on disability, and race and gender respectively, and argue that resilience justifies and conceals exploitative social and economic relations. James, in particular, provides a rare, and vigorous racialised analysis of resilience discourse, arguing that it incites individuals and groups to perform the emotional labour of getting over the injuries and harm caused by white supremacist capitalist patriarchy. Her critical point is that such emotional labour reproduces white supremacist capitalist patriarchy. In particular, she argues that resilience discourse encourages white women to perform the emotional labour of 'overcoming' racism and sexism in order to produce a good white femininity. The performance of such a good resilient, strong femininity generates human capital for white women—for example, political or moral goodness, proper femininity, etc.— and in so doing, buttresses neoliberalism because emotional labour does not change structures. A key structure within resilience discourse for James is that we are actually invited to expose ourselves to the damage of sexism so that we can bounce back and prove our resilient, strong, postfeminist subjectivity. Hence, she argues, resilience discourse does not propose the elimination of harm but the 'active production of specific populations as damaged and damaging' (James, 2014). This means minoritised groups such as those racialised, queer, non-cis gendered and non-able-bodied. Thus, in a provocative but incisive argument, she puts forward the view that white women's resilience grounds 'the sexism and racism hiding behind the appearance of postfeminist, post-race multiculturalism' (James, 2016). To understand this complex and somewhat counter-intuitive claim in relation to coaching means clarifying how race and psy practices in organisations are entangled, and what is meant by whiteness.

Whiteness and Psy

There are few studies on how organisational practices such as Human Resource Development (HRD), Human Resources (HR) and coaching reproduce whiteness. In contrast, historians highlight the cultural and historical gendered and racialised specificities of the psychological. For instance, Stephanie Coontz (2003) argues that feminine expertise in dominant forms of emotional labour is a product of a distinctive historical mix of race and class dynamics, associated with the type of gender relations that predominate in the white middle class. Furthermore, other writers show that HR practices are not gender or race neutral. For example, in a fascinating historical analysis of Taylorist experiments on fatigue in early twentieth century France, Laura Levine Frader (1999) shows how white French workers and workers of colour were gendered and racialised differentially. She argues the working body was separated from its racialised meanings although these meanings saturated so-called objective experiments in work science. The scientists argued that Moroccans were 'sturdy' and 'energetic', and suitable for industrial work, Arabs more fit for to agricultural work, and the Indochinese 'soft and submissive', therefore better positioned in unskilled work in factories or agriculture. Thus, apparently objective work techniques reproduced and constituted racialised, gendered hierarchies and stereotypes.

In recent years, scholars have attended to the racialisation and racism of psychology and its whiteness (Riggs and Augoustinos, 2005). For example, several theorists argue that white, middle-class Euro Americans are seen to have more psychological 'depth' than other social groups (Coontz, 2003). Psychology historian, Joel Pfister is one of the few theorists to suggest that the types of psychology we see in the workplace is white. He writes,

> What still needs to be investigated is the degree to which . . . modern 'therapeutic' discourses, while often presuming to fathom and repair universal 'human nature,' have in fact contributed ideologically to the normative racial construction of whiteness.
>
> (1997: 36)

He argues that North American psychology, in particular, has been constructed through racist notions of the 'Native American Indian', cast as primitive and close to nature, and used as a figure to structure racialised constructions of psychology. The subfields of counselling and therapy have had a sustained debate about the racism of the professions. Jennifer Wallis and Reenee Singh (2014) and Eunjung Lee and Rupaleem Bhuyan (2013) argue that white therapists reify whiteness as an unmarked norm, which then non-white clients have to negotiate or resist. And even in the field of performance art, artist Miranda July explores self-help practices and argues that self-help belongs to the cultural practices of whiteness (Czudaj, 2016).

These brief examples illustrate the complexity and multifaceted nature of the category of whiteness. Indeed, critical race and whiteness scholars use the term 'whiteness' to cover a wide range of social, embodied, economic and cultural practices, ideologies, values and discourses. For instance, philosopher Charles Mills (1997) differentiates between the idea of whiteness as a phenotype, a set of power relations and a commitment to white supremacy. Whiteness studies theorise white privilege and show how it is 'repetitious mundane practices which reinforce and mask the power of privilege' (Zhang, Gajjala, and Watkins, 2012: 205). Thus, 'whiteness' does not mean phenotype. Rather whiteness is a position of high status within a racialised hierarchy. Whiteness constitutes and demarcates ideas, feelings, knowledge, social practices, cultural formations and systems of intelligibility that are identified with or attributed to white people and that are invested in by white people as 'white'. And the interconnections between the experiential lives of white people, structures of power and privilege and socio-cultural and legal context creates, and maintains the power of whiteness (Zhang et al., 2012).

Critical race theorists are unanimous that whiteness is unmarked and largely invisible to people who have access to white privilege. This is because whiteness claims universal normalcy against which racialised people are judged (Dyer, 1997; Shome, 2000). Hence, 'many white people imagine their lives to be run of the mill, normal and average and yet ideal, setting the standards for humanity and the apogee of civilisation' (Goudge, 2003: 49) As Raka Shome writes, this makes whiteness difficult to name and destabilise. Indeed, many white people cannot see how whiteness has shaped institutions, economics, politics, morals, and spaces and structures how society at large perceives reality (Mills, 1997). Through the lens of so-called colour-blindness or the postracial, many white people are ignorant of the causes and implications of racialisation. Accordingly, whiteness becomes a refusal to acknowledge how white people are implicated in social relations of privilege, domination and subordination (Goudge, 2003; Mills, 1997; McLaren, 1997).

Other theorists focus on how the body produces and performs whiteness. Thus, Anoop Nayak reminds us that whiteness is achieved through 'repetition, stylised gestures, parodic reiterations and corporeal enactments' (2003 173). Whiteness is embedded in codes of speech, inflection, and modes of thought. It can take the form of whites 'interests', 'points of view', 'material well-being', 'self-image' and notions of 'appropriate behaviour' portrayed as the norm (Thompson, 2004: 30). In a work context, Nirmal Puwar, extending Joan Acker's notion of the gendered ideal worker's body, coins the term 'the somatic ideal' to refer to organisations valorisation of white middle-class masculinity as the ideal worker. She shows how the white, masculine somatic ideal is reproduced through practices, systems, representations, customs, and behaviour within organisations. 'Whiteness and masculinity are embedded in the character and life of organisations' (Puwar, 2004: 32). Furthermore, in institutions such as the British Civil Service, 'the timing, working procedures, rituals and bodily performances endorse specifically classed notions of masculine Englishness' (2004: 36). As a result of these organisational processes, black workers are required to 'whitewash' gestures, speech patterns, interests and value systems in order to conform to the behavioural 'norms' of the workplace. More broadly speaking, whiteness works to 'normalize civility, instil rationality, erase emotion, erase difference, impose middle-class values and beliefs with an assumption of heterosexual matrix' (Villaverde, 2000: 46). In structuring ideas of the ideal worker, their form of embodiment, proper ways of behaving, and organisational emotional behaviours, I argue that whiteness inflects the ideals and techniques of workplace coaching.

Postfeminist analyses of postfeminism and popular or workplace psychology have yet to take up such important ideas. So whilst Gill's work underlines the significance of the psychic makeovers and labour in postfeminist culture, she does not examine how psy ideals and practices reconfigure workplace femininity and emotionality, and how these maybe described as white.

Method

To start to explore these imbrications, I provide an analysis of websites and documents which focus on resilience coaching, and in particular, resilience coaching aimed at women. From my review of the feminist and critical race literature on resilience and coaching, my research question became how do the web pages for resilience coaching for women represent postfeminist work femininities? How are they racialised?

My sample includes web pages on resilience coaching, web pages on resilience coaching aimed at women in the workplace, and references to resilience coaching in reports located on web pages. I located the websites through a Google search for resilience coaching for women accessed in the period from November 2016 to February 2017. My criteria for selecting websites for analysis in this article is that they specialised in resilience coaching, provided extensive verbal text, and exemplified a number of themes in the academic literature. The websites analysed specifically for this chapter are as follows:

- The 'School of Life' founded by popular philosopher Alain Boton
- The UK Department for Health
- The UK Chartered Institute of Personnel and Development (CIPD)
- UK 'resilience coach' Dr Carole Pemberton who has written a book on resilience coaching
- UK Shapiro coaching (coach wrote the Tough at the Top report on women's resilience)
- UK businesssake coaching
- Internationally based, The Coaching Federation
- UK Pathway Coaching
- US The Resilience Group
- US Tiara International Coaching
- A report entitled *Tough at the Top? New Rules of Resilience for Women's Leadership Success* commissioned by UK companies, Nationwide Building Society and Vodafone
- A book entitled *Coaching Women to Lead*, by Averil Leimon, Francois Moscovici, and Helen Goodier (2010)

Unlike other studies where I undertake a close, fine-grained reading of visual, textual and interactive semiotic resources, in this chapter, I examined verbal text, and not on the production, consumption, interpretation or distribution of the site (Swan, 2010, 2017; Flowers and Swan, 2016). Although web pages are image-led and so typography, layout and colour become important in meaning-making and a sole focus on textual analyses is limited, it can still illuminate significant discursive themes and point to wider cultural trends. I selected a sample of these pages as the data for the present study and undertook a textual analysis of specific references to resilience coaching on the web pages and texts. My method entailed several stages of analysis including viewing web pages, selecting screenshots, preliminary coding and secondary coding. The websites and texts are from US and UK coaching organisations. There are national, historical and cultural specificities around the representation of coaching in the United States and in the United Kingdom, and their constructions of work femininities. For instance, neoliberal feminism and postfeminism take particular forms given the political, economic, social contexts, and popular psychology and psy discourses have a long history in constructing gender and advice for women (Cameron, 1995; Swan, 2010). In particular, they recommend work femininities which fit with US and UK discourses and representations of neoliberalism and postfeminism. The preliminary and secondary coding enables descriptions of analytic categories but theoretical approaches are needed to facilitate wider social and political interpretations (Jewitt and Oyama, 2001). Thus, my analytical strategies were informed by theories on postfeminism, sociological and cultural theories of resilience and critical studies of coaching.

Psy-resilience

Turning now to my survey of psy-resilience on my sample of US and UK websites, it is clear that psy-resilience aims at different populations from children, students, unemployed people, women executives, leaders, workers in the private, educational and public spheres. For example, the 'School of Life' founded by popular philosopher Alain Boton, is running a 'Resilience Bootcamp' 'promoting emotional intelligence in the world'. But it is the workplace that demands resilience most vigorously. For example, the UK Department for Health website offers a free 'emotional resilience toolkit' for employers on how to help workers 'survive and thrive' at work. The UK CIPD produced a guide called *Developing Resilience* aimed at HR practitioners to develop training to improve resilience skills (CIPD, 2013a). A final example derives from the influential US executive magazine *Harvard Business Review* which in 2010 published a lead article by Joshua D. Margolis and Paul G. Stolz entitled 'How to Bounce Back from Adversity'. This contained a section called 'Spotlight on Reinvention', an example of the self-work discourse prevalent in many workplaces. Just a brief glance at these titles show that it is imagined that psy-resilience can be taught, is connected with emotional labour, self-transformation and overcoming difficulties and helps you 'succeed' at work. As Pat O'Malley puts it,

> In recent years discourses of 'resilience' have emerged in which elements formerly identified as human 'attributes', such as courage, will-power, fortitude and character, have been reconfigured as 'coping strategies' or 'skills' that can be learned by anyone.
>
> (2010: 489)

Thus, new resilient subjectivities are responsible for capacitating and skilling their emotions, psyches and interiorities for a world of uncertainty and anxiety (Joseph, 2013; Welsh, 2014). Psychologies have to be worked on and managed. And as Aubrecht (2016) notes, success is understood as a capacity or trait rather than as a relational socio-cultural practice.

Indeed, psy-resilience is a mini industry with specialist coaches and their books, seminars and leadership models. For example, UK-based 'resilience coach', Dr Carole Pemberton has published a book on *Resilience Coaching: A Practical Guide for Coaches* with activities and checklists to teach coaches how to perform and coach resilience. Part of the work of coaching is defining resilience. For Pemberton resilience is 'the capacity to remain flexible in our thoughts, feelings, and behaviours when faced by a life disruption, or extended periods of pressure, so that we emerge from difficulty stronger, wiser, and more able' (2015: 2). Pemberton insists that resilience is not about getting 'toughened' nor is it simply 'bounceback' but transformation and learning, what she calls bouncing forwards, 'mov[ing] forward with insight' (Pemberton, 2016). In an often-used metaphor in the coaching industry, she describes resilience as being like a slinky toy, which 'extends and stretches over a challenging step, then springs forward, gathering itself together again' (Hall and Ellinson, 2015).

Resilience then is beyond flexibility and calls forth a new kind of subject. Being like a slinky suggests properties of pliability, elasticity, stretch, expansion and shrinking, morphing but returning and wholeness in that all the parts stretch and retun (Turner, 2010). As Emily Martin (2000) writes in the twentieth century, workers were supposed to be adaptive, moulding their capacities to be in tune with the environment. But resilience suggests that the environment may be toxic or painful and therefore a new form of adaption is needed where the environment's damage can be a source of learning and resource for exchange in the workplace.

Definitions of coaching on websites and related texts emphasise this never-ending need for flexibility. Two large UK companies, the Nationwide Building Society and Vodafone, commissioned two UK women coaches to write a report about women, leadership and resilience. The report was taken up by other coaching websites and media outlets. One of the coaching websites is a leading provider of women's leadership and maternity coaching, Executive Coaching. The report is entitled *Tough at the Top? New Rules of Resilience for Women's Leadership Success*. The authors note that resilience is 'not just coping with life's ups and downs, twists and turns' but 'more long-term, not just about reacting to crisis, but about tenacity and the ability to adapt well to constant change'. They continue, 'resilience required of people at work, is not just every now and then, but every day'. In similar vein, The Coaching Federation suggests that resilience is a coping process which means growing, being transformed. In their words, 'Thriving involves growth beyond the pre-adversity baseline level of functioning and is often a conscious choice people can make when faced with tough times'. In these definitions, resilience is not just a reaction, a way of coping from time to time, but a transformation of one's capacities and subjectivity in the face of duress. Such capacitation, they suggest, requires intentional decisions about how to behave. Or what we might see as a hyper-reflexivity to micromanage 'absolutes' (Sedgwick, 1994).

James (2014, 2015a) stresses that resilience discourse asks white women and minorities not only to cope with injuries caused by capitalism, patriarchy, sexism and racism but also to overcome them. Thus, white women and people of colour are expected to repair the damage caused by femininity and patriarchy and become stronger as a result. The injuries caused by patriarchy and neoliberalism are acknowledged and adapted to in ways that are imagined to make us better workers. Like the slinky, we are supposed to stretch and accommodate to the injuries or damage, changing but also bouncing back in ways which mean we have made ourselves more capacitated for future harm.

It is notable that resilience coaching targets white middle-class women. There are no companies offering resilience coaching specifically for white middle-class men. For instance, *Pathway Coaching* are running a seminar for women on influence and resilience for women and *The National College for Teachers* in the United Kingdom wants to recruit women to coach women 'to increase confidence, unlock potential and build resilience'—the holy postfeminist trinity. Coaches vary in the reasons they give for why women need to develop resilience. For example, hints are made about the inequalities of the uneven division of labour and women's gendered workload. In this vein, *Pathway Coaching* suggests,

> As women we may have many things draining our energy'. Intimations about sexism are made on various websites in phrases such as women need 'resilience tools' so they can 'step up into the next level of performance more easily' given the 'inevitable challenges in the leadership journey.

Rather than simply being good at their job, women need 'persistence, perseverance, and stubborn determination to get on'. The report *Tough at the Top* notes that 'women are "bracing themselves"' for 'a tough time en route to the top'. And once women are in senior roles, the Coaching Federation suggests that many experience 'derailing'—a coaching term for when women are promoted and then seen as failing to live up to expectations. The report stresses that 'Resilience is absolutely vital to career success' and speculates that more women than men want to be resilient because 'women understand the challenges they're likely to face and think, 'I'm going to need to be resilient to make it'. As feminists write, postfeminist culture acknowledges and repudiates gender inequalities and in these comments, we can see how resilience coaching discourse codes 'archetypal feminist questions' about sexism and inequality in psychologised language and as individual psychological function (Gill, Kelan, and Scharff, 2016; Gill and Donaghue, 2016). In this way, the feminist call to action the personal is political becomes the political is individualised, atomised, emotionalised and technologised (Gill and Donaghue, 2016).

Whilst wider social and political contexts such as neoliberalism and austerity—'challenging times'—are alluded to by the websites, reports and books, women are seen as having essentialised gendered 'resilience challenges'. Hence, women are seen as less curious or experimental unwilling to 'step out of comfort zones'. In a book called *Coaching Women to Lead*, authors Averil Leimon, Francois Moscovici, and Helen Goodier (2010) suggest women need resilience coaching because they have the wrong emotionality, being too traditionally 'feminine'. Thus, 'women can be too "touchy feely" ', 'create too much guilt for themselves' and the report *Tough at the Top* adds that 'taking things too personally is more of a struggle for women in the pipeline to the top than for men'. The report notes that women talk more than men 'about the tension they experienced between having to appear resilient and the emotional turmoil underneath'.

The wrong emotionality also means being 'negative'. The book explains that senior women as a result of travelling, not eating or sleeping properly, and other difficulties, 'can lose it' and become 'sullen, moody or aggressive'. To address these 'wrong feelings', produced no doubt from overwork, the unfair division of labour at work and home, and exhaustion, the coaching experts suggest building optimism and positivity and emotional literacy. The book does acknowledge women have to cope with the pressures of work, their own insecurities and the extra work they have to do at home. But the authors suggest without any irony, whilst these demands could make one feel exhausted, 'women especially need to be resilient in order to keep functioning at the peak of their ability'. There is no idea that women should slacken off and not work so hard. Indeed, coaching itself needs to be challenging, confronting women's 'constructive and destructive approaches to resilience'. To achieve this, women's transformation to become more resilient has to go beyond just the emotional, to include a full root and branch transformation including behavioural and physical resilience. Resilient coaches offer new modalities of emotional control, and as Aubrecht puts it, 'resilience mediates perception of adversity with professional knowledge' (2012: 270). Such professional knowledge includes techniques which transmute feelings and their expression. For example, US organisation, *The Resilience Group* offers a full-blown, all singing, all dancing 'Resilient Leadership Model'. This teaches 'strategies for inner coaching™', at the heart of which is 'counteract[ing] negativity'. The website explains that 'Inner coaching™ expands emotional intelligence (EI), promotes positive self-talk, decreases stress, promotes strengths, builds productive work environments and increases successful outcomes'. In this way, psy-resilience becomes a hyper-individualised technology of the self involving emotional control through internal management of feelings and cognitions. This requires that we submit our emotionality to the 'gaze of expertise, to be corrected, reconciled, normalised' (Hughes, 2010: 49). Internalising these psy practices inoculates us against neoliberal and capitalist injuries and enables us to carry on, and even transcend our circumstances. The effects claimed are more than individual and amplify to the organisation and its productivity.

This thinking is underpinned by the idea that we become tougher through experiencing and overcoming capitalism and white patriarchy injuries. To exemplify, US-based *Tiara International Coaching* 'brought together a panel of women leaders to share their wisdom about resilience on our Global Women's Leadership Roundtable', available as a downloadable podcast, on which women were asked how they kept going, and how tough situations made them stronger. In the broadcast, the contributors emphasise strength and toughness as critical characteristics of psy-resilience. Thus, the women leaders interviewed shared how they continued working even in the face of critical illness, moving jobs, working in different countries, and having over-work. Keeping going is key: the show must go on. Indeed, resilience become capital, as they 'harness' challenges and difficulties to enable them to 'build resources' and learn lessons.

In these ways, resilience is a makeover which as James (2015a) states requires the overcoming of challenges and is based on a 'structure of sub-jectivity' which encourages women to reject traditional white middle-class feminine fragility for strength. In short, good postfeminists are strong, not pretty (James, 2015a). Thus, individual women are expected to overcome the injuries wrought by traditional femininity through sexism, exploita-tion, inequality and oppression. Fragility is no longer the neoliberal ideal for femininity. Thus, 'good girls' need to be resilient, 'lean in' and be tough' (James, 2015a).

A central technique in overcoming and strengthening is performing the specific emotional labour of being positive. As one of the coaches in the round table puts it, women need to 'stay grounded in positivity even when times are dark'. *Pathway* Coaches, Hilary Danelian and Ruth Morris who run coaching and resilience events for women say that women need to 'feel energised and optimistic, as we manage all the elements of our lives and work' (2017). Positivity draws on tropes from positive psychology and the happiness industry. Several commentators critique the conservatism of posi-tivity as it inoculates us from negativity (Frawley, 2015), pacifying us so that we adapt and perpetuate the status quo: building 'walls of protection from the outside world so that it never reaches the inside of the self or affects the mood' (Mentinis, 2013: 369). Coaches encourage us to use our minds and emotions to make us feel better, 'relocate[ing] social problems into individ-ual's cognitive, behavior or moral failing' (Scanlon and Adlam, 2012: 101). Suffering becomes privatised (Ehrenreich, 2010) and positivity is seen as the cause of success not the other way around (Cabanas, 2016).

But whilst scholars lambast the proliferation of positivity as a psy tech-nique and basis for a new subjectivity, very few examine its gendered asso-ciations. Feminists associate positive thinking, optimism, being upbeat, cheerful and helpful, persevering and coping with white middle-class fem-ininity (Layton, 2004; Swan, 2010), and for Diana Negra (2009), many of these are postfeminist neoliberal affects, all as far removed from what she calls the 'rough emotions' such as anger, and disappointment, linked to black and working-class women. As Martin (2013) argues the classifica-tion of emotions into good and bad produces a hierarchisation of 'good'

and 'bad' femininities and good and bad workers. Thus, not everyone is fit
for neoliberalism. To illustrate: UK coach Jo Painter (2013) who coaches
women in resilience, cites Barbara Fredrickson, the author of a self-help
book called *Positivity* in an online article: 'Resilient people are able to
experience positive and negative emotions in difficult or painful situations.
Whereas when non-resilient people face misfortune their emotions are all
negative'. If you are not positive, you are harmful to yourself, others and
the workplace (Ehrenreich, 2010; Frawley, 2015). The ability to produce
the right kind of emotional state associated with resilience is producing new
hierarchies based on emotions (Adkins and Lury, 1999). Renyi Hong argues
that having the wrong emotionality can mean we are pathologised as emotionally defective and not having the right 'professional personality' (2015:
197). In this view, so-called negative emotions are seen as 'backwards and
stultifying', leading to inaction (Hong, 2015: 197). James suggests that it
is white women and their emotional 'labor of overcoming' which is a form
of human capital that translates into tangibles such as employment, recognition, reward, legitimacy and status. In this way, resilience is a 'form of
subjectification and investment: it makes individuals legible as legitimate
members of society who are entitled to the benefits of living in that society'
(2015: 168).

But coaches stress that white women are not necessarily innately positive.
White middle-class women can learn to be more positive through emotional
labour and coaching techniques. Some of these are represented as quite mundane. For instance, Painter (2013) suggests that you can practice 'positivity
every day on life's everyday small stresses, for example, when stuck in a
traffic jam or if your child is off sick. Good luck!' Such an approach is imagined to produce a cumulative emotional capacity capable of bigger things
through changing daily habits. The recommending of individualised techniques to find solutions to structural issues again underlines Eve Sedgwick's
(1994) term, the 'micromanagement of absolutes', the never-ending attempt
to control the impossible through small steps and individual choices.

As well as trying to feel positive, *Pathway Coaching* suggests, 'It is critical
we learn how to keep pressure positive'. This means that women should not
avoid stress or pressure but turn it into something upbeat and cheery. Doing
this means that we don't just survive but have 'greater ability to *sustain*
peak performance'. Moreover, women's resilience is not just about 'maintaining their own optimism and positivity but inspiring others'. Positivity
is imagined to be contagious and to create new forms of bodily reactions,
changing how we think and feel, helping us prepare for future challenges
and even making us more productive. Being tired, taking a break, slacking
off, taking it easy, moaning, criticising, changing work practices are not
on the coaching agenda. As James (2014) argues, resilience 'makes women
responsible for fixing sexism, and treating the effects of sexism as individual women's failure'. What is most shocking is her claim that patriarchy
and neoliberalism do not fix injuries but solicit them (2015a: 84). Thus,

we are left vulnerable to 'threats' so that we 'can demonstrate our agency, our independence, our postfeminist subjectivity in bouncing back from and eliminating that threat' (2014). This means that psy-resilience is not the 'elimination of existing damage, but the active production and maintenance of specific populations as damaged and damaging' (2014). In her view, it is people of colour in particular who are seen as damaged and damaging and whose inability to access productive resilience enables white women to capitalise their resilience. Next, I discuss more on whiteness and resilience.

Psy-resilience, Positivity and Emotional Labour

In the next two sections, I discuss the imbrications of resilience, whiteness and postfeminism, starting with a discussion of emotional labour. First, it can be seen that psy-resilience requires emotional labour and more specifically what coaches call emotional intelligence or EI. As Jason Hughes (2010) explains EI promulgates the view that 'the degree and pattern of control exercised over emotions is something that is learned, developed, enhanced, and can be harnessed for (predominantly commercial) competitive advantage' (2010: 30). More specifically, Alicia Grandey (2000) reminds us that Arlie Hochschild (1979) writes of three techniques through which emotional labour is performed:

1 Cognitive which entails changing our thoughts;
2 Somatic: changing our bodily responses; and
3 Expressive: changing our expressions.

As we have seen, resilience coaching requires the regulation of positive and deactivation of negative emotions through all three of these. Women are being asked to regulate their situation or their sense of situation so that their perception changes or their emotions are transformed. This involves trying to change an emotion cognitively through thinking good thoughts or reappraising the event (Grandey, 2000). Emotions can be calibrated, suppressed and produced. The aim is to achieve certain states of feeling and in particularly, optimism and positivity.

But such emotional labour—being positive and optimistic—means ignoring injury, damage, hurt, tiredness, exhaustion, overwork, difficulties, illness, pain and trauma. It means modifying or sidelining feelings which feminist theorists understand as signs of inequality and harm in social structures and systems (Ahmed, 2010; Pedwell and Whitehead). For instance, Sara Ahmed writes, 'feelings may be how structures get under our skin' (2010: 216) and Hong, feelings can be 'diagnostics for the injuries of capital' (2015: 203). Thus, resilience coaching advocates that structurally produced feelings of exploitation, inequality, injustice, stress and distress should be suppressed, and their socio-political meanings marginalised, undervalued and misread. Psy-resilience calls for women to regulate and control their emotional and bodily responses to sexism, racism, inequalities, austerity and the unequal division of labour at work and in the home.

Another aspect of being positive in resilience coaching means women should learn to look for positive information or produce and amplify positive feelings that contradict signs of hurt or harm. So-called negative emotions are understood as a catalyst for non-productivity, hindering action, whereas it is imagined that positivity has an energy or life force which springboards action and inoculates against future injuries and difficulties. But as Ahmed argues, feelings are not self-evident, but need to be read. Thus, rather than the consciousness raising of feminism in which feelings are read as signs of power, exploitation and oppression, and sites of resistance, psy-resilience calls for feelings not to be read.

Furthermore, critical race and feminist authors take issue with the specific postfeminist and neoliberal emotionality for women to be friendly, cheerful and positive. In a discussion on the way that emotions can be seen to circulate, with some emotions valorised and some denigrated in what she calls an economy of emotions, Ahmed (2004) argues that we can conceive of emotions as forms of intensity, body orientation and direction. Emotions are not inherent in a body or sign but they are social and intentional. In this understanding, sensations and impressions are transformed into judgments as emotions are produced through bodily movements towards or away from others or objects.

Hence, we can understand positivity as an orientation. Thus, glossing Ahmed's discussion of happiness, we can say that positivity is 'to face the right way' such that social goods and objects, are 'aligned not alienated' (2010: 41). Resilience is about correcting our feelings, to be affected in the right way. We have to convert bad feelings into good feelings by scanning our lives and workplace for signs of positivity: 'look on the bright side' and ignore realities of life (Ahmed, 2010). The assumption in resilience coaching is that positive people have a better consciousnessness of the world. So-called negative people are seeing the wrong things and spreading their bad feelings, hindering action and change.

This stands in contrast to feminist consciousness raising which is about reading the violence and power concealed in positivity (Ahmed, 2010). Ahmed insists that 'the act of saying no or pointing out injuries as an ongoing present affirms something' (2010: 207). But resilience discourse suggests that this is the wrong reading. Hong (2015) argues that positivity diverts attention from deep seated social problems and hinders our ability to understand social structures of inequality. The 'coercively imposed' positivity forecloses the potential in galvanising bad feelings to reveal social problems. She adds, 'To produce an alternative affective imaginary, the possibilities in bad feelings need to be resuscitated, given an opportunity to air as a collective recognition of pain' (2015: 203). Instead, resilience discourse creates the idea that feminism is over and there is no need for feminism if we can overcome through resilience capacities and techniques (James, 2015).

Whitening Psy-resilience

Having outlined how psy-resilence relates to postfeminism, I now discuss how its elements in coaching can be understood as reproducing whiteness. I suggest three ways: emotional control, white enterprise and positivity. First, it is important to stress that emotionality and emotional control are unevenly distributed by race. Historians of race and colonialism show us that white people saw themselves as more emotionally in control and therefore more civilised. Indeed, emotions have been used to justify who is seen as culturally and morally refined and fit to lead (Illouz, 2007; Dyer, 1997; Puwar, 2004). For Nirmal Puwar (2004), this becomes embodied in the somatic ideal of white, middle-class masculinity in organisations. In relation to femininity, bell hooks (1994) and Dreama Moon (1998) emphasise how middle-class white femininity is associated with a contained, controlled emotionality related to ideals of bourgeois decorum, respectability and civility. In similar vein, Jennifer Roth-Gordon (2011) synthesises the work of a number of critical race theorists to insist that constructions of race are based on an ability to 'exhibit proper bodily control'. As she writes,

> White bodies are defined by their "natural" proclivity towards discipline and their capacity for refinement and control, in contrast to non-white bodies that can be defined by excessive (or overly restrictive) consumption practices, unregulated (or overly regulated), expressions of one's sexuality, tendencies towards uncontrollable violence, a lack of intellectual rigor, and, especially, a lack of personal hygiene or bodily cleanliness.
>
> (2011: 213)

Whilst she does not explicitly mention emotions here, scholars have argued that non-whiteness is culturally associated with over-emotionality and expressivity (Martin, 2013; Moon, 1999; Puwar, 2004).

Secondly, psy-resilience is founded on having the mental and bodily strength to keep going: 'not miss a beat', as one of the roundtable respondents described it. In this way, psy-resilience can be linked to long-standing historic ideas about 'white enterprise'. According to whiteness theorist Richard Dyer (1997), the cultural representation of whiteness links to ideals, will power, enterprise and control. These assumed attributes of white people were used to motivate and justify European colonialism and imperialism. As Dyer writes,

> Enterprise . . . energy, will, ambition, the ability to think and see things through—and its effect—discovery, science, business, wealth creation, the building of nations. . . . Enterprise as an aspect of spirit is associated with the concept of will—the control of self and the control of others. . . . Thus white people lead humanity forward because of their

temperamental qualities of leadership: will power, far-sightedness, energy.

(1997: 31)

Building on this work in an organisational studies context, Puwar (2004) makes clear that these attributes mean that white men and to a lesser extent, white women are seen to fit the category of leader. In relation to this ideal, minoritised workers excluded, discriminated against and if they do manage to take up a leadership postion, intensely surveilled and policed.

Thirdly, psy-resilience in its call for emotional control and strength demands a specific emotionality—optimisim, enthusiasm, positivity, cheerfulness—the core emotions of postfeminism (Negra, 2009). Indeed, Ana Ramos-Zayas (2012) writes that affective disciplining is often tied up with the interests of the state and the market. Thus, she argues that a particular kind of emotional 'style' based on being 'friendly' is critical to the formation of neoliberalism. To produce such a performance means to self-manage according to the feeling rules and normative emotional regimes of flexible capitalism and neoliberalism (Ramos- Zavas, 2012).

But the performance of a postfeminist style of emotions in unevenly distributed. For example, so-called EI is positioned as a prerogative of the white middle-class professional (Illouz, 2007). Furthermore, not everyone can shield her or himself from negativity. Some aspects of work and life are just not possible to overcome and be positive about and require collective support and community support (Gill and Orgad, 2015; Heyes, 2014; Swan, 2010). Lisa Adkins (2005) argues that such emotionality is only valued in relation to its effects on customers and their feeling content, satisfied and 'well-treated'. Postfeminist emotionality requires access to certain resources to produce a successful 'audience reception' and this is not available to everyone. For instance, the ability to be friendly and be seen as friendly by others, is profoundly classed, racialised and gendered (Tolia-Kelly, 2006). Audience reception of emotions is racialised. As Ahmed (2004) shows feelings such as being friendly or being frightening stick to some bodies and not others. Culturally circulating stereotypes and histories of different racial groups shape expectations about emotional expressionality, for example 'the angry black'.

Moreover, this 'economy of emotions' means that distinct normative feeling rules for racialised minorities exist in workplaces, inflected by class and gender (Wingfield, 2010; Ramos-Zayas, 2012; Srivastav, 2005; Froyum and Stalp, 2012). These rules shape expectations about what racialised minorities are expected to feel, how they should express emotion and how their emotions are interpreted (Froyum, 2012; Wilkins, 2012; Wingfield, 2010). Moreover, white workplaces and workers create distinctive emotional demands on racially minoritised men and women (Froyum, 2012; Wingfield, 2010). For example, research shows how racialised men and women are expected to suppress criticism of inequality and racism (Wilkins, 2012;

Froyum, 2012). As Carolyn Pedwell puts it: "subjects who feel are differentially embedded and produced" (2012: 176). Emotions are 'differentially felt, constructed and mobilised' (2010: 281). Thus, not all emotions can be turned into economic, cultural and social capital (Skeggs, 2004).

Finally, James argues that psy-resilience is used to discriminate between those that can profit and benefit from damage and injury and those who do not bounce back enough or in the right way. Indeed, she argues that whilst 'feminised, queered, disabled, racially blackened damage are the building blocks of resilience discourse' not every can overcome to create new identities and surplus value (2015: 125). Whilst some racialised women can recover and profit, it is much more difficult because inclusion into 'multiracial white supremacist patriarchy' is conditional and instrumental, with black people seen as much less reformable. Furthermore, white middle-class women can turn damage into capital more than black women, using resilience as proof of their good postfeminist femininity. Indeed, she asserts that it is black women and men who are seen to cause some of the damage that white women have to overcome.

Conclusion

In this chapter, I have brought concepts of postfeminism, psy-resilience, whiteness and coaching in dialogue to address gaps in current studies of coaching and postfeminist analyses of organisations. Arguing that coaching is not race neutral, I have shown how psy-resilience coaching can be understood as a form of whiteness, working through postfeminist emotionality, emotional labour and enterprise. In so doing, I contribute to critiques of postfeminist psy makeovers and organisational psy practices such as coaching by showing how femininity is being reconfigured at the level of the subjective, psychological and organisational. More specifically, I have extended current analysis of postfeminist psy culture by bringing in an analysis of whiteness. My discussion augments our understanding of how postfeminism both acknowledges and repudiates feminism through the practice of coaching and its specific ideals and techniques. In particular, my analysis of resilience coaching illustrates how a specific postfeminist emotionality is being reproduced which attempts to sideline negative feelings which feminists argue are signs of sexism, racism, oppression in organisations, etc.

What is so important about James's feminist and critical race analysis of resilience is that she insists that resilience benefits hegemonic institutions more than it benefits us. She is very critical of the politics of psy-resilience because she argues it is 'designed to get individuals to perform the superficial trappings of recovery from deep, systemic and institutional issues, all the while reinforcing and intensifying the very systemic issues it claims to solve' (James, 2015b). Hence, postfeminist culture valorises women who are resilient and strong and can show they have overcome racism and sexism. In this way, resilience discourse requires women to fix the mess of sexism and racism in organisations and wider society, like women are expected to clean up the mess in the home. If people of colour or white women are not resilient, positive or strong and do not show they have overcome racism and sexism, they are seen as failures.

The implications of the concept of psy-resilience and associated practices such as coaching are that women are responsibilised to deal with sexism and racism through practices such as coaching and its ideals of postfeminist emotionality, emotional labour and enterprise. But as James insists, these very solutions consolidate sexism and racism. In relation to people of colour, this means additional taking on burdens in organisations. People of colour and white women are expected to overcome the demands, challenges, inequalities and exploitation in paid and unpaid work through developing exhausting skills like being positive. An important consequence is that white feminists in organisations and in academia need to learn how to hear so-called negative feelings of anger and frustration from people of colour. In particular, white feminists should not call for people of colour to be positive in relation to white feminism. As part of this, discussions on emotional labour need to attend to race as critical race theorists have emphasised. Furthermore, organisations and organisational theorists need to find ways to understand how psy-resilience in its various incarnations reproduces and consolidates whiteness and white privilege. In particular, we need to examine James's assertion that in resilience discourse, black women and men are seen to cause some of the damage that white women then have to overcome. Finally, we need to study how other kinds of organisation practices, like diversity work, require people of colour and white women to perform the social and organisational housework which cleans up the mess of social injuries caused by racism, neoliberalism and sexism.

Acknowledgements

Thanks to the editors for encouraging my thinking in postfeminism, whiteness and coaching, and particularly to Yvonne Benschop for pushing my argument and clarity.

References

Adkins, L. (2001). Cultural feminization: "Money, sex and power" for women. *Signs: Journal of Women in Culture and Society*, 26(3): 669–695.

Adkins, L. (2005). The new economy, property and personhood. *Theory, Culture and Society*, 22(1): 111–130.

Adkins, L., and Jokinen, E. (2008). Introduction: Gender, living and labour in the fourth shift. *NORA—Nordic Journal of Feminist and Gender Research*, 16(3): 138–149.

Adkins, L., and Lury, C. (1999). The labour of identity: Performing Identities, performing economies. *Economy and Society*, 28(4): 598–614.

Ahmed, S. (2004). *The Cultural Politics of Emotion*. Edinburgh: Edinburgh University Press.

Ahmed, S. (2010). *The Promise of Happiness*. Durham, NC: Duke University Press.

Aubrecht, C.K.M. (2012). *Surviving Success, Reconciling Resilience: A Critical Analysis of the Appearance of Student "Mental Life" at One Canadian University* (Doctoral dissertation, University of Toronto).

Aubrecht, K. (2012). The new vocabulary of resilience and the governance of university student life. *Studies in Social Justice*, 6(1): 67.

Aubrecht, K. (2016). Psy-times: The psycho-politics of resilience in university student life. *Intersectionalities: A Global Journal of Social Work Analysis, Research, Polity, and Practice*, 5(3): 186–200.

Baker, J. (2010). Claiming volition and evading victimhood: Post-feminist obligations for young women. *Feminism & Psychology*, 20(2): 186–204.

Blackman, L. (2004). Self-help, media cultures and the production of female psychopathology. *European Journal of Cultural Studies*, 7(2): 219–236.

Blackman, L. (2005). The dialogical self, flexibility and the cultural production of psychopathology. *Theory and Psychology*, 15(12): 183–206.

Blackman, L. (2007). Inventing the psychological. In J. Curran and D. Morley (Eds.), *Media and Cultural Theory* (pp. 209–220). London: Routledge.

Boulton, C. (2015). Under the cloak of whiteness: A circuit of culture analysis of opportunity hoarding and colour-blind racism inside us advertising internship programs. *TripleC: Communication, Capitalism & Critique: Open Access Journal for a Global Sustainable Information Society*, 13(2): 390–403.

Cabanas, E. (2016). Rekindling individualism, consuming emotions: Constructing "psytizens" in the age of happiness. *Culture & Psychology*, 22(3): 467–480.

Cameron, D. (1995). *Verbal Hygiene*. London: Routledge.

Chartered Institute of Personnel and Development (CIPD) (2013). *Developing Resilience: An evidence-based guide for practitioners*. London: CIPD

Coontz, S. (2003). Diversity and communication values in the family. *Journal of Family Communication*, 3(4): 187–192.

Czudaj, A. (2016). *Miranda July's Intermedial Art: The Creative Class Between Self-Help and Individualism* (Vol. 93). Bielefeld, Germany: Transcript Verlag.

Dosekun, S. (2015). For western girls only? *Feminist Media Studies*, 15(6): 960–975.

Dyer, R. (1997). *White*. London: Routledge.

Ehrenreich, B. (2010). *Smile or Die: How Positive Thinking Fooled America and the World*. London: Granta Books.

Flowers, R. and Swan, E. (2016). *Food Pedagogies*. London: Routledge.

Frader, L.L. (1999). From muscles to nerves: Gender, "race" and the body at work in France 1919–1939. *International Review of Social History*, 44(S7): 123–147.

Frawley, A. (2015). Happiness research: A review of critiques. *Sociology Compass*, 9(1): 62–77.

Froyum, C.M. and Stalp, M.C. (2012). Constructing a colour line in the twenty-first century. *Journal of Contemporary Ethnography*, 41(3): 3–6.

George, M. (2013). Seeking legitimacy: The professionalization of life coaching. *Sociological Inquiry*, 83(2): 179–208.

Gill, R. (2007). Postfeminist media culture: Elements of a sensibility. *European Journal of Cultural Studies*, 10: 147–166.

Gill, R. (2008). Culture and subjectivity in neoliberal and postfeminist times. *Subjectivity*, 25(1): 432–445.

Gill, R., and Donaghue, N. (2016). Resilience, apps and reluctant individualism: Technologies of self in the neoliberal academy. *Women's Studies International Forum*, 54: 91–99.

Gill, R., Kelan, E.K. and Scharff, C.M. (2017). A postfeminist sensibility at work. *Gender, Work and Organization*, 24(3): 226–244.Gill, R., and Orgad, S. (2015). The confidence cult (ure). *Australian Feminist Studies*, 30(86): 324–344.

Gill, R., and Scharff, C. (Eds.). (2011). *New Femininities: Postfeminism, Neoliberalism, and Subjectivity*. London: Palgrave.

Goudge, P (2003). *The Whiteness of Power: Racism in Third World Development. Dagenham.* London: Lawrence and Wishart.

Graf, E.M., and Pawelczyk, J. (2014). The interactional accomplishment of feelings-talk in psychotherapy and executive coaching. In E.M. Graf, M. Sator, and T. Spranz-Fogasy (Eds.), *Discourses of Helping Professions* (Vol. 252, pp. 59–90). Amsterdam: John Benjamins Publishing Company.

Grandey, A.A. (2000). Emotional regulation in the workplace: A new way to conceptualize emotional labor. *Journal of Occupational Health Psychology*, 5(1): 95.

Grimes, D.S. (2002). Challenging the status quo? Whiteness in the diversity management literature. *Management Communication Quarterly*, 15(3): 381–409.

Hall, L., and Ellinson, R. (2015). *Resilience: Think of a Slinky.* Available at: www.coaching-at-work.com/2015/09/03/resilience-think-of-a-slinky/ Accessed 13 December 2016.

Heyes, C. (2014). Anaesthetics of existence. In K. Zeiler and K.L. Folkmarson (Eds.), *Feminist Phenomenology and Medicine* (pp. 263–284). New York: Sundy.

Hochschild, A.R. (1979). Emotion work, feeling rules and social structure. *The American Journal of Sociology*, 85(3): 551–575.

Hochschild, A.R. (1983). *The Managed Heart: Commericialization of Human Feeling.* Berkeley: University of California Press.

Hong, R. (2015). Finding passion in work: Media, passion and career guides. *European Journal of Cultural Studies*, 18(2): 190–206.

Hooks, Bell (1994). *Outlaw Culture: Resisting Representations.* London: Routledge

Hughes, J. (2010). Emotional intelligence: Elias, Foucault, and the reflexive emotional self. *Foucault Studies*, 8: 28–52.

Hunter, S., Swan, E., and Grimes, D. (2010). Introduction: Reproducing and resisting whiteness in organizations, policies, and places. *Social Politics*, 17(4): 407–422.

Ilouz, E. (1997). Who will care for the caretaker's daughter? Toward a sociology of happiness in the era of reflexive modernity. *Theory, Culture & Society*, 14(4): 31–66.

Illouz, E. (2007). *Cold Intimacies: The Making of Emotional Capitalism.* Cambridge: Polity.

Ilouz, E. (2008). *Saving the Modern Soul: Therapy, Emotions, and the Culture of Self-help.* New York: University of California Press.

James, R. (2014). *Toxic: On Race, Gender and Resilient Labor on Social Media.* Available at: https://thesocietypages.org/cyborgology/2014/02/17/toxic-on-race-gender-and-resilient-labor-on-social-media/ Accessed 10 December 2016.

James, R. (2015a). *Resilience & Melancholy: Pop Music, Feminism, Neoliberalism.* John Hunt Publishing. www.johnhuntpublishing.com

James, R. (2015b). *Resilience an Ideal That Hurts More Than It Helps.* Available at: www.prindlepost.org/tag/coping/ Accessed 14 December 2016.

James, R. (2016). *Women's Resilience and Postfeminist Sexism.* Available at: www.prindlepost.org/2016/05/womens-resilience-and-post-feminist-sexism/ Accessed 13 December 2016.

Jewitt, C. and Oyama, R. (2001). Visual meaning: A social semiotic approach. In T. Van Leeuwen and C. Jewitt (Eds.), *Handbook of Visual Analysis* (pp. 134–156). London: Sage.

Joseph, J. (2013). Resilience as embedded neoliberalism: A governmentality approach. *Resilience*, 1(1): 38–52.

Kauppinen, K. (2013). "Full power despite stress": A discourse analytical examination of the interconnectedness of postfeminism and neoliberalism in the domain of work in an international women's magazine. *Discourse and Communication*, 7(2): 133–151.

Lawler, S. (2005). Disgusted subjects: The making of middle-class identities. *The Sociological Review*, 53(3): 429–446.

Layton, L. (2004). Dreams of America/American dreams. *Psychoanalytic Dialogues*, 14(2): 233–254.

Lazar, M.M. (2006). Discover the power of femininity! Global "power femininity" in local advertising. *Feminist Media Studies*, 6(4): 505–517.

Lee, E., and Bhuyan, R. (2013). Negotiating within whiteness in cross-cultural clinical encounters. *Social Service Review*, 87(1): 98–130.

Leimon, A., Moscovici, F., and Goodier, H. (2010). *Coaching Women to Lead*. London: Routledge.

Lewis, P. (2014). Postfeminism, femininities and organization studies: Exploring a new agenda. *Organization Studies*, 35(12): 1845–1866.

Liu, H., and Baker, C. (2016). White knights: Leadership as the heroicisation of whiteness. *Leadership*, 12(4): 420–448.

Martin, E. (2000). Flexible survivors. *Cultural Values*, 4(4): 512–517.

Martin, E. (2007). *Bipolar Expeditions: Mania and Depression in American Culture*. New York: Princeton University Press.

Martin, E. (2013). The potentiality of ethnography and the limits of affect theory. *Current Anthropology*, 54(S7): S149–S158.

McFadden, C.R. (2011). *Critical White Feminism: Interrogating Privilege, Whiteness, And Antiracism in Feminist Theory* (Doctoral dissertation, University of Central Florida Orlando, Florida).

McLaren, P (1997). *Revolutionary Multiculturalism Pedagogies of Dissent for the New Millennium*. Boulder, CO: Westview Press.

McRobbie, A. (2009). *The Aftermath of Feminism*. London: Sage.

Mentinis, M. (2013). The entrepreneurial ethic and the spirit of psychotherapy: Depoliticisation, atomisation and social selection in the therapeutic culture of the "crisis". *European Journal of Psychotherapy & Counselling*, 15(4): 361–374.

Mills, C. (1997). *The Racial Contract*. Ithaca, NY: Cornell University Press.

Moon, D.G. (1998) Performed identities: "Passing" as an inter/cultural discourse. In J.N. Martin, T.K. Nakayama, and L.A. Flores (Eds.), *Readings in Cultural Context* (pp. 322–330). Mountain View, CA: Mayfield.

Moon, D. (1999). White enculturalism and bourgeois ideology: The discursive production of "good identity". In T.K. Nakayama and J.N. Martin (Eds.), *Whiteness: The Communication of a Social Identity* (pp. 177–197). London: Sage.

Moreton-Robinson, A. (2000). *Talkin' up to the White Woman: Indigenous Women and Feminism*. St. Lucia: University of Queensland Press.

Nayak, A. (2003). "Ivory Lives": Economic restructuring and the making of whiteness in a post-industrial youth community. *European Journal of Cultural Studies*, 6(3): 305–325.

Negra, D. (2009). *What a Girl Wants? Fantasizing the Reclamation of Self in Postfeminism*. London: Routledge.

Neocleous, M. (2012). "Don't be scared, be prepared": Trauma-anxiety-resilience. *Alternatives*, 37(3): 188–198.

Nkomo, S.M. (1992). The emperor has no clothes: Rewriting "race in organizations". *The Academy of Management Review*, 17(3): 487–513.

Nkomo, S.M., and Al Ariss, A. (2014). The historical origins of ethnic (white) privilege in US organizations. *Journal of Managerial Psychology*, 29(4): 389–404.

O'Malley, P. (2010). Resilient subjects: Uncertainty, warfare and liberalism. *Economy and Society*, 39(4): 488–509.

Painter, J. (2013). *The Secret of Resilience*. Available at: www.lifecoach-directory. org.uk/lifecoach-articles/the-secret-of-resilience/ Accessed 10 December 2016.

Pawelczyk, J., and Graf, E.M. (2011). Living in therapeutic culture. In I. Lassen (Ed.), *Living with Patriarchy: Discursive Constructions of Gendered Subjects Across Cultures* (pp. 273–300). Amsterdam: John Benjamins Publishing Company.

Pedwell, C. (2010). *Feminism, Culture and Embodied Practice: The Rhetorics of Comparison*. London: Routledge.

Pedwell, C. (2012). Affective (self) transformations: Empathy, neoliberalism and international development. *Feminist Theory*, 13(2): 163–179

Pemberton, C. (2015). *Resilience Coaching: A Practical Guide for Coaches*. Milton Keynes: Open University Press.

Pemberton, C. (2016). *Resilience Coaching: Working with the Wobble and the Fall*. Available at: http://carolepemberton.co.uk/wp-content/uploads/masterclass_flyer_ carole_pemberton_web.pdf/ Accessed 29 December 2016.

Pfister, J. (1997). Glamorizing the psychological: The politics of the performances of modern psychological identities. In J. Pfister and N. Schnog (Eds.), *Inventing the Psychological: Toward a Cultural History of Emotional Life in America* (pp. 17–59). New York: Yale University Press.

Puwar, N. (2004). Thinking about making a difference. *The British Journal of Politics and International Relations*, 6(1): 65–80.

Ramos-Zayas, A. (2012). *Street Therapists: Race, Affect and Neoliberal Personhood in Latino Newark*. Chicago: University of Chicago Press.

Reid, J. (2012). The disastrous and politically debased subject of resilience. *Development Dialogue*, 58(April): 67–80.

Riggs, D.W. and Augoustinos, M. (2005). The psychic life of colonial power: Racialising subjectivities, bodies and methods. *Journal of Community and Applied Social Psychology*, 15(6): 461–477.

Ringrose, J., and Walkerdine, V. (2008). Regulating the abject. *Feminist Media Studies*, 8(3): 227–246.

Rose, N. (1989). *Governing the Soul: The Shaping of the Private Self*. London: Routledge.

Rose, N. (1996). Governing advanced liberal democracies. In A. Barry, T. Osborne and N. Rose (Eds.), *Foucault and Political Reason: Liberalism, Neoliberalism and Rationalities of Government* (pp. 37–64). London: UCL Press.

Roth-Gordon, J. (2011). Discipline and disorder in the whiteness of mock Spanish. *Journal of Linguistic Anthropology*, 21(2); 211–229.

Salmenniemi, S., and Adamson, M. (2015). New heroines of labour: Domesticating post-feminism and neoliberal capitalism in Russia. *Sociology*, 49(1): 88–105.

Samaluk, B. (2014). Whiteness, ethnic privilege and migration: A Bourdieuian framework. *Journal of Managerial Psychology*, 29(4): 370–388.

Scanlon, C., and Adlam, J. (2012). The recovery model or the modelling of a cover-up? *Groupwork*, 20(3): 100–114.Sedgwick, E.K. (1994). *Tendencies*. Durham: Duke University Press.

Shome, R. (2000). Outing whiteness. *Critical Studies in Media Communication*, 17(3): 366–371.

Skeggs, B. (2002). Techniques for telling the reflexive self. In T. May (Ed.), *Qualitative Research in Action* (pp. 349–375). London: Sage.

Skeggs, B. (2004). *Class, Self, Culture*. London: Routledge.

Skeggs, B. (2005). The making of class and gender through visualising moral subject formation. *Sociology*, 39(5): 965–982.

Srivastava, S. (2005). "You're calling me a racist?": The moral and emotional regulation of antiracism and feminism. *Signs: Journal of Women in Culture and Society*, 31(1): 29–62.

Steedman, C. (2002). Enforced narratives. In T. Coslett, C. Lury, and P. Summerfield (Eds.), *Feminism & Autobiography: Texts, Theories, Methods* (pp. 25–39). London: Routledge.

Stoler, A., and Cooper, F. (1997). *Between Metropole and Colony: Rethinking a Research Agenda in Tensions of Empire: Colonial Cultures in a Bourgeois World*. Thousand Oaks, CA: Sage.

Sullivan, S. (2014). *Good White People: The Problem with Middle-class White Antiracism*. Albany, NY: State University of New York.

Swan, E. (2006). Gendered leadership and management development: Therapeutic cultures at work. In D. McTavish and K. Miller (Eds.), *Women in Leadership and Management* (pp. 52–70). Cheltenham: Edward Elgar.

Swan, E. (2008). "You make me feel like a woman": Therapeutic cultures and the contagion of femininity. *Gender, Work and Organization*, 15(1): 88–107.

Swan, E. (2010). States of white ignorance, and audit masculinity in English higher education. *Social Politics: International Studies in Gender, State & Society*, 17(4): 477–506.

Swan, E. (2017). Postfeminist stylistics, work femininities and coaching: A multimodal study of a website. *Gender, Work & Organization*, 24: 274–296. DOI: 10.1111/gwao.12162

Thompson, A. (2004). Gentlemanly orthodoxy: Critical race feminism, whiteness theory and the APA manual. *Educational Theory*, 54(1): 27–57.

Tolia-Kelly, D.P. (2006). Affect-an ethnocentric encounter? Exploring the "universalist" imperative of emotional/affectual geographies. *Area*, 38(2): 213–217.

Turner, G. (2010). Approaching celebrity studies. *Celebrity Studies*, 1(1): 11–20.

Villaverde, L.E. (2000). Border crossing: The act and implications in the production of art vis-à-vis patriarchy and whiteness. In N.M. Rodriguez and L.E. Villaverde (Eds.), *Dismantling White Privilege: Pedagogy, Politics, and Whiteness* (pp. 41–58). New York: Peter Lang.

Walkerdine, V. (1996) Working-class women: Psychological and social aspects of survival. In Wilkinson, S. (Ed.) *Feminist Social Psychologies: International Perspectives* (pp. 145–162). Buckingham: Open University Press.

Wallis, J., and Singh, R. (2014). Constructions and enactments of whiteness: A discursive analysis. *Journal of Family Therapy*, 36(S1): 39–64.

Welsh, M. (2014). Resilience and responsibility: Governing uncertainty in a complex world. *The Geographical Journal*, 180(1): 15–26.

Wilkes, K. (2015). Colluding with neo-liberalism: Post-feminist subjectivities, whiteness and expressions of entitlement. *Feminist Review*, 110(1): 18–33.

Wilkins, A. (2012). "Not out to start a revolution": Race, gender and emotional restraint among Black university men. *Journal of Contemporary Ethnography*, 41(1): 34–65.

Wingfield, A.H. (2010) Are some emotions marked "whites only"? Racialized feeling rules in professional workplaces. *Social Problems*, 57(2): 251–268.

Zhang, Y., Gajjala, R., and Watkins, S. (2012). Home of hope: Voicings, whiteness, and the technological gaze. *Journal of Communication Inquiry*, 36(3): 202–221.

4 Postfeminism, Queer and Work

Nick Rumens

Introduction

This chapter explores how a postfeminist sensibility shapes the discursive deployment of 'queer' in the workplace. Of note here is Butler's (2013: 53) observation that, 'with a few exceptions, scholars of postfeminism seem to have sidestepped questions of sexuality, even as queer theorists continue to emphasize the central role of heterosexism in the reproduction of inequality'. To date, the connection between postfeminism and queer has largely been articulated in analyses of how queer is animated within postfeminist media culture (Cohan, 2007; Gerhard, 2005; Gill, 2008; LeMaster, 2015; Sender, 2006), although some scholars of postfeminism have highlighted queer theory as an important resource for interrogating the inequalities postfeminist discourse reproduces (Genz and Brabon, 2009; LeMaster, 2015; McRobbie, 2009). This limited body of research has examined, among other things, how queer can function as an aesthetic (e.g. 'queer chic', Gill, 2008), as a catalyst for rehabilitating heterosexual men in TV shows such as *Queer Eye for the Straight Guy* (Sender, 2006) and as a narrative structure in the television series *Sex and the City* (Gerhard, 2005). Taken together, this literature has established links between postfeminism and queer, with some analyses using queer theory as a conceptual resource to interrogate how sexual and gender binaries are reinforced in postfeminist media culture (LeMaster, 2015).

Adding to the writing that seeks to bring postfeminism and queer into dialogue, this chapter examines how a postfeminist sensibility is connected to the discursive construction of queer in the workplace, illustrated empirically by drawing on the perspectives of gay men. Relying, in part, on Gill's (2007) conceptualisation of postfeminism as a sensibility and how this collaborates with neoliberal discourses, this chapter also engages with queer theory to examine how queer is discursively mobilised by gay men and their employers. As the empirical sections of this chapter show, another discursive formation, the notion of a 'post-gay' culture, mirrors postfeminist discourse in how it re-secures gender and sexual hierarchies. As such, the analysis that follows hopes to show how postfeminist, neoliberal and queer discourses intermingle, producing a variety of effects. To begin, this chapter outlines the various ways postfeminism has been conceptualised by feminists, elaborating in particular Gill's (2007) notion of a postfeminist sensibility. Turning next to elucidate how queer is mobilised as a theoretical resource, the discussion then proceeds to review briefly how queer is invoked within postfeminist media culture. The chapter then presents the empirical data to examine the discursive deployment of queer in the workplace before concluding.

Postfeminism

Postfeminism is a polysemic term. It has been written about and deployed in different and sometimes contradictory ways, making it a slippery and vague concept to grasp. However, the burgeoning literature on postfeminism, mostly originating within cultural studies, media and feminist studies (Butler, 2013; Gill, 2007, 2008, 2009, 2014, 2016; Gill and Scharff, 2011; McRobbie, 2009; Negra, 2009; Tasker and Negra, 2007), has given postfeminism a bibliographic shape from which it is possible to discern patterns in how it has been mobilised and the kinds of meanings it has been ascribed. Providing an overview of the field, Gill and Scharff (2011) argue that postfeminism tends to be deployed in three broad ways. First, the term has been used to signal an 'epistemological break within feminism' (2011: 3), whereby feminism is said to intersect with other theoretical movements concerned with difference such as postmodernism, poststructuralism, queer theory and postcolonialism. In this sense, postfeminism is understood as an 'analytical perspective' that indicates a transformation within feminism (2011: 3), one that challenges the hegemonic conceptions of womanhood and femininity promulgated in white, Anglo-America feminist theory. As such, postfeminism is seen to confront the challenge of theorising difference by abandoning the binary thinking of second-wave feminist theory and focusing on plurality, fluidity and hybridism.

Second, postfeminism has been used to signal an historical shift in feminism. Gill and Scharff (2011) reason that postfeminism may be articulated as a set of assumptions about the 'pastness' of feminism that Negra and Tasker (2007: 1) suggest can be 'noted, mourned or celebrated'. For example, Negra's (2009) analysis of postfeminist media culture reveals how cultural discourses celebrate the passing of feminism, illustrated by instances of female achievement in male dominated workplaces, women's ability to treat men as sexual objects and the seemingly unencumbered freedoms women enjoy in respect to career choice, parenting and domesticity. Third, the term has been drawn on to indicate a backlash against feminism. Here, postfeminist media culture has played an influential role in claiming that feminism is moribund and irrelevant in the contemporary lives of women (Faludi, 1992, 1999). Various permutations of backlash discourse include, that feminism has achieved its goals and is no longer required and that feminism is responsible for unhappiness in women's lives. As Negra (2009) contends, in postfeminist media culture, feminism is almost forgotten or, when it is visible, it is represented as a threat to the family and a modern woman's capacity to choose and sustain an expressive lifestyle.

It is not altogether surprising that postfeminism has been interrogated by feminist scholars and been pulled up short for its conceptual cloudiness, becoming ever more overburdened with meanings and interpretations (Lumby, 2011; Whelehan, 2010). Noting this disquiet among feminist theorists, Gill (2016) argues that we need to scrutinise existing feminist vocabularies to assess if they are 'up to the task of reading and engaging with change' (2016: 613). As such, Gill (2016: 614) holds that postfeminism retains power as a term within feminist critical vocabulary, not least given the complicated, highly nuanced and contradictory nature of 'the new visibility of feminism'. The media is a crucial site for locating and questioning the visibility of feminism, for Gill (2008) points out that it is the media that plays a key role in shaping much of what counts as feminist debate. Indeed, Gill and other writers on postfeminism and media culture (McRobbie, 2009; Projansky, 2001) have paved the way for reading postfeminism as a set of shifting discursive assemblages, in which different discourses of feminism co-exist, even if they do not do so amicably.

Commenting on the complicated nature of feminist discourses in and outside the media, McRobbie (2009) refers to discursive processes of disarticulation that take feminism into account but suggest there is no longer any need for feminist politics within women's lives. Disarticulation then is a potent discursive force that decouples feminism from politics, as it severs feminism from its political and philosophical roots, thereby working to erode and 'undo' the cultural purchase of feminism within the contemporary lives of women. Disarticulated in this way, feminism is (re)modified into various forms that are diluted or drained of their political vigor. For instance, media and corporate friendly formulations of contemporary feminism, as can be seen in the self-help/autobiographies of female leaders and entrepreneurs such as Sheryl Sandberg (*Lean In*, 2013), exemplify this more palatable reconstitution of feminism. Versions of 'corporate feminism', dubbed as such by Gill (2016: 617), bear out McRobbie's (2009) disarticulation thesis because they acknowledge feminism by taking it into account in how women are positioned as empowered and able to make individual choices, while simultaneously concealing and installing a 'whole repertoire of new meanings which emphasis that [feminism] is no longer needed, it is a spent force' (2009: 12). In this sense, postfeminism can be understood in terms of competing, overlapping and sometimes contradictory discourses that, as Lewis (2014: 1850) puts it, 'shapes our thinking, attitudes and behaviour towards feminism and women's changing position in contemporary society, not entirely linked to an "actual" historical event or moment'. Seen in this way, postfeminism is not essentialised as a specific set of beliefs, ideas or theories that stabilise its meaning. Developing the concept of postfeminism as an unstable, shifting and historically patterned discursive formation, I turn now to Gill's (2007) seminal work on postfeminism as a sensibility, which forms part of the theoretical scaffolding for this chapter.

Postfeminism as a Sensibility

The concept of a postfeminist sensibility has been adopted as an object of analysis among scholars interrogating postfeminist media culture (Agirre, 2012; Blue, 2013; Gerhard, 2005; Kissling, 2013). Many of these studies take as their launch pad Rosalind Gill's seminal article on postfeminist sensibility (2007). Conceived of as a sensibility, Gill argues that postfeminism is said to comprise a number of distinct but overlapping themes: the

> notion that femininity is a bodily property; the shift from objectification to subjectification; an emphasis upon self-surveillance, monitoring and self-discipline; a focus on individualism, choice and empowerment; the dominance of a makeover paradigm; and a resurgence of ideas about natural sexual difference.
>
> (2007: 147)

For example, in regard to the theme of individualism, choice and empowerment, Gill points out that 'notions of choice, of "being oneself" and "pleasing oneself" are central to a postfeminist sensibility that suffuses contemporary Western media culture' (2007: 153). While achieving heterosexual desirability is still considered important for many women, it is re-framed within postfeminist media culture as a case of women pleasing themselves, not men, thereby seemingly offering 'new' representations of women as sexually agentic rather than passive objects of sexual desire for men. However, the constitution of the self within postfeminist media culture is, as Gill (2008) insists, an exercise in gendered power relations, demanding attention is trained to examining the discursive processes of subjectification. Gill (2008) draws on Foucault and his writing on the discursive construction of the individual subject (i.e. subjectification), to demonstrate how power can be creative, in how the self is formed, and repressive in how the formation of the self is also constrained by norms.

In this chapter, elements of a postfeminist sensibility are treated as objects of critical analysis, thereby countering the tendency to reduce postfeminism to a distinct theoretical orientation, historical shift in feminism or a one-dimensional form of feminist backlash. Furthermore, and germane to the analysis that follows, is the link between a postfeminist sensibility and neoliberalism (Gill, 2007; Gill and Scharff, 2011). Like postfeminism, neoliberalism is another contested term, but it is generally understood as a mode of political and economic rationality that has been characterised by deregulation of labour markets and privatisation. As Harvey (2005: 2) argues, it is a 'theory of political and economic practices that proposes that human well-being can be best advanced by liberating individual entrepreneurial freedoms and skills within an institutional framework characterised by strong private property rights, free markets and free trade'. The sovereignty currently given to economic factors and the privileging of a neoliberal agenda exerts tremendous influence on how we understand ourselves and relate to others. Neoliberalism encourages us to consider our work and lives in economic terms, as consumers and entrepreneurs, and that this economic hue is imbued into our relations with the self and others. In other words, neoliberalism can be read as a technology of power, in the Foucauldian sense, whereby subjects are governed as autonomous and enterprising.

As Gill (2007) elaborates, postfeminism is intimately bound up with neoliberal discourses on a number of fronts. One of these relates to how both emphasise individualism, in particular the role of the individual in changing themselves (e.g. bodies, behaviours, attitudes) in order to succeed at home and work. As such, the argument that the social, political and economic contexts in which individuals are enmeshed exert influence, both positive and negative, is subdued. Neoliberal discourses that promote the subject as self-regulating and enterprising adhere closely to postfeminist discourses that circulate a notion of the individual unaffected by power relations and gender inequalities, who can engage freely in activities of self-invention, where free choice is a recurring leitmotif. Another front concerns the pressure placed on women, far more so than men, to engage with the self-regulation and self-invention components of neoliberal and postfeminist discourses respectively. As Gill (2007) sums up, a postfeminism sensibility is partly constituted through discourses of neoliberalism that establish an individualistic mode of governance that characterises significant aspects of contemporary Western cultures. With this in mind, Gill's (2007) notion of a postfeminist sensibility informs part of the framework for examining the discursive deployment of queer within the workplace. Additionally, this chapter draws on queer theory as a conceptual resource, discussed in the next section.

Queer and Postfeminist Media Culture

Queer has been understood in different ways including a term of insult for lesbian, gay, bisexual and transgender (LGBT) subjects, something that is odd, a position, an umbrella identity under which LGBT identities may be subsumed and as a theory (Butler, 1993; Halperin, 1995; Sedgwick, 1990; Sullivan, 2003). Queer's conjunction with theory is of particular relevance to this chapter, since it is the intellectual project of queer theory that enables the articulation of queer as a mode of critique that 'chafes against normalization' (Edelman, 2004: 6). In other words, queer theory questions what is 'normal', challenging taken-for-granted wisdom about what is 'natural' and destabilising normative regimes (Halberstam, 2011; Halperin, 1995; Jagose, 1996; Warner, 1993). Queer theory is usefully understood as a constellation of ideas and conceptual resources that have links with gay and lesbian studies, feminism and poststructuralism. It is also multi-branched but central to queer theorising is an anti-normative impulse that aims to upend and exceed the norms that narrowly constitute subjects as 'culturally intelligible' within a heteronormative regime (Butler, 1990). In this regard, queer theory works at the site of ontology, such as problematising humanist ontologies that essentialise sexuality and gender within binaries such as heterosexual/homosexual, male/female and masculine/feminine (Sullivan, 2003). Queer theory enables us to examine how ontologies operate as 'normative injunctions', setting the 'prescriptive requirements' whereby, for instance, bodies are constituted as culturally ineligible in terms of sex, gender and desire (Butler, 1999: 148). Heteronormativity is an important category of analysis for queer theorists as a normative regime that constrains how LGBT sexualities and genders can be lived, not least because they are typically judged as 'abnormal' against heterosexuality which is ascribed a normative and privileged status (Warner, 1993). Queer then has sometimes been used as an umbrella for those sexualities and genders which are 'abnormal' and 'unintelligible', that fail to demonstrate coherence between sex, gender and desire (Sullivan, 2003). In this chapter, queer is not reduced to an identity; rather, it is treated as a politically charged set of conceptual resources that hold discursive formations of what is 'normal' within its analytical grip. Furthermore, the chapter's focus on gay men does not indicate that queer operates here as code for gay male.

Queer theory can be used as a conceptual resource to examine how elements of a postfeminist sensibility can shape the discursive deployment of queer within media culture (Butler, 2013; LeMaster, 2015). Typically, research has explored queer visibility within postfeminist media (Cohan, 2007; Gerhard, 2005; Gill, 2007; LeMaster, 2015; Sender, 2006). For example, Jane Gerhard analyses queer in the context of the phenomenally successful US television show *Sex and the City* (SATC), arguing that 'queerness figures as a narrative structure that directs Carrie and her friends to solutions beyond postfeminist individualism' (2005: 42). Gerhard mobilises queer in its theoretical capacity to examine how queer and postfeminism coalesce in the media. One prominent instance of this in SATC is how the show depicts friendship between women. Being a central theme of the show, the friendship bonds between the female protagonists offer them a relational context for pleasure, love and intimacy. Contra to a postfeminist sensibility that emphasises individualism over collective understandings and solutions, female friendship offers the women an alternative relational context for pleasure and intimacy that grants them 'options different from those traditionally signified as "heterosexual" (where women satisfy their desires with one man, serially or monogamously)' (2005: 44). In this sense, we might be witness to, as Gerhard implies, a queering of female heterosexuality that treads a tightrope between 'never tipping the women into outright gayness' and acknowledging that heterosexual women have 'desires that sometime defy the simple equation between genital contact and sexuality' (2005: 46).

A markedly different media representation of queer is observed in Bravo's successful US makeover show *Queer Eye for the Straight Guy*, later shortened to *Queer Eye*. The show departed from the usual makeover format by taking heterosexual men rather than women as the subjects in need of being made over by the show's experts, five gay men referred to as the 'Fab Five'. *Queer Eye* has been critiqued by academics who berate the gay stereotyping and heteronormativity the show reinforces (Ramsey and Santiago, 2004; Westerfelhaus and Lacroix, 2006). For example, the Fab Five engage routinely in delivering withering one-liners to the heterosexual male being made over, while the show grants visibility to queer through an association with gay men as 'natural experts' in the style professions. These critiques are well pitched, but one notable analysis examines how the show collaborates with neoliberalism. Sender (2006) points out that while the Fab Five conform to a stereotype of bitchy gay men, they are acutely aware that heterosexual men, as well as women, must make the 'right' choices to succeed at home and at work. On this basis, the show betrays its neoliberal goal—the revamping of the heterosexual male subject so he is suitable for heterosexual coupledom and business-ready for the world of work. *Queer Eye* is daring in several respects: for acknowledging that men also must engage in the neoliberal project of self-regulation and management, and employing gay men as experts in reformulating male heterosexuality, despite the fact that gay men have for years been cast as deficient in masculinity. In other ways, the show reinforces heteronormativity. Consumerism is the primary catalyst for positive change that is structured by a queer eye whose expert gaze is based on gay men's supposed penchant for consumption rather than reproduction. Ultimately, the show does not discursively deploy queer as a politics to transform heteronormativity but to uphold and sustain it through the endorsement of discourses that emphasise personal responsibility, individualism and consumption. This necessarily brief discussion of queer within postfeminist media culture inspires the question that structures the remainder of this chapter: how is the discursive deployment of queer in the workplace shaped by a postfeminist sensibility?

Postfeminist Sensibility and the Discursive Deployment of Queer in the Workplace

Gill, Kelan, and Scharff (2017) argue that postfeminist sensibilities are already at work in the workplace, placing emphasis on individuals, in particular women, to make the *right* choices, to self-discipline, to be confident and to please themselves, all in a corporate landscape where it is said that all the major equality battles have been won. In light of this and the discussion earlier, this section presents empirical illustrations of the discursive deployment of queer at work based on previous published research (Rumens, 2011). Following Gill et al. (2017) and Lewis (2014) in this approach, focusing on specific examples from prior research, is fruitful for reading how a postfeminist sensibility has and continues to permeate the world of work. A brief methodological note is useful here (for a fuller account, see Rumens, 2011). The empirical data has been drawn from an interview-based study on gay men's workplace friendships which has spanned 8 years (2005–2013), involving 35 study participants based in the United Kingdom. Although the study explored the role, place and meaning of gay men's workplace friendships, interviews were conducted iteratively and covered a wide range of topics including employment background, career aspirations, identity disclosure and management, discussion of equality and inclusion, and LGBT and queer politics. Discourse analysis techniques were used to analyse the interview data. A Foucauldian approach to discourse analysis was adopted (Jørgensen and Phillips, 2002), which demonstrates a concern with how relations of power are enmeshed within language and discourse, in particular focusing on the meaning of discourses within the interview texts. This involved reiterative readings of the interview texts to identify, compare, contrast and interpret emergent data categories within the interview findings. One data category to emerge from this re-analysis process was the discursive deployment of queer in regard to work, presented next.

Repudiating LGBT Inequality in a 'Post-Gay' Culture

One component of a postfeminist sensibility that threads its way unevenly through my interview data is the repudiation of LGBT inequality. Specific discourses were drawn upon to convey the pastness of LGBT inequality, the most notable being a post-gay discourse. The idea of living in a 'post-gay' era was proffered by some interviews to capture the current progress in LGBT equality and inclusion. 'Post-gay' is a term that has entered into common parlance in recent times to describe how LGBT sexualities and genders are visible but not necessarily used by LGBT people as the primary means by which they identify. Emerging research on the notion of a post-gay culture suggests that LGBT people are integrating within a heteronormative culture, socialising in venues and districts outside 'gay villages' and emphasising their similarities with rather than differences from heterosexuals (Alderson, 2016; Nash, 2013). This is reflected in mainstream forms of LGBT activism that are structured around a logic of bridge building into straight worlds, where boundaries between LGBT and heterosexual subjects are blurred (Ghaziani, 2011), giving rise to forms of gay and lesbian normativity (Duggan, 2002; Seidman, 2002).

In the context of the interview data, 'post-gay' discourse was apparent in accounts of contemporary gay life by older gay men who had lived through

the turbulent years following the Stonewall riots of 1969 and the homo-
phobic Reagan-Thatcher political regime that was at its zenith during the
1980s.

> Sure in the 60s, 70s and 80s it was bad . . . homophobia was rife, there
> was the whole AIDS thing going on and people could fire you at will.
> They were dangerous times.Nowadays it's different. It's post-gay . . .
> you can live an openly gay life if you want to, no one gives a shit.
>
> (Hugo, academic)

> Gay liberation has done its job. We're at the table now, people listen to
> us. The last thing you want now is to rock the boat, to get all radical
> and queer . . . it just pisses off society.
>
> (Jack, director)

The two quotes, from gay men in their fifties, describe aspects of what
Hugo labels a 'post-gay' culture. Hugo constructs a clear distinction between
a time when being openly gay was 'dangerous' in a way it is seemingly not in
the present. Notably, Hugo's comments reveal how it is up to the individual
to live an openly gay life, if they *want* to, which implies there is both unfettered agency and choice in how an openly gay life can be lived and how it
is met with indifference. As such, the influence of heteronormativity and
the material circumstances of gay men's lives in shaping the possibilities for
an 'openly gay life' are glossed over. Yet heteronormativity in the United
Kingdom persists in the workplace (Einarsdóttir, Hoel, and Lewis, 2015;
Rumens, 2016), with studies showing how opportunities for gay visibility
at work are structured by conformity to hetero-norms that emphasise fitting
into heteronormativity (Ozturk and Rumens, 2014; Williams, Giuffre, and
Dellinger, 2009).

Jack offers another perspective on the current 'post-gay' landscape for
LGBT people at work. Acknowledging that the gay liberation movement
'has done its job', Jack sounds a warning to those LGBT people who might
wish to 'rock the boat' by sustaining a mode of queer politics that is radical
and transformative, unprepared to accept 'the modest goals of tolerance
for diverse lifestyles' (Bersani, 1995: 76). Here Jack discursively constructs
queer as a redundant mode of politics and commits it to the past, indicating
that its presence might risk the world of work that has been won for LGBT
subjects. As with Jack, these sentiments overlook the persistence of heteronormativity as an organising principle and element in LGBT people's lives in
and outside work. If anything, Jack's insistence that queer is abandoned as
a form of disruptive politics is underwritten by an impulse to maintain the
current status quo at work, where in his work context 'no one cares if you're
gay' or, in the words of Hugo, 'no one gives a shit . . . if you like sucking
cock as long as you do your job'.

Alex, a younger man in his late twenties, also located LGBT inequality as an issue that largely affected a previous generation:

> I feel for the older generation you know, the guys that had to endure homophobia, lurking in the shadows for sex, the dingy bars . . . being closeted. That world isn't familiar to me, but they had to put up with it. Thank god it's alright now.

Alex's quote reveals how a postfeminist sensibility is at work. LGBT discrimination is minimised as a contemporary workplace issue by noting that generational change has occurred. In this excerpt, sexual prejudice against LGBT people is simultaneously acknowledged but discursively framed as a phenomenon of the past, experienced by an older generation who ought to be admired for soldering through it. Homophobia is framed as a generational issue, allowing Alex to assert that being openly gay is not a barrier to employment or 'getting ahead' in the workplace.

At the time of interview, Alex was employed by a small advertising agency and excited to be working for a company full of 'hipsters', a label he used to identify the affluent, white, middle-class, fashion and music conscious youth employed there. Within this creative setting, LGBT inequality was not 'on [his] radar', either as an issue the agency was currently addressing or as something he had experienced. Nonetheless, his description of work life within the agency revealed other facets to a postfeminist sensibility that emphasises choice. For Alex, it was up to the individual to 'fit into' the workplace in order 'to get on'. Making the 'right' choices is crucial, as Alex revealed when he spoke about fitting into the hipster work culture of the advertising agency. This entailed 'wearing the right clothes' (e.g. 'vintage clothing'), listening to the 'right kind of music' (produced by 'indie labels'), drinking and eating the 'right stuff' (e.g. 'artisan bread from the local bakery') and conveying an 'anti-mainstream attitude'. In this hipster work culture, 'being gay' was framed by Alex as a 'non-issue'. Yet his commentary revealed that he had another set of choices about how to present himself as 'gay' at work. He seemed anxious to convey a 'good impression' of 'being gay' to his 'straight' colleagues by showing them that 'gay men are like straight people'. Here, Alex adopted a discourse of gay normativity to elucidate his capacity to approximate hetero-norms through performing a 'straight acting' masculinity, suggesting, 'People were surprised I was gay when I told them . . . I just blend in with everyone else'. Also, he intended to invite his colleagues to his forthcoming civil partnership, discursively framing the event in heteronormative terms: as an opportunity to show 'straight people that it's normal for a couple of gayers to get hitched, like a straight couple going to the register office'. Alex's commentary is notable in revealing how gay men seek to conform to hetero-norms that grant them recognition as 'normal' gay subjects. Ironically, in a work culture where displaying an anti-mainstream attitude appears de rigueur, it is conforming to rather than departing from the heteronormative mainstream that is a necessity, enabling Alex to fit in.

Queer as Adding Value

In stark contrast to the interview accounts presented earlier, the excerpts analysed next reveal how queer can be discursively mobilised in terms of adding value, both to organisations and individuals. Relating this to a post-feminist sensibility, interview accounts suggest that queer can be a site at which postfeminism and neoliberal discourses converge, whereby individuals are required to self-manage queer as a part of themselves that may also be desirable to others within the organisation. One way to read this is as an instance of what Meg Wesling refers to 'queer value': how the 'inter-actional performance of sexuality and gender constitutes a form of labor, accruing both material and affective value' (2012: 108). Although limited, prior research has explored the notion of 'queer value' within the work-place. For example, David (2015) examined Filipino transgender women in a call-centre work environment, finding that the basis on which they expe-rienced inclusion was contingent on how they could meet organisational expectations about how 'trans' should be put to work in the expansion and accumulation of global capital. David found that some transwomen were expected to 'produce queer value through their performance of a specifi-cally Filipino queerness, a lightheartedness that yields comfort among work-place teams' (2015: 188). The queer value yielded from the performances of stereotypical notions of femininity (through bodily appearance, conduct and dress) reinforced the status of some transwoman employees as 'proper transgender subjects' (2015: 189) who could do workplace appropriate per-formances of gender. But the production of queer value in this way also created new hierarchies among transgender people, disadvantaging those transgender subjects who lacked the ability or skills (e.g. education and flu-ency in English) to engage in narrowly defined organisationally desirable gender performances. As such, David's study brilliantly exposes the ten-sions that arise when transgender subjects are normalised in the workplace, creating new opportunities for recognition as transgender subjects at the same time as playing 'valuable' and productive work roles but within tightly defined performances of gender that reinforce harmful gender hierarchies.

Similarly, re-analysis of the interview data yielded insights into how queer can be reformulated as an organisational resource to enhance customer service relations, sell products to clients and improve interactions within the workplace. In these instances, the reiterative performances of gay male sexuality compose a type of labour that produces value for the organisation, which may be coded as 'queer', as demonstrated in the following:

> So my office manager tells me to do my queer thing every time we have a SWF [single white female) who wants to view a property . . . I get

assigned to her, to arrange viewings . . . during which I mention I'm gay to put her at ease, so she doesn't feel like she's going to get hassled from a straight guy trying to do a hard sell. I tell you, they love it. I camp it up a bit, do my queer eye for the straight woman thing which helps to keep the buying process smooth.

(Oliver, estate agent)

Once I was introduced to a prospective client as the guy with the queer eye, you know that programme with the five queers . . . the client later told me he felt more comfortable with a gay designer because he reckoned gay men are naturally more creative, and I guess my manager knew that before he introduced me like that.

(Dean, graphic designer)

In these examples, organisations are seen to insist from their gay male employees a performance of 'queer' to improve relationships with clients. Notably, queer is invoked not as a disruptive mode of identifying, relating or organising, but as a productive identification from which a set of assumptions unfold about the gay male subject performing queer. For Oliver, queer is mobilised as a way to improve how men relate to single white female clients. In this case, the organisation exploits the heteronormative cultural assumption that gay rather than heterosexual men relate more easily to women in a work context, and incites Oliver to do his 'queer thing', to engender a client relationship that yields affective and material value. Similarly, Dean finds himself discursively positioned by his manager as 'queer', the co-ordinates of which are drawn directly from media presentations of queer; in this example, the US makeover show *Queer Eye*. Again, queer is demanded as a performance that constitutes Dean as a desirable organisational subject—a naturally talented creative expert. In these examples, the incitement to constitute queer performatively render both men as organisationally viable subjects who can add value by pleasing and satisfying client expectations. Crucially, the effort undertaken by the men to perform organisationally desirable performances of queer appeared to go unacknowledged, as Dean indicated when he told me how 'pissed off' he was sometimes at 'playing up to the queer eye stereotype . . . he [Dean's manager] just thinks I can turn it on and off like a tap'. That such performances of queer are asserted to be natural to both Dean (as suggested by his client) and Oliver (by his manager) because they are gay men, helps explain why their employers seem to have little inclination in formally recognising the performance of queer as a form of paid labour.

Elsewhere, interview data regarding the role and meaning of gay men's workplace friendships shows how queer can be been appropriated to add value outside interactions that constitute forms of paid labour. This was apparent in quite a conspicuous way in the workplace friendships struck up between gay and heterosexual men. In a cultural context that is said to celebrate the sexually ambiguous and acknowledges the multiplicity of LGBT sexualities and genders (Weeks, 2007), interviewees often discursively fixed their own and their friend's sexual identities as polar opposites. On this basis, Austin's account of his close friendship with Dominic (both are occupational therapists) is illuminating because it highlights some of the tensions arising from overlapping and competing components of discourses of gender and sexual difference:

> Dominic and I agree that we have two sides to us . . . a feminine side and a masculine side. I'm mostly aware of my feminine side because I'm gay, but straight guys are more aware of their masculine side, so there's a big difference between us. I give [Dominic] a more feminine perspective on the world, and I think he likes that coming from a gay man, rather than a straight guy. I think he feels he can open up to me without any worry of being chastised for being soft.

By essentialising sexuality and gender within a hetero/homo binary, hetero and homo subject positions are invoked to open up opportunities for organising cross-sexuality workplace friendships between the men, on a principle of 'opposites attract' according to Austin. Drawing on a heteronormative discourse that polarises sexuality and gender, Austin generates two subject positions that emphasise distinct and desirable gendered perspectives and qualities such friendships are said to occasion. Austin provides Dominic with a 'feminine perspective' on the world, such as when Austin found himself acting as a confidante to Dominic about 'girlfriend problems', 'what clothes are fashionable' and how to perform a 'softer masculinity' expected of him from his line manager. Likewise, Dominic advises Austin on how to 'use the dipstick' to test the oil level in his car and how to 'toughen up' so he avoids getting too emotionally involved with patients. In this exchange of gender based perspectives, Austin and Dominic strive to rehabilitate the other in the hope that each will become 'a better man', as Austin put it.

Both men appear to conform to a neoliberal project of self-regulation and management that is required of men as well as women in a postfeminist culture (Sender, 2006). They recognise that gay and heterosexual masculinity requires maintenance and fixing from time to time, an observation that was not lost on Austin: 'It's like that TV show, I give Dom a queer eye on life and Dom gives me a straight man's eye'. Striking here is the quirky twist on the concept of the queer eye having a recuperative effect on male heterosexuality. In this example, a 'straight man's eye' is also put to work as a restorative resource, to enable Austin to be a more 'masculine' gay man in the workplace. Indeed, the appropriation of both 'queer' and 'straight' discourse within the relational context of friendship is driven by a recognition of the possibilities for improving forms of organisational gay and straight masculinities. Austin is better equipped to manage the professional self in his interactions with patients, while Dominic is schooled in how to do a softer version of hetero-masculinity that is expected of him by his manager. As such, both men are cognisant of the shortfalls in their gender performances, and how these performances are linked to the sexual categories they identify with. Here, a tension surfaces. Realising the value of the 'queer' and 'straight' eye is premised on the assumption that gay and heterosexual men are fundamentally different. Discursive boundaries are established that have the effect of representing cross-sexuality friendship between men as a worthwhile and pleasurable enterprise that has affective and material value. From one perspective, this has a disruptive (in a queer sense) effect since it unsettles heteronormative discourses on men's friendships that routinely characterise them as emotionally hollow and difficult to establish across the hetero-homo binary (Nardi, 1999). The rise of queer visibility within postfeminist (media) culture may be seen to have a positive influence, offering co-ordinates for understanding male friendships that were once taboo at worst and difficult to formulate at best. Still, as this example testifies, in order to bring such friendships into life, both men adopt essentialist discourses of gender and sexual difference that fail to bring the hetero/homo binary to a point of collapse, leaving a heteronormative regime intact.

Concluding Discussion

This chapter has explored postfeminist sensibilities at work, in particular how they shape how queer is understood and experienced in the workplace. To that end, this chapter has discussed how queer has been variously animated in postfeminist media culture before examining how this occurs in organisational settings by drawing on previous empirical research with gay men. As such, this chapter highlights the value of continued scholarly attention to postfeminism, not least of all within organisation studies which has only started to explore the potential of postfeminism as a critical object of inquiry (Gill et al., 2017; Kelan, 2009; Lewis, 2014). What is more, this chapter underscores the importance of exploring how postfeminism intermingles with discourses on neoliberalism and those that surround queer. One benefit of importing queer into the site of debate on postfeminism is that it can be deployed as a conceptual resource to examine postfeminist sensibilities as objects of analysis (Genz and Brabon, 2009; McRobbie, 2009). For example, queer theory can help us to address questions of sexuality that seem to have been circumnavigated by scholars of postfeminism (Butler, 2013).

For the purposes of this chapter, I have engaged critically with queer theory to expose how queer is variously invoked by gay men and the organisations that employ them, and to what end. In so doing, we may observe, for instance, how employers discursively deploy queer as an organisational resource that adds value. In these instances, queer is evacuated of any political valence. It is also the case that we may come across queer moments in how gay men organise with other men in friendship, moments in which heteronormative discourses are simultaneously contested and buttressed. Such illustrations are, in one respect, remarkable given the persistent attempts made by organisations over the years to expel and/or manage 'queer' out and within the workplace (Colgan and Rumens, 2014). In another respect, that queer should be seized upon by employers as a potential valuable organisational resource is not altogether surprising. More than ever it seems sexuality is subject to intense control, organisation and regulation (Hearn, 2011). How queer is discursively deployed by employers and by gay men such as Austin reveals another set of meanings that may be attributed to what is widely recognised by scholars as a very slippery term (Sullivan, 2003). As this chapter shows, rather than get tangled up in extricating the 'real' meaning of queer, more productive is to scrutinise the conditions of possibility for discourses on queer to enter the corporate realm, and what are the consequences for reconstituting 'queer' bodies, identities, selves and relationships in the workplace. Of interest is how postfeminist and post-gay discourses permeate the study participants' interpretive repertoires of queer. As the interview data demonstrates, post-gay discourse chimes in with a postfeminist sensibility in how its annexes LGBT inequality to the past, emphasises individualism and choice over collective action and maintains the heteronormative status quo. The implications of this are problematic.

First, the reading of queer by some interviewees as a spent political force that is no longer needed in the current LGBT equalities landscape firmly locates the locus of change within the individual. Here, the interview data exposes the collaboration of postfeminist, neoliberal and post-gay discourses that, together, militate against and seek to neutralise queer as a form of anti-normative critique and politics. This does mean to say that all these discourses align harmoniously; rather, it might be that specific discursive arrangements carry sensibilities that may be traced to each of these discourses. In this way, elements from within and across these discourses may have a mutually reinforcing effect. For example, the invocation of 'post-gay' as an imprecise descriptor for a 'new' era in the equality landscape for LGBT people functions in a similar way to postfeminist discourses, in how the contributions of political movements are acknowledged, but also repudiated as no holding contemporary relevance. In a post-gay culture, as in a postfeminist culture, undue emphasis is placed on the individual to forge their own way through the world of work. As one of the earlier interviewees suggests, a gay man can *choose* to live an openly gay life if he wants to, implying that such choices are unimpinged by the constraints of hetero-norms. In this vein, younger gay men such as Alex might be said to be the heirs of a post-gay culture hard won by a previous generation. However, as noted earlier, Alex's interview extracts suggest that he cannot choose how to be gay in whatever fashion or expression he elects; it is carefully managed and regulated within the confines of heteronormativity.

Second, as McRobbie (2009) points out, neoliberal discourses mask how social groups continue to be disadvantaged and discourage collective action, especially political organising developed through alliances (e.g. feminism and LGBT activist groups). As some of the interview accounts reveal, there is a neoliberal endorsement of 'gay normality' which has supplanted queer or, where queer is manifest, reduces it to a sanitised form that has aesthetic and commercial appeal, as in those instances of 'queer value' (Wesling, 2012). For example, Alex's account shows how fitting into trendy 'hipster' work cultures, supposedly anti-mainstream in their attitude and tastes, recirculate heteronormative expectations about how gay male visibility is manifest. Again, it is the individual, not the organisation, who is freighted with the responsibility to change, in order to fit into a heteronormative work context. Of additional concern is how the neoliberal elements of postfeminist discourses that promulgate choice and change through the individual obscure those LGBT subjects who do not or cannot meet the expectations placed on them to fit into a post-gay culture. If we were to give any credence to the postfeminist assertion that all the equality battles have been won, then it is a world that only *some* have won. As commentators have pointed out, it is white, middle-class, affluent gay men and lesbians, typically domiciled in gentrified urban areas, who are the winners in a 'post-gay' age of gay and lesbian normativity (Duggan, 2002; Seidman, 2002). Such observations remind us that intersectional analyses are important to examine how postfeminist and post-gay discourses reproduce inequalities of race, gender, sexuality and so on. Indeed, it is crucial to acknowledge that the emergence of post-gay discourse at this socio-historical moment is not arbitrary. It has surfaced precisely at a time when LGBT visibility has heightened over the last few decades (Alderson, 2016; Nash, 2013), particularly within Western societies. As more LGBT people participate openly in everyday life, including the sphere of work, post-gay discourse emerges to fulfil an important role: to secure the heteronormative regime. A parallel can be drawn with postfeminist discourse. Just as a postfeminist sensibility has re-emerged at a time when more women have entered higher education and employment (McRobbie, 2009), so post-gay discourse is another example of how certain discourses mutate to ensure normative regimes remain intact. In this context, post-gay discourses reaffirm the status quo. This is voiced by Hugo who suggests that LGBT people should not 'rock the boat' for fear of losing the investments they and others have made in a neoliberal politics of gay normativity.

In conclusion, my point is that, despite the postfeminist and neoliberal overtones associated with the discursive deployment of queer in the workplace, it must not be dismissed as lacking political valance or the potential for disruption. Queer is ripe for reinvigoration, to retain its capacity to startle, unsettle and disrupt. Indeed, it is my hope that this chapter inspires others to engage critically with postfeminism as an object of study using the conceptual resources queer theory provides, so that we might further advance critique of the discourses that shape how queer is understood and experienced within a post-gay culture.

References

Agirre, K. (2012). Whenever a man takes you to lunch around here: Tracing post-feminist sensibility in "Mad Men". *Catalan Journal of Communication & Cultural Studies*, 4(2): 155–170.

Alderson, D. (2016). *Sex, Needs, and Queer Culture: From Liberation to the Post-Gay*. London: Zed Books.

Bersani, L. (1995). *Homos*. Cambridge: Harvard University Press.

Blue, M.G. (2013). The best of both worlds? Youth, gender, and a post-feminist sensibility in Disney's "Hannah Montana". *Feminist Media Studies*, 13(4): 660–675.

Butler, J. (1990). *Gender Trouble: Feminism and the Subversion of Identity*. London: Routledge.

Butler, J. (1993). *Bodies That Matter*. London: Routledge.

Butler, J. (1999). *Gender Trouble: Feminism and the Subversion of Identity*. New York and London: Routledge Classics.

Butler, J. (2013). For white girls only? Postfeminism and the politics of inclusion. *Feminist Formations*, 25(1): 35–58.

Cohan, S. (2007). Queer eye for the straight guise: Camp, postfeminism and the Fab Five's makeovers of masculinity. In Y. Tasker and D. Negra (Eds.), *Interrogating postfeminism: Gender and the Politics of Popular Culture* (pp. 176–200). Durham and London: Duke University Press.

Colgan, F., and Rumens, N. (2014). *Sexual Orientation at Work: Contemporary Issues and Perspectives*. New York: Routledge.

David, E. (2015). Purple-collar labor: Transgender workers and queer value at global call centers in the Philippines. *Gender & Society*, 29(2): 169–194.

Duggan, L. (2002). The new homonormativity: The sexual politics of neoliberalism. In R. Castronovo and D. Nelson (Eds.), *Materializing Democracy: Toward a Revitalized Cultural Politics* (pp. 175–194). Durham, NC: Duke University Press.

Edelman, L. (2004). *No Future: Queer Theory and the Death Drive*. Durham, NC: Duke University Press.

Einarsdóttir, A., Hoel, H., and Lewis, D. (2015). "It's nothing personal": Anti-homosexuality in the British workplace. *Sociology*, 49(6): 1183–1199.

Faludi, S. (1992). *Backlash: The Undeclared War Against Women*. London: Vintage.

Faludi, S. (1999). *Stiffed: The Betrayal of the American Man*. New York: W. Morrow and Company.

Genz, S., and Brabon, B.A. (2009). *Postfeminism: Cultural Texts and Theories*. Chippenham: Edinburgh University Press.

Gerhard, J. (2005). Sex and the city: Carrie Bradshaw's queer postfeminism. *Feminist Media Studies*, 5(1): 37–49.

Ghaziani, A. (2011). Post-gay collective identity construction. *Social Problems*, 58(1): 99–125.

Gill, R. (2007). Postfeminist media culture: Elements of a sensibility. *European Journal of Cultural Studies*, 10(2): 147–166.

Gill, R. (2008). Culture and subjectivity in neoliberal and postfeminist times. *Subjectivity*, 25(1): 432–445.

Gill, R. (2009). Mediated intimacy and postfeminism: A discourse analytic examination of sex and relationships advice in a women's magazine. *Discourse & Communication*, 3(4): 345–369.

Gill, R. (2014). Unspeakable inequalities: Post feminism, entrepreneurial subjectivity, and the repudiation of sexism among cultural workers. *Social Politics*, 21(4): 509–528.

Gill, R. (2016). Post-postfeminism? New feminist visibilities in postfeminist times. *Feminist Media Studies*, 16(4): 610–630.

Gill, R., Kelan, E.K. and Scharff, C.M. (2017) A postfeminist sensibility at work. Gender, Work and Organization, 24(3): 226–244.

Gill, R., and Scharff, C. (Eds.). (2011). *New Femininities: Postfeminism, Neoliberalism and Subjectivity*. Basingstoke: Palgrave Macmillan.

Halberstam, J. (2011). *The Queer Art of Failure*. Durham, NC: Duke University Press.

Halperin, D. (1995). *Saint Foucault: Towards a Gay Hagiography*. New York: Oxford University Press.

Harvey, D. (2005). *NeoLiberalism: A Brief History*. Oxford: Oxford University Press.

Hearn, J. (2011). Sexualities, work, organizations, and managements: Empirical, policy, and theoretical challenges. In E. Jeanes, D. Knights, and P.Y. Martin (Eds.), *Handbook of Gender, Work and Organization* (pp. 299–314). Chichester: Wiley.

Jagose, A. (1996). *Queer Theory: An Introduction*. New York: New York University Press.

Jørgensen, M.W., and Phillips, L.J. (2002). *Discourse Analysis as Theory and Method*. London: Sage.

Kelan, E.K. (2009). Gender fatigue: The ideological dilemma of gender neutrality and discrimination in organisations. *Canadian Journal of Administrative Sciences*, 26(3): 197–210.

Kissling, E.A. (2013). Pills, periods, and postfeminism: The new politics of marketing birth control. *Feminist Media Studies*, 13(3): 490–504.

LeMaster, B. (2015). Discontents of being and becoming fabulous on RuPaul's Drag U: Queer criticism in neoliberal times. *Women's Studies in Communication*, 38(2): 167–186.

Lewis, P. (2014). Postfeminism, femininities and organization studies: Exploring a new agenda. *Organization Studies*, 35(12): 1845–1866.

Lumby, C. (2011). Past the post in feminist media studies. *Feminist Media Studies*, 11(1): 95–100.

McRobbie, A. (2009). *The Aftermath of Feminism: Gender, Culture and Social Change*. London and Thousand Oaks, CA: Sage.

Nardi, P.M. (1999). *Gay Men's Friendships: Invincible Communities*. Chicago: University of Chicago Press.

Nash, C.J. (2013). The age of the "post-mo"? Toronto's gay village and a new generation. *Geoforum*, 49(6): 243–252.

Negra, D. (2009). *What a Girl Wants? Fantasizing the Reclamation of Self in Postfeminism*. London: Routledge.

Ozturk, M.B., and Rumens, N. (2014). Gay male academics in UK business and management schools: Negotiating heteronormativities in everyday work life. *British Journal of Management*, 25(3): 503–517.

Projansky, S. (2001). *Watching Rape: Film and Television in Postfeminist Culture.* New York and London: New York University Press.

Ramsey, E.M., and Santiago, G. (2004). The conflation of male homosexuality and femininity in Queer Eye for the Straight Guy. *Feminist Media Studies*, 4(3): 353–355.

Rumens, N. (2011). *Queer Company: The Role and Meaning of Friendship in Gay Men's Work Lives.* Aldershot: Ashgate.

Rumens, N. (2016). Towards queering the business school: A research agenda for advancing lesbian, gay, bisexual and trans perspectives and issues. *Gender, Work & Organization*, 23(1): 36–51.

Sandberg, S. (2013). *Lean In: Women, Work and the Will to Lead.* London: WH Allen.

Sedgwick, E.K. (1990). *Epistemology of the Closet.* Berkeley, CA: University of California Press.

Seidman, S. (2002). *Beyond the Closet: The Transformation of Gay and Lesbian Life.* New York: Routledge.

Sender, K. (2006). Queens for a day: *Queer Eye for the Straight Guy* and the neoliberal project. *Critical Studies in Media Communication*, 23(2): 131–151.

Sullivan, N. (2003). *A Critical Introduction to Queer Theory.* New York: New York University Press.

Tasker, Y., and Negra, D. (Eds.). (2007). *Interrogating Postfeminism: Gender and the Politics of Popular Culture.* Durham, NC: Duke University Press.

Warner, M. (Ed.). (1993). *Fear of a Queer Planet: Queer Politics and Social Theory.* Minneapolis: University of Minnesota Press.

Weeks, J. (2007). *The World We Have Won.* London: Routledge.

Wesling, M. (2012). Queer value. *GLQ: A Journal of Lesbian and Gay Studies*, 18(1): 107–125.

Westerfelhaus, R., and Lacroix, C. (2006). Seeing "straight" through Queer Eye: Exposing the strategic rhetoric of heteronormativity in a mediated ritual of gay rebellion. *Critical Studies in Media Communication*, 23(5): 426–444.

Whelehan, I. (2010). Remaking feminism: Or why is postfeminism so boring? *Nordic Journal of English Studies*, 9(3): 155–172.

Williams, C.L., Giuffre, P.A., and Dellinger, C. (2009). The gay-friendly closet. *Sexuality Research and Social Policy*, 6(1): 29–45.

5 Contested Terrain

The Power to Define, Control and Benefit From Gender Equality Efforts

Elisabeth K. Kelan

The Dynamics of Postfeminism and Gender Equality in Organisations

83% of companies cite gender equality among their strategic priorities (McKinsey, 2012). Sheryl Sandberg encourages women to 'lean in' (2013) and Anne-Marie Slaughter (2015) asks women to find happiness through work-life balance. Men are encouraged to become champions for gender equality change efforts which is visible in the United Nations #HeforShe campaign (United Nations, 2016), and the *Esquire* special issue on men's role in gender equality (Esquire, 2016). There is a plethora of awards for gender equality (Business in the Community, 2016; The Times, 2016) and corporate websites regularly contain information on what the companies are doing for women. Yet it is evident that not only is the number of women in senior leadership roles moving at a snail's pace but also that work-life balance is not any easier to achieve. Gender inequality is still prevalent in organisations and society (World Economic Forum, 2016). While the gendered nature of organisations remains largely unaddressed (Acker, 1990), some organisations are competing to appear as engaging on gender equality. The attempt by organisations to appear as good employers for women can therefore be understood as a 'glossification' of diversity and inclusion (Gatrell and Swan, 2008). This raises the question of in how far being a change agent for gender equality in those organisations might yield some prestige for individuals involved in that work.

In order to understand the recent changes in the discursive configurations of gender equality in organisations, it is therefore useful to draw on the notion of a postfeminist sensibility (Gill, 2007). Postfeminism is a fairly recent addition to the lexicon of gender, work and organisation (see Kelan, 2008; Kelan and Dunkley Jones, 2010; Lewis, 2014) although it has been used in media and cultural studies and the humanities for a longer period of time. There are at least four competing definitions of postfeminism which have been outlined elsewhere (Gill, Kelan, and Scharff, 2017). In this chapter, postfeminism is conceptualised as a sensibility or a specific discursive formation. Postfeminism is used to understand how the contemporary common sense on gender is structured and what the winning arguments on gender are at any given time. This does include notions of the 'overing' of feminism where feminism is repudiated by taking it into account (McRobbie, 2008). This version of postfeminism analyses how the individual is constructed as in charge of their own destiny and how that relates to neoliberalism. As Lewis and Simpson (2017) have shown, Hakim's preference theory can be seen as an expression of this version of postfeminism where structural and cultural barriers are downplayed and gender equality is seen as a choice. Using post-feminism as a sensibility also means that postfeminism is not understood as an identification. While it has been acknowledged that postfeminism is closely related to neoliberalism and in fact that choosing subject of postfemi-nism is closely aligned with the ideals associated with the subject of neolib-eralism (Gill, 2007), using postfeminism as a lens does not attempt to map different forms of feminisms. Instead postfeminism is here understood as an analytical tool to understand the contemporary common sense on gender.

In an earlier article with Rosalind Gill and Christina Scharff (Gill et al., 2017), we identified the current expressions of postfeminism centre on the repudiation of sexism and gender fatigue. We show that in empirical research participants regularly claim that they have never encountered any sexism, although they do notice the low number of women in certain fields of work. Research participants also regularly minimise any experience of sexism or they provide alternative explanations for why there are few women in spe-cific areas. This expression of postfeminism is supported by four ways of accounting for gender inequalities. First, gender inequalities are located in the past and are constructed in such a way that they could not happen today. Second, gender inequalities are spatially located elsewhere; they hap-pen in other organisations or other countries. Third, we also noticed that many research participants talked about a 'female advantage' where women simply cannot be discriminated against because the labour market is stacked in their favour; their skills are in high demand and they have the right type of education to succeed. Finally, many research participants just accept gen-der inequalities as the way the world is; this reasoning does not allow much questioning for why the world is that way or if it could be different. In this work, postfeminism is put to work by exploring the patterning of the com-mon sense of how gender is constructed.

This patterning of the common sense seems to shift since the much dis-cussed books by Sheryl Sandberg (2013) and Anne-Marie Slaughter (2016). While much of this work is very much in line with the choosing and self-reinventing subject of postfeminism, it has also been observed that this cur-rent formation of postfeminism is closely associated with treated gender inequalities as obvious and self-evident (Gill and Orgad, 2016). While in earlier postfeminist formations gender inequality has been 'overed' and experiences of gender discrimination have firmly been located in the past (Kelan, 2009a), there is a specific knowingness around gender inequality which constructs gender inequality as obvious and as a fact of life (Kelan and Dunkley Jones, 2010). The tools suggested to deal with this obvious gender inequality are however highly individualised and focus on empowering the individual rather than changing systems and structures (Gill and Orgad, 2016).

An interesting juncture to explore this dynamic is in relation to how gender inequality is treated within organisations. While research has explored how individuals deal with gender inequality (Kelan, 2009a, 2009b), this questions concerns how organisations attempt to change individuals, systems and structures. The particular interest here is on change agents who try to implement gender equality alongside other equalities in organisations (Kirton, Greene and Dean, 2007; Meyerson and Tompkins, 2007; Tatli, 2011). As organisations are increasingly in public competition to appear as 'good citizens' in regard to gender equality, it could well be imagined that those who define and shape gender equality conceptualisations in organisations are getting some credit for it. With this, who can define the parameters of gender equality and who gets credit for it, is becoming a contested terrain. In many organisations, the contest for who has the power to define gender is already entailed in the structure of gender equality efforts. Most organisations have a function responsible for equal opportunities or diversity and inclusion which depending on size might include various individuals who fulfil this function either full or part time often on top of existing responsibilities. In addition, most organisations have an employee resource group like a women's network which hosts events on gender equality topics and often works closely with the equal opportunities or diversity and inclusion professionals. The women's networks normally have a more voluntary character, in that members organise events on top of their daily duties and often in their free time. Organisations would regularly support these women's networks by providing space and a budget for catering and speakers. In most organisations, the women's network and the diversity and inclusion function work side by side but it is evident that both groups might have a very different outlook on, and responsibilities for, gender equality. This is partly a function of the role the two groups play in the organisation but might also be dependent on individual strategies to achieve gender equality. It is for instance possible that both groups compete for getting credit for working towards gender equality. Another area of tension could potentially be if men are included in gender equality efforts.

This chapter will consider how in one organisation the women's lobby and the equal opportunities officer are struggling to pursue their own vision of what gender equality should look like and who is rewarded for it. This example provides the opportunity to explore how different interpretations of gender equality are competing in one workplace and how this could be conceptualised against the backdrop of a postfeminist sensibility. It is argued that in the organisation, the women's lobby and the equal opportunities officer are competing with each other about who defines the boundaries of gender equality and who gets credit for gender equality efforts. This indicates that gender equality has become a desired resource that different organisational actors are competing for. As analysts of postfeminism have shown, gender inequality is regularly minimised, denied and repudiated in conversations but with gender equality being seen as a desired outcome, it appears that gender equality has also become a prized resource which is worth competing for. This chapter will offer an interpretation of this dynamic through a postfeminist lens.

Researching Information Media

Before outlining the contested terrain between the women's lobby and the equal opportunities officer, I would like to explain how the research was conducted. The material I draw on for this chapter form part of a wider research project. This project explored how men in middle management positions can be change agents for gender equality. In prior research I had explored how CEOs talk about gender equality (Kelan and Wratil, 2014) and one of the key insights from that research was that it is often middle managers who are roadblocks for gender equality. Using 'doing gender' as a framework (Nentwich and Kelan, 2014), I presumed that many of the ways in which men support gender equality are going to be subconscious and would be hard to articulate. I, therefore, selected ethnographic methods to explore men's involvement in gender equality (Czarniawska, 2014; McDonald, 2005) and set out to job shadow middle managers. I decided to approach organisations that I had known were at the forefront of implementing gender equality because I presumed that I would be most likely to find middle managers there who would be doing gender equality well. I approached a range of organisations and most responded positively to my request. This is fairly unusual for ethnographic work due to the invasive nature of this approach. However, finding men who are in middle management positions and good at gender equality was a different issue. I defined middle management position broadly as having direct report and reporting to senior management (Harding, Lee, and Ford, 2014; Rouleau, 2005). Most organisations struggled to suggest a middle manager who would be willing to be shadowed and who they felt was good at gender equality. Even when they suggested someone, it was often through the initial conversation with the middle manager that it became evident that this person was not suitable for the research. I was able to shadow three men in middle management positions in three organisations. In each organisation, I conducted supplementary interviews with the shadowee and co-workers. The interviews were transcribed and I noted my observations in field notes, which were later coded.

For this chapter, I will particularly explore how gender equality is a contested terrain in one organisation. The organisation is a public sector organisation working in the media field. I have selected the pseudonym Information Media for the organisation (all names of interviewees are pseudonyms as well). Like many organisations, there is not one single cataclysmic event that started the focus on gender equality at Information Media. Instead, there was a range of intertwined approaches that over time contributed to the fact that gender equality was institutionalised at Information Media.

On Information Media's website, gender equality is described as 'equal opportunities and the advancement of women'. This shows that the focus is on creating equal opportunities between women and men, but equally to advance women into positions where they are currently not present. The rationale provided by Information Media on their website for their engagement in gender equality is that they are a public organisation and as such have a role model function to influence changes in society such as achieving greater gender equality. In addition, new equalities legislation from the government meant that Information Media had to develop a strategy for achieving equal opportunities. As a consequence, the organisation created a commission for equal opportunities and the position of an equal opportunities officer. The organisation had developed an equal opportunities strategy, which aimed at reducing any potential disadvantages for women to reduce the underrepresentation of women. The organisation therefore draws on push factors like the new legislation, as well as pull factors through being a role model for gender equality in society to justify its engagement in gender equality efforts. The framing also makes clear that the gender equality strategy focuses on women with the explicit aim to end women's underrepresentation and to remove any forms of discrimination.

Following the legal requirement as well as the role model function Information Media holds, the organisation established a range of equal opportunities officers in different organisational units that would work closely with the main equal opportunities officer to remedy existing inequalities within the organisation. The CEO appoints the main equal opportunities officer after a consultation with the gender equality commission. The network of equal opportunities officers, who perform this role on top of their daily responsibilities, are the first point of contact for any grievances individuals might have about gender equality. Often those issues are then relayed to the main equal opportunities officer who dedicates most of his/her time to advancing equality in Information Media. The main equal opportunities officer reports to the senior team and one member of the senior team is responsible for briefing the CEO on the state of gender equality in the organisation.

While this is the formal structure of gender equality in the organisation, there is a parallel structure which is more informal. A group of senior women within Information Media have put pressure on the organisation to become more gender equal. This group of influential women formed a women's lobby, which predates the gender equality programme. This women's lobby is a networking group for women who get together to discuss issues of mutual relevance. The women's lobby is—as the name implies—also a lobby group, which brings pertinent issues to the attention of senior management.

The women's lobby is a voluntary grouping, meaning that members give up their private time to join group activities and discussions. Membership appears fairly stable, although not all members are equally involved all the time.

Traditionally, there was a strong overlap between the office of the equal opportunities officer and the membership of the women's lobby—i.e., the function of the equal opportunities officer had been occupied by a member of the women's lobby. This meant that the agendas of the two groupings were perceived as aligned and the personal union of being the equal opportunities officer and being a member of the women's lobby ensured that. However more recently a woman who had not been part of the women's lobby was appointed as the equal opportunities officer for the organisation. It is not clear what prompted this decision by the CEO to appoint an equal opportunities officer who is not a prominent member of the women's lobby but it is evident that being part of the women's lobby is not a requirement *de jure* or *de facto* to be the equal opportunities officer. In conversations I had during the fieldwork, it was suggested that the fact that the equal opportunities officer was also a member of the women's lobby has been a historical coincidence. This appointment cast the unity of vision between the women's lobby and the equal opportunities officers into question. Very quickly after entering the field, I noticed the emergence of some friction between the two groupings, and the majority of this chapter will explore how the terrain of gender equality was contested between the women's lobby and the equal opportunities officer.

Gender Equality, Change Agents and Postfeminism

Before unfolding how the terrain of gender inequality is contested in Information Media, it should be highlighted that part of the struggle around gender inequality was entailed in the different functions the change agents for gender equality play in an organisation. The women's lobby wants more radical change whereas the equal opportunity officer is working in and through an existing structure which makes her more of a tempered radical (Meyerson and Scully, 1995). Tempered radicals embody ambivalence as they aim to change the organisation while also being different themselves and as such experience inequality (Meyerson and Scully, 1995). They are radical as they aim to change the status quo but tempered because they feel unfairly treated by aim to control this feeling. Equal opportunities officers and diversity practitioners generally often occupy the space of tempered radicals (Kelan and Wratil, 2017; Kirton et al., 2007; Tatli, 2011).

As a consequence, one might argue that the women's lobby has a more radical agenda that might be more aligned with radical feminism, whereas the equal opportunities officers are closer to a neoliberal understanding of feminism. It was however notable that the actual ideological content of the debates around gender equality were in the background. The conceptualisations of how to achieve gender equality were rather driven by the structural positioning where the women's lobby could make more radical demands whereas the equal opportunities officer had to find a consensus to ensure that gender equality measures are in place. What makes this an interesting scenario to explore as an expression of a postfeminist sensibility is the fact that the women's lobby and the equal opportunities officers agreed that gender inequality is obvious and self-evident. The disagreement over how to achieve gender inequality was partly related to the structural positioning but more importantly for a postfeminist analysis is that the disagreement was used to exert power. As the main protagonists in this definitional struggle are women, this could be read as a specific intra-gender relationship (Mavin and Grandy, 2016; Mavin, Grandy, and Williams, 2014), it is also an expression of a specific postfeminist moment where gender equality is seen as a desired currency to which different actors lay claim.

In the following section, I will discuss two discursive formations where the different organisational actors vied for power over who controls and defines gender equality and who is rewarded for it. The first discursive formation evolved around who received credit for an award for gender equality and the second explores how the inclusion of men in gender equality became a discursive ideological struggle. Both of those discursive formations are understood as a specific expression of a postfeminist sensibility where gender equality is seen as priced and therefore becomes worthwhile to struggle over. This expression of the postfeminist sensibility is a specific example of how gender equality is made sense of in a unique context. Rather than constructing gender as passé or appealing to individuals to reinvent themselves (Gill and Orgad, 2016; Kelan, 2009a), it is shown that achieving gender equality is seen as the obvious objective and that how prestige is bestowed on those who are seen as in charge of gender equality in an organisational context.

The Award for Gender Equality

Shortly before I started the fieldwork, the CEO of Information Media received an award for gender equality. This prestigious award was a public recognition of the equality efforts the organisation had undergone and was handed out to the CEO in a ceremony. The award was given to the CEO directly to value his leadership on gender equality. The equal opportunities officer, who had also written the submission for the award, was allowed to travel with the CEO to the award ceremony. The CEO's award was widely celebrated in the media as a major achievement.

The equal opportunities officer, Brunhilde, and I had been in touch through a mutual contact. She was extremely helpful in supporting my research, and she introduced me to Benjamin, my shadowee, for further discussions and arrangements. I had never met Brunhilde in person, but she stopped by Benjamin's office:

Brunhilde comes to Benjamin's office to introduce herself to me. We have a brief conversation and arrange an interview for later this week. She also mentions to Benjamin that he should stop by her office later on. . . . Benjamin and I walk back from a meeting and knock on Brunhilde's door. She is in and tells us that she is glad to see us. She also gives a box of chocolates to Benjamin. She had purchased them on her recent trip aboard when the CEO received the award for gender equality.

When I conducted the fieldwork, the CEO receiving the award for gender equality was still very fresh in people's minds, I asked Brunhilde in the interview directly how the award was perceived internally and externally:

Brunhilde: I did not really have time to speak with many people [since I returned] but I think that everyone should be proud. Because we made an effort . . . particularly in comparison to other organisations. And of course, it could always be more but if you see where we started . . . And we try to move things forward by talking about them. And course it is always not enough for the women's lobby. In the media, the award was discussed in a positive way. There was a report in [one of the newspapers], where the president [of a women's network], I do not know this lady, there are many women's networks here and she said, 'I don't know why Information Media received the award. They are not that great'. That was the only critical comment and I was a bit surprised by this and asked myself 'why are women so critical yet again'. . . . We are not where we want to be [in regard to gender equality] but to talk everything down?

Brunhilde constructs the media coverage of the award as largely positive but also mentioned that the president of an external women's network was a bit critical about the award and questioned what Information Media had done to deserve it. Brunhilde appears disappointed that women are not more supportive of one another. This goes back to an earlier part of the interview where Brunhilde explained to me how the women's lobby group and the equal opportunities officer have developed different approaches to achieving gender equality. Brunhilde described how being part of a panel with a member of the women's lobby was challenging for her:

Brunhilde: Well, the most friendly, the most friendly label, that I have been given so far, was by a colleague from the women's lobby. We were invited to appear at an event and I thought that will not go well. But we somehow made it. But when she introduced me, she introduced me, that was crazy, she really usurped the presenting role and she said 'she [Brunhilde] always see the glass half full and I see it half empty'. That was a friendly description of our relationship.

Brunhilde reflected on a public interaction she had with a member of the women's lobby which was indicative of the different approaches that both groups take: the women's lobby seemed to be more critical and the equal opportunities officer more positive. However, in the short description of the interaction the frictions are becoming evident.

In spite of those problems, Brunhilde talked very positively about the efforts of a precursor of the women's lobby, which meant that women in the 1990s already lobbied for greater gender equality at Information Media. Later on, the women's lobby emerged from this group, which particularly focused on and consists of women in leadership positions.

Brunhilde: And the women's lobby really ensured that the gender strategy was put into place because they put a lot of pressure on. Our problem is now, well, we do not have a problem that the women's lobby exists, but we would prefer a proper lobby group not a group that, well, sees itself as a watchdog. We [the equal opportunities officers] are in the process of emancipating ourselves. We are institutionalised, and our approach is a different one to a pure lobbying group. . . . Our approach is a different one and we would want the women's lobby to be a partner. And, I don't know if that is a women's problem or a men's problem as well but it is this mentality 'I invented it and it is mine and I do not want to hand it over'. And that is where we are now. And when we try to make a point, then we get back 'who invented it?'. We then say that we totally agree and we would not want to question that and we value that. . . . And that is where we are at the moment.

Brunhilde clearly articulates how she sees that the women's lobby and the equal opportunities officers have a fundamentally different role—the lobby group puts pressure onto the organisation and the equal opportunities officers that make gender equality happen. Later, Brunhilde goes on to describe how her predecessor in the main equal opportunities role was at the same time a member of the women's lobby and that she was torn apart between the institutional requirements and the requirements of the women's lobby. As discussed earlier, the nature of the change agency that both groups engage in are fundamentally different. This relates to the structural difference in the nature of the change agency that both groups have but Brunhilde goes further. Brunhilde points out that the women's lobby behaves as if it owned the topic of gender equality and no one else is allowed to intervene. Brunhilde describes how she attempted to give credit to the women's lobby for their work, and in fact, she talks about them in complementary ways, but it is also evident that the women's lobby challenges much of Brunhilde's work. This indicates that Brunhilde thinks that the women's lobby is possessive of the issue of gender equality and aims to dominate it, allowing other perspectives or functions not to exist. It indicates the struggle over who is in charge of gender equality. Brunhilde herself described the difficulty of working with members of the women's lobby because they sit on the gender equality commission and say that 'everything we [the equal opportunities officers] do is bad'.

Brunhilde: You have to fight all the time, and then you have to fight against the women as well. That is hard.

Brunhilde here articulates the difficulty of being a change agent on gender equality in that one has to fight everyone—even those who presumably should be on your side. The idea here is that the organisation is resistant to change and she has to fight for gender equality to be recognised. However, she appears particularly hurt by the fact that she also has to fight the women's group. Although both sides aim to make gender equality a reality, this shows that both sides fight to have the power to control gender equality.

When I asked Brunhilde, why she thinks that the women's lobby is behaving in the way, she says,

Brunhilde: They [the women's lobby] might see its success evaporate and they maybe see their hopes dashed. I mean it is well, it is a bit like cutting the proverbial umbilical cord, the child does not want to do anymore what you want and finds its own path. (. . .) There are many ways to help me to understand but it is still unacceptable.

What we see here is that Brunhilde tries very hard to find a positive explanation for why the women's lobby might be reacting negatively and she suggests that it has to do with the fact that a different agenda is being developed but there also seems to be a sense that the women's lobby might feel that they did not get enough credit for gender equality. At the core of the conflict seems to be who has the right to decide on what actions are taken for gender equality and who is rewarded for it.

My access to the organisation has come through Brunhilde, and I was embedded within the official gender equality structure rather than the women's lobby, which might explain why my research project became an area of interest. A researcher conducting an academic project in the organisation can potentially be seen as an expert validating a certain perspective in this case presumably of the equal opportunities officer. It is therefore not surprising that getting to speak with the women's lobby members has been difficult. I was able to speak with Bianca, a prominent member of the women's lobby and one of its co-founders. Before agreeing to be interviewed, she first wanted to speak with me informally and we arranged a brief meeting. After this 'vetting', she agreed to an interview. Although I prompted her several times to talk about the women's lobby and the equal opportunities officer, she was fairly guarded and talked about the formal structure rather than differences in opinion. However, what became apparent in the interview but also the informal conversation beforehand is that the women's lobby wants change in regard to gender relations fast and they perceive the official structure as too slow which echoes a more radical view on change agency.

Bianca was already a member of a women's network and was then approached by the CEO to see if she wanted to support him on gender equality alongside other women. They then went on to invite all the women who work for Information Media to a meeting where the strategic plan they wanted to implement was discussed. According to Bianca, 'The CEO was fabulous. He really created an advisory role for us'. She also talked about how the women's lobby got the CEO to sign a public declaration for gender equality which played an important role in the CEO receiving the gender equality award. In the interview, Bianca clearly tries to establish that she has a close connection with the CEO through her advisory role as part of the women's lobby and she also was instrumental in ensuring that the CEO made the public declaration on gender equality which was then one of the influential factors for the award that the CEO received.

What seems to have happened in this situation is that Bianca and the women's lobby must have felt that they laid the groundwork for the CEO's award but were then not attending the award ceremony and the CEO took the equal opportunities officer instead. The equal opportunities officer of course had completed the application form for the award and also driven the agenda on gender equality forward. However, the fact that the CEO did not take a representative from a women's lobby but the equal opportunities officer made it seem like the award was due to the effort of the CEO and the equal opportunities officer. This undoubtedly did not contribute to an amelioration of the relationship between the women's lobby and the equal opportunities officer and goes right to the heart of what this struggle is about not only defining gender equality at Information Media but also being rewarded for it.

This first discursive formation is indicative of the struggle that the women's lobby and the equal opportunities officer seem to engage in. While both have different functions in the organisation, the core debate is not about those different roles or even how radical one can be or not be. It is not simply the conflict between tempered radicals and radicals. Instead, the struggle is about who can define gender equality and who is rewarded for it. This is an expression of a specific postfeminist sensibility where gender inequality is accepted as a fact but the struggle is about who gets to define how gender equality is achieved and who is given credit for it. The sense making around gender that exists in this specific context therefore sees gender equality as a prized good and different sides want to claim the spoils. The spoils in this case are the prestige that radiates from the award.

A Diverging Ideology on Including Men

The second discursive formation centres on the role of men in gender equality change processes. As I described previously, the CEO of Information Media had recently been honoured for his commitment to gender equality before I started the fieldwork. I had selected a company specifically for the purpose of researching what men can do to support gender equality. However, the role of men in gender equality turned out to be a central point of contention between the women's lobby and the equal opportunity officer as I discovered swiftly. One might presume that there was a particularly strong focus on men in the organisation. This was not the case. The overall equal opportunities agenda tries to achieve balance between women and men. From my experience in the organisation, most activities and evaluations were specifically focusing on women and ensuring that women are not disadvantaged in any shape or form in the organisation. While many activities were targeted at women such as around career advancement, there was also a programme to encourage female and male journalists to use gender-aware language. Most programmes on work-life integration seemed to specifically focus on women's responsibilities in the home. During the research, I only came across one initiative, which attempted to ensure that men are taking parental leave, which was targeted specifically at men. While most activities in the organisation did not focus on men, the inclusion of men in gender equality is another example of how the aim to control and shape gender equality is equated with power in this specific context.

Throughout the field visit at Information Media, I noticed that the CEO's award was an issue not only from the perspective that the women's lobby had not been included in the award but also that there were questions raised as to why a man would be given this award. I heard comments and remarks either first hand or reported from a range of individuals in informal conversations of how 'strange' it is to give a man an award for gender equality. This specific CEO award is given to CEOs of either gender following the idea that leadership support is central to achieve gender equality (Thomas, 2004). However, on this occasion a male CEO received the award, which created some discussion on why a man would receive such an award.

Bjorn saw this award as a great motivator for the CEO but also for other men:

Bjorn: It is a special recognition and he notices, yes, that makes sense. (. . .) It is good for the cause, because he gives a new impetus. (. . .) It is also good for others to see that if one engages with the topic and supports it that pays off. That is not a disadvantage but that is good. And it is a good thing for managers to get such awards.

Bjorn thereby sees such awards as inspirational for other men to take gender equality seriously, but also acknowledges that it might give the CEO a clear signal that he should continue and potentially even intensify his efforts on gender equality.

One initiative through which the organisation tries to encourage men to change roles is paternity leave. There was a specific campaign targeted at men to ensure that they start taking parental leave, which was widely advertised across the organisation.

Bjorn: You can see that in the daddy campaign, that we ran, well, for many that is not a big topic but you see it on the intranet, and you see posters on the wall and maybe something sticks with individuals and they develop an understanding, bit by bit, that 'yes, if men take parental leave, well, that is okay'. That changes the mindset.

Talking about the paternity leave campaign within Information Media, Bjorn suggests that people who are exposed to this message slowly accept the fact that fathers should take parental leave as well. However, later in the interview Bjorn suggests that the campaign was not well received and some people were highly critical of it:

Bjorn: In regard to the daddy campaign, it was questioned 'why is there no campaign for all the poor single mothers, who have to master their life like true champions. Not only half a year or two months, like daddies, who then tell you how lovely it was, but who have to plan the entire time, the entire life from early to late in great detail'. That is totally right. That is terrible. But against the backdrop of 'I want to ensure that more men take parental leave and achieve gender equality' that is completely wrong. But this narrow mindedness starts swiftly.

Bjorn here defends the initiative to ensure that more men participate in parental leave by saying that one needs to see the bigger picture. He does not deny the fact that single mothers have a tough life, but he maintains that focusing on men taking parental leave is a necessary requirement for gender equality to be achieved. However, this points to some of the pushback that exists within the organisation around focusing on men and gender equality.

Brunhilde described the stance of the women's lobby towards men as rather antagonistic ('these evil men do not want to give up [power]'). Brunhilde, however, was of the opinion that one has to work with men to achieve gender equality, but that was not a viewpoint that seemed shared with the women's lobby. The women's lobby was described in the conversation as constructing men as enemies who have to give up the power in favour of women. The women's lobby appears to resist the move to include men and instead seems to prefer to focus on women.

This also transpired in some of the comments I received about my research. While I have not heard open criticism of my project directly, it was reported to me by Brunhilde as well as Bjorn that my choice of research subject has been questioned. Brunhilde told me that some members of the women's lobby apparently had remarked something along the line of 'what's the point of it'. Bjorn also mentioned that my wish to study men's involvement in gender equality, together with my choice of person to follow, had raised some eyebrows. This indicates that not only the idea to explore men's involvement in gender equality is supposedly questionable—if not flawed—but also that the person that Brunhilde and I selected was not an appropriate choice.

Bianca was also once the boss of my shadowee, Benjamin. Both had fallen out at one point. Although it was difficult to reconstruct what had happened at the time, it appears that the fallout concerned Benjamin missing a work meeting to be with his child and Bianca resenting this. From what I understand from Bianca, she thought that Benjamin played the caring father to get out of the meeting while Benjamin felt that his wish to be with his child was not respected. While this appears as a minor incident it still had repercussions many years after which it occurred, which led to the women's lobby questioning my choice of research subject.

It also touches on a similar point to what Bjorn described in regard to parental leave for fathers. Men who want to be involved fathers face the criticism of women, presumably mothers, maybe even single mothers, who potentially had their requests for flexibility ignored for many years and now men can profit from those benefits that women never enjoyed. Focusing on men as fathers is therefore seen as a distraction for gender equality which just allows men to have an excuse to be absent from work while women not only have to cover for them at work but also still carry the main responsibility for childcare. Men prioritising childcare is thereby seen as a convenient excuse and the real issues that working mothers face remain ignored. This seems to be the opinion of many members of the women's lobby. However, the opposing view that men need to be involved in gender equality efforts means that giving voice to men's caring issues is relevant and important. Such a perspective was more in line with Brunhilde's, Bjorn's and the official gender equality strategy that Information Media pursued.

These tensions were also visible in respect to the mentoring scheme that Information Media set up. The mentoring scheme aimed to advance women which would happen through them receiving advice from more senior members of the organisation. One central point of contention was whether or not men can be mentors for women. One point of view was that women should be mentored by women, but another point of view was that mentors could be men or women as long as the mentees are women. The former clearly presumed that women can only learn from other women. However, the scarcity of women in senior positions means that there are fewer senior women around which effectively means that the few senior women have to mentor many junior women. This was the perspective that many members of the women's lobby had. The latter presumes that women can learn from senior women as well as senior men, but it also implies that the senior individuals, particularly men, can learn something from the junior women as well. This was what the equal opportunities officer preferred. It is another example of how the women's lobby and the equal opportunities officer had different ideas about how to advance gender equality.

The diverging ideology in regard to the inclusion of men often meant that the women's lobby and the equal opportunity officer pursued different strategies for gender equality. The women's lobby questioned why men should be involved in gender equality efforts from why the CEO received an award over who is seen as a parent, to who can mentor. They were against including men and often questioned and pushed back when they perceived that men had an advantage from engaging in gender equality that women did not enjoy. The equal opportunity officer and the official organisational perspective in contrast followed an approach of including men to ensure that they are on board when it comes to achieving gender equality. Rather than seeing men as an enemy who get credit for things that women have fought for, this perspective sees men as an important part of achieving gender equality by addressing them directly.

As in the previous example, one could read this as different forms of feminism trying to pursue their own set of politics. In turn, this could be understood as a difference between second-wave feminism, which often argued for a focus on women and women-only spaces against a more neoliberal feminism where men are seen as partners on the way to gender equality. However, there is also another dynamic that lurks underneath the surface and that dynamic is an expression of a postfeminist sensibility. As discussed earlier, the award in itself or that the (male) CEO received it was not an issue as such, but the women's lobby disliked not being included in the award ceremony. Similarly, the focus on men was not only an issue because some members of the women's lobby wanted to empower women rather than men; part of the issue seems to be that this was not something that had emerged from the women's lobby. If the focus on men and gender equality gains traction, this could be equated with the women's lobby losing some of its power to define how gender equality looks. In this expression of the postfeminist sensibility gender equality is seen as something that awards prestige and not having defined a specific focal area, in this case engaging men in gender equality, means that the own ability to shape gender equality is diminished. Rather than being the result of different versions of feminism, some of the contention seems to relate to the power to shape gender equality and the risk of losing control over it.

Gender Equality Work and Postfeminism

The fact that the equal opportunities officer and the women's lobby competed for the direction and rewards of gender equality is indicative of the fact that gender equality is contested terrain. Those who define and control gender equality can also reap rewards from it; not in the sense that gender equality has been progressed or indeed is achieved but rather through the prestige that is associated with being involved in that work. While most work on gender equality is rather unthankful and does not come with the reward of prestige, it appears that in this organisation, the external and internal recognition through legal frameworks, awards and senior leadership responsibility has made gender equality a resource for potential prestige. The examples discussed in this chapter and the struggle for gender equality was structured around who can claim credit for gender equality and who can define what is included in gender equality. The former related to an award the organisation won and the latter related to if men are included in gender equality and who came up with the idea. The struggles for who has the power to define gender equality moved beyond debates of different forms of feminism and how to achieve gender equality. The discussions did not unfold around whether there is an equality of outcome or opportunity (Jewson and Mason, 1986) or which different instruments are used to achieve gender equality, such as the benefits of mentoring over sponsoring that is often discussed (Ibarra, Ely, and Kolb, 2013). Instead, the contest was entirely about who had the right to define gender equality and who was rewarded for it.

This contest did not unfold around actual achievements in regard to gender equality but around representations of success in regard to gender equality such as an award. While awards are normally judged in comparisons to other entries, they cannot be taken as the basis that gender equality has actually been achieved. As a matter of fact, many of the awards reward those who have engaged in specific initiatives to advance gender and can point to some specific outcomes but in most cases the awards do not claim that gender equality has been achieved. The struggle to compete for the power to define gender equality is therefore only partly rooted in actual gender equality and related much more to the perception that gender equality has been advanced.

This is an interesting moment for analysts of postfeminism for several reasons. First, it indicated that gender equality has moved from a topic that is 'overed' and repudiated to something that carries prestige (at least in some areas). This can in part be explained by the fact that the new types of corporate feminisms are reinvigorated debates on gender equality, albeit from an individualistic and neoliberal perspective. If gender equality is constructed as desired, it is not surprising that individuals compete for it in terms of defining the boundaries of gender equality and getting credit for it.

Second, the competition for gender equality seems to be detached from actually achieving gender equality. The competition is largely around the symbolic capital and the prestige that comes with the issue, rather than the moral argument that achieving gender equality is important and that there is progress on gender equality. The competition for the power to define and control gender remains abstract on a political level leaving the equality of men and women out of sight. This becomes particularly visible in the fact that the women's lobby and the equal opportunities officer essentially want to achieve equality between women and men and while it might be understandable that one takes a different approach to achieving gender equality, the competition and undermining of the women's lobby and the equal opportunities officer is not furthering the goal of gender equality. It rather leads to fraction and infighting that ignores the fact that joining forces albeit with different agendas might be a more effective change strategy. However, what gender equality actually is and how it can be achieved is hidden and disguised.

Questioning how gender is discussed using a postfeminist lens made it possible to show how gender equality has become something that appears worthwhile to compete for. In this chapter, I have analysed how in one organisation, the struggle for the power to define and control gender equality was expressed through who has the power to define the boundaries of gender equality, who is included in it and who received credit for gender equality. The chapter thereby shows that a newer facet of a postfeminist sensibility no longer only aims to repudiate gender equality and construct it as something no longer required but that the opposite is true: gender equality has become so central that it is worth competing over it because of the symbolic capital attached to gender equality. This competition for the perceived prestige of gender equality is however detached from actually achieving gender equality which might be better served by working together rather than competing for different definition and rewards attached to gender equality. The chapter shows how postfeminism is a complex and multifaceted issue that can take different expressions in different contexts. It also pointed to the ever changing dynamics of how postfeminism takes shape (Gill, 2016), which makes it a useful resource for the analysis of gender relations.

Acknowledgement

The research was supported by a British Academy Mid-Career Fellowship [MD130085]. Thanks to Jayne Ashley for proofreading the chapter. Due to the ethically sensitive nature of the research, no participants consented to their data being retained or shared.

References

Acker, J. (1990). Hierarchies, jobs, bodies: A theory of gendered organizations. *Gender & Society*, 4(2): 139–158.
Business in the Community. (2016). *Workplace Gender Equality Awards 2016-Winners and Finalists*. Available at: http://gender.bitc.org.uk/awards-benchmarking/workplace-gender-equality-awards-2016-winners-and-finalists/ Accessed 21 October 2016.

Czarniawska, B. (2014). Why I think shadowing is the best field technique in management and organization studies. *Qualitative Research in Organizations and Management: An International Journal*, 9(1): 90–93. Available at: http://doi.org/10.1108/QROM-02-2014-1198/

Esquire. (2016). Special Issue: Women and men-We need to talk. April.

Gatrell, C., and Swan, E. (2008). *Gender and Diversity in Management: A Concise Introduction*. London: Sage.

Gill, R. (2007). Postfeminist media culture: Elements of a sensibility. *European Journal of Cultural Studies*, 10(2): 147–166.

Gill, R. (2016). Post-postfeminism? New feminist visibilities in postfeminist times. *Introduction: Feminism, Postfeminism and Generation*, 16(4): 610–630. Available at: http://doi.org/10.1080/14680777.2016.1193293/

Gill, R., Kelan, E.K., and Scharff, C.M. (2017). A postfeminist sensibility at work. *Gender, Work & Organization*. Available at: http://doi.org/10.1111/gwao.12132/

Gill, R., and Orgad, S. (2016). The confidence cult(ure). *Australian Feminist Studies*, 30(2015): 324–344.

Harding, N., Lee, H., and Ford, J. (2014). Who is "the middle manager"? *Human Relations*, 67(10): 1213–1237. Available at: http://doi.org/10.1177/0018726713516654/

Ibarra, H., Ely, R., and Kolb, D. (2013). Women rising: The unseen barriers. *Harvard Business Review*, 91(9): 60–67.

Jewson, N., and Mason, D. (1986). The theory and practice of equal opportunities policies: Liberal and radical approaches. *The Sociological Review*, 34(2): 307–334.

Kelan, E.K. (2008). The discursive construction of gender in contemporary management literature. *Journal of Business Ethics*, 18(2): 427–445.

Kelan, E.K. (2009a). Gender fatigue-The ideological dilemma of gender neutrality and discrimination in organisations. *Canadian Journal of Administrative Sciences*, 26(3): 197–210.

Kelan, E.K. (2009b). *Performing Gender at Work*. Basingstoke: Palgrave.

Kelan, E.K., and Dunkley Jones, R. (2010). Gender and the MBA. *Academy of Management Learning & Education*, 9(1): 26–43.

Kelan, E.K., and Wratil, P. (2014). *Winning Hearts and Minds-How CEOs Talk About Gender Parity*. Available at: www.kpmg.com/UK/en/IssuesAndInsights/ArticlesPublications/Documents/PDF/About/kpmg-kcl-gender-parity-study.pdf/

Kelan, E.K., and Wratil, P. (2017). Post-heroic leadership, tempered radicalism and senior leaders as change agents for gender equality. *European Management Review*. DOI: 10.1111/emre.12117.

Kirton, G., Greene, A.-M., and Dean, D. (2007). British diversity professionals as change agents-radicals, tempered radicals or liberal reformers? *The International Journal of Human Resource Management*, 18(11): 1979–1994. Available at: http://doi.org/10.1080/09585190701638226/

Lewis, P. (2014). Postfeminism, femininities and organization studies: Exploring a new agenda. *Organization Studies*, 35(12): 1845–1866.

Lewis, P., and Simpson, R. (2017). Hakim revisited: Preference, choice and the postfeminist gender regime. *Gender, Work & Organization*, 24(2): 115–133. Available at: http://doi.org/10.1111/gwao.12150/

Mavin, S., and Grandy, G. (2016). A theory of abject appearance: Women elite leaders intra-gender 'management of bodies and appearance. *Human Relations*. Available at: http://doi.org/10.1177/0018726715609107/

Mavin, S., Grandy, G., and Williams, J. (2014). Experiences of women elite leaders doing gender: Intra-gender micro-violence between women. *British Journal of Management*, 25(3): 439–455. Available at: http://doi.org/10.1111/1467-8551.12057/

McDonald, S. (2005). Studying actions in context: A qualitative shadowing method for organizational research. *Qualitative Research*, 5(4): 455–473.

McKinsey. (2012). *Women Matter 2012: Making the Breakthrough*. Available at: www.mckinsey.com/client_service/organization/latest_thinking/women_matter/

McRobbie, A. (2008). *The Aftermath of Feminism: Gender, Culture and Social Change*. London: Sage.

Meyerson, D., and Scully, M.A. (1995). Tempered radicalism and the politics of ambivalence and change. *Organization Science*, 6(5): 585–600.

Meyerson, D., and Tompkins, M. (2007). Tempered radicals as institutional change agents: The case of NSF's gender equity project in higher education. *Harvard Journal of Law and Gender*, 30(2): 303–322.

Nentwich, J.C., and Kelan, E.K. (2014). Towards a topology of "doing gender": An analysis of empirical research and its challenges. *Gender, Work & Organization*, 21(2): 121–134.

Rouleau, L. (2005). Micro-practices of strategic sensemaking and sensegiving: How middle managers interpret and sell change every day. *Journal of Management Studies*, 42(7): 1413–1441.

Sandberg, S. (2013). *Lean in-Women Work, and the Will to Lead*. London: Random House.

Slaughter, A.-M. (2015). *Unfinished Business: Women Men Work Family*. London: Oneworld Publications.

Tatli, A. (2011). A multi-layered exploration of the diversity management field: Diversity discourses, practices and practitioners in the UK. *British Journal of Management*, 22(2): 238–253.

The Times. (2016). Top 50 employers for women. Available at: http://gender.bitc.org.uk/TTT502016/ Accessed 21 October 2016.

Thomas, D.A. (2004). Diversity as strategy. *Harvard Business Review*, (September): 98–108.

United Nations. (2016). *#HeforShe*. Available at: www.heforshe.org/ Accessed 21 October 2016.

World Economic Forum. (2016). *Global Gender Gap Report 2016*. Available at: http://www3.weforum.org/docs/GGGR16/WEF_Global_Gender_Gap_Report_2016.pdf/

6 Postfeminism and the Performance of Merit

Savita Kumra and Ruth Simpson

Introduction

This chapter examines the postfeminist logic that underpins practices and discourses of 'merit' and presents the argument that, while the allocation of rewards according to merit is emblematic of the so-called success of equal opportunities, the *recognition* of merit and worth relies on traditionally masculine embodied performances and displays. We show how meritocratic principles that define a shift from ascription to achievement as the primary basis for social selection, underpin and reflect postfeminist understandings of the realization of equality in the workplace and how new embodiments of femininity undermine claims to 'masculine' merit-based success. As we seek to demonstrate, the performance of merit is gendered 'masculine', and while women are expected as postfeminist subjects to participate in merit-based achievement at work, their ability to engage successfully and persuasively with its regime is compromised by the requirement to also enact an embodied femininity—preventing the recognition of their ability, skills and talents as being valued, rewarded and 'deserved'.

Heavily influenced by liberal-democratic ideals, merit is seen in most Western organizations as an 'objective' measure of ability and achievement and is generally accepted, both morally and practically, as the dominant and appropriate criterion determining progression within organizations. This is predicated upon a postfeminist sensibility whereby merit can be seen as the practice and articulation of individual effort and agency based on a self-managing and self-motivated female subject. This subject willingly and unconstrainedly invests in self-improvement and neoliberal entrepreneurial careerism that translate persuasively into aspirations and attitudes of potential. Young women in particular, influenced by postfeminist discourses of female success, articulate a trust in meritocracy despite widespread evidence of gender based disadvantage and see their own organizations as 'blameless' even when their senior ranks are heavily male dominated. Education, skills and past achievements, comprising key criteria for the distribution of rewards, are seen as gender neutral attributes with the suggestion that women must work hard—in Sheryl Sanberg's terms that they should '*lean in*'—to overcome any challenges faced.

As we discuss in the chapter, this is to not only overlook the social and cultural limits placed on women's access to self-determination (e.g. through gendered constructions of aspirations and ambition) but also to deny the significance of merit's subjective, 'performed' dimensions namely, the gendered as well as contextual factors that may underpin how merit is recognized and given value. In other words, merit has to be demonstrated and displayed in day-to-day activities and practices—e.g., through dress, language, comportment as well as self-presentations and impression management so that others can be persuaded of value and worth. As we suggest, merit is conveyed through embodied performance and the extent to which it is seen as 'deserved' is profoundly gendered where some embodiments of the new postfeminist subject (sassy, sexy, feminine) fail to 'fit' with gendered notions of what is appropriate for a leadership and/or management role.

We locate this tension within a postfeminist gender regime where women are required to 'do masculinity' through agentic self-determination and the forging of a successful merit-based career while at the same time 'doing femininity' by conforming to a re-articulation of traditional expectations and traditional gender stereotypes around attractiveness and female sexuality (Lewis, Benschop, and Simpson, 2017). Merit—through its performance—can there be seen to be gendered masculine with women in a postfeminist regime 'required' to do masculinity whilst the recognition of merit is undermined by new feminine embodiments in the workplace. This highlights some of the contradictions within postfeminism that signal gender-neutral choice and agency against a backdrop of persistent and pervasive gendered power. Women are unable to 'shed' the detrimental implications of their gender as they seek to demonstrate merit-based 'deservingness' at work. Deeply insinuated into Human Resource Management (HRM) rationales and procedures, such as recruitment and reward practices, we show how the inflated discursive configurations of merit leave the traditional gender order undisturbed and how they articulate and reflect both a neoliberal market-based ideology and postfeminist cultural regime.

Our chapter firstly considers how merit is constructed and perceived within a neoliberal socio-economic context and a postfeminist gender regime—manifest in part through a shared focus on individual choice, agency and empowerment as key characteristics of an 'objective', meritocratically based organizational system, as well as through a common requirement to 'work on oneself' and self-improve. We critically evaluate, from a gendered perspective, the idea that individuals, armed with choice, can be autonomous agents and 'authors' of their destinies and show how merit must be performed appropriately—e.g., according to pre-existing gender norms and scripts, in order to be recognized and given value. Finally, we point to contradictions and inconsistencies within postfeminism and merit—whereby the new postfeminist subject is expected to be ambitious and agentic while traditional re-articulations of (groomed, sexual) embodied femininity may undermine, in a power laden and patriarchal organizational context, claims to a meritorious and deserving self.

Postfeminism, Neoliberalism and Constructions of Merit

Supported by neoliberal principles of self-management, individual responsibility and enterprise, the merit-based ranking and rewarding of individuals are seen to create a 'level playing field'. Here, in a 'free market', aspirations of individuals are 'brought in line' with the objectives of the organization (Sommerlad, 2011) and where 'fair chances' are ensured through 'energy, aspirations and ambition' (Rose, 1990). This, however, is to overlook the contingent nature and characteristics of merit and how its operation and constitution are determined in a context of prevailing power relations (DeSario, 2003; Thornton, 2007) dependent on the perception of what is 'good' and/or appropriate in a particular society or social context.

Kumra (2014) for example points to how organizations evolve so that rewards are allocated in expected and accepted ways, rendering other manifestations of merit invisible (see also Brink and Benschop, 2012). In this respect, the neoliberal market-based, meritocratic system can be seen to conceal a gender bias in that what counts as merit is endorsed by prevailing power elites who stand to gain most from maintaining the gendered status quo (Sommerlad, 2012; Brink and Benschop, 2012). Given that the top of most organizational hierarchies are dominated by men, ideal constructions of the 'best person' for the job are often based upon a masculine model. In support, Kumra and Vinnicombe (2008) have exposed the masculinized, highly individualistic and 'self-managed' nature of career development in the promotion-to-partner process in professional services. This supposedly meritocratic process undervalued the more collaborative approach of women, who were more used to advocating on behalf of others than operating from a traditionally masculinist individualistically self-interested position. This highlights the 'plasticity' of merit and how it may serve to construct understandings that are more aligned with masculinity and men's practices helping to 'naturalize' male authority and entitlement. Despite these imperfections, as Sommerlad suggests, merit represents what is generally seen as an 'unassailable moral order' and is rarely contested in mainstream accounts—partly because of the ways it underpins and is underpinned by neoliberal philosophies (e.g. deregulation, laissez-faire) that have created perceptions of the market as the 'natural, universal, core organizational form' (Sommerlad, 2015: 2340).

These understandings of merit find purchase within particular notions of a 'postfeminist sensibility' (Gill, 2008; Gill and Scharff, 2013) seen as a 'cultural discourse' that 'shapes our thinking, attitudes and behaviour towards feminism and women's changing position in contemporary society' (Lewis, 2014: 1850). This sensibility or cultural regime is based on personal empowerment, choice, sexual agency and assumptions of emancipation through, as example, the supposed success of second-wave feminism in terms of equal opportunities in the context of a functioning merit-based allocative system. Gill (2007) identifies key modalities of postfeminism as a prominence given to individualism, choice and empowerment as a substitute for collective gender politics; femininity as a bodily property through an emphasis on self-surveillance and 'makeover'; the revival and reappearance of 'natural' sexual difference; the resexualization of women's bodies and finally the retreat to home as a matter of choice not obligation (see also Lewis, 2014). Upholding the principle of feminist success in the context of equality of opportunity, postfeminism at the same time denigrates feminism as an outdated political movement (McRobbie, 2011). Feminism is, therefore, both taken into account, through discourses of feminism's success, and understood to have passed away. Writers such as Gill (2008) and McRobbie (2009) have referred to the 'entanglement' of feminist and ant-feminist discourses where feminist ideas are both articulated and repudiated. As Gill writes,

> On the one hand, young women are hailed through a discourse of "can-do" girl power, yet on the other their bodies are powerfully re-inscribed as sexual objects; on the one hand women are presented as active, desiring social subjects, yet on the other they are subject to a level of scrutiny and hostile surveillance that has no historical precedence. The patterned nature of the contradictions is what constitutes a sensibility—a sensibility in which notions of autonomy, choice and self-improvement sit side by side with surveillance, discipline and vilification of those who make the 'wrong' choices.
>
> (Gill, 2008: 442)

Here, women's entry into the work force has underpinned notions of 'girl power', signalling a postfeminist era in which women's equality is seen to have been achieved. Thus, as Kauppinen (2013) suggests, the 'masculine' world of work—a key domain for neo-liberalist ideas and practices based on market principles and on a self-regulating entrepreneurial self—has at the same time allowed expression of a postfeminist sensibility in the form of the aspirational and ambitious career woman. Through a discourse analysis of the woman's magazine *Cosmopolitan*, she shows how readers are guided to construct themselves, through various "self-help strategies, into a neoliberal and postfeminist self—drawing on a language of entrepreneurial self-management and aspiration and offering strategies for women to get ahead in their careers". A postfeminist discourse of self-management and an ethos of engagement are accordingly moulded upon a version of the entrepreneurial self, required by the neo-liberalized workplace. Postfeminism is, therefore, 'partly constituted' through neoliberal ideas (Gill and Scharff, 2013).

As Gill and Scharff (2013) argue, there is a 'powerful' resonance' between neoliberalism and postfeminism at three levels. First, as we have seen, they are both structured around an individualistic fundamental that has largely replaced the social or the political as a source of influence or constraint. Choice, agency and empowerment—where the individual bears full responsibility for their life biography irrespective of external constraints—are accordingly central to neoliberalism and postfeminism. Secondly and relatedly, the autonomous, self-regulating subject of neoliberalism bears a 'strong resemblance to the active, freely choosing, self-reinventing subject of postfeminism' (Gill and Scharff, 2013: 7)—requiring that women to 'work on themselves' in appearance, attitudes, skills and behaviour to achieve success. As Kauppinen (2013) comments, the logic of the discourse of postfeminist self-management is that of neoliberal governmentality that produces disciplined enterprising selves, participating enthusiastically in the 'neoliberalized order' of the world of work. Finally, with clear parallels with postfeminism, it is women who within a neoliberal regime are called upon to self-manage and self-regulate to a greater extent than men and to present their actions as freely chosen. Neoliberalism can be accordingly be seen as profoundly gendered, presenting women as its 'ideal subjects' and where, in McRobbie's (2009) terms, female participation by well-qualified young women in particular (depicted as unconstrained and freely choosing) is seen as critical to the 'new' economy's success.

As Gill (2008) points out, it is difficult to overestimate the extent to which discourses of choice, empowerment and agency have become central to both neoliberalism and postfeminism—underpinning the rational self-regulating entrepreneurial self (with ability to choose maximum material gain) and the self-monitoring and disciplined postfeminist subject, where performances and practices around achieving 'perfectibility' and success are presented as having been freely chosen. Here, to reach full potential, individuals must embrace attitudes of self—belief and of endless possibilities, particularly in the area of paid work. In this respect, meritocracy provides the underpinning rationale for belief that hard work, effort and ambition can lead to endless potential within a gender neutral labour market, encompassing neoliberal ideas of the rational, enterprising self and the postfeminist view of feminism's 'success'. This can be seen in the faith that many young women in particular place in the meritocratic system and in the denial of gender as an issue in their organizational lives, preferring to rely on personal narratives of self-determination and of unbounded potential—referred to by McRobbie (2011) as a 'disidentification' with feminism. The consistency of the narrative of self-empowerment is despite clear evidence of gender-based disadvantage at work (Chen, 2013)—such as a paucity of women in senior roles—indicating the extent to which the merit-based agendas of equal opportunity, gender neutrality and achievement have been absorbed. Thus, Simpson, Ross-Smith, and Lewis (2010) found in a study of Australian managers that women drew on a meritocratic rhetoric of equal chance, hard work and effort in explaining career success and distanced themselves from gender as a source of constraint, despite the lack of women in senior positions in their organizations and the evident privileging and community of men. Kelan (2010) highlighted how women often failed to recognize discrimination and instead positioned systemic disadvantage as surmountable through individual strategies. As Gill (2007) points out, women often invest in a meritocratic discourse even though it implicitly pathologizes them: if they are doing less well than male peers, it must be their fault.

Thus, Kevin Roberts the chairman of Saatchi and Saatchi claimed in a recent interview that the debate about gender bias in his organization "is over" and that the lack of women in senior positions was because they lacked "vertical ambition" (BBC news online, 2016: www.bbc.co.uk/news/business-36963686). This attitude was also articulated by Sandberg (2013)—chief operating officer of Facebook—in her popular text based on the exhortation that women should 'lean in' and, through a variety of strategies, create their own success. As Gill (2007) argues, the choice (and by implication, the merit) agenda ignores complexity and refuses to address how power works through subjects: how we make socially constructed ideals (e.g. around the efficiency of the market and the fairness of merit) our own. Rather than identifying structural or cultural constraints, 'losers' in the merit-based competitive market are urged to keep working on the project of the self through investment and self-improvement. Therefore, while a merit-based system does not directly coerce the choices made, it provides the conditions of possibility for a choosing, self-managing self—both in terms of the belief in personal effort and choice as the core ingredients for achievement and success and in the presentation of the context (the labour market; the workplace) as gender neutral and fair.

Gender, Merit and the 'Project of the Self'

From the aforementioned, central to both neoliberalism and postfeminism is the notion of individualization namely, that individuals endowed with choice are authors of and have responsibility for their own biographies. Underscored by postfeminist assumptions that equality has been achieved and by a faith in equal opportunities and merit to deliver a fair outcome in terms of the allocation of rewards, we have seen that women often fail to recognize gender-based disadvantage at work, preferring to believe that individual energy and drive will overcome challenges faced.

This, however, is to ignore the gendered nature of the individualization ethic where being ambitious, autonomous and 'self-made' have historically been associated with men (Lewis, 2014). In this respect, women must take up a male subjectivity in the unfettered project of the self (Lewis and Simpson, 2017). McRobbie (2009) coined the phrase 'female individualization' to highlight the idea that while women are now required to 'write' their own biographies, they must do so within a gendered terrain. Thus, as Tincknell (2011) points out, the priority given to the seemingly gender neutral rational, autonomous and highly individualized subject overlooks the ways in which women's ability to produce themselves has always been compromised. The 'ideal' is therefore implicitly gendered in that women's autonomy and self-determination are constrained by social and cultural factors such as prescriptive and gendered attitudes and behaviours and assumptions of women's responsibility for domestic care.

Benschop et al. (2013), for example, highlight some of the power dimensions and gendered practices associated with ambition—a key component of the new aspirational subject position. Rather than an individual trait, they see ambition as a gendered, social and relational construct bound up with notions of hegemonic masculinity. Ambition is therefore not a neutral concept but is saturated with power based on explicit and implicit norms and rules. Not only are the achievements of women afforded less value but also they must present their ambition carefully so as not to violate gender based norms that dictate, as example, that women focus on others rather than on the self in the form of an 'open' careerism. As they show, ambition conforms in particular to understandings of the 'ideal worker' (Acker, 1990) as a specific manifestation of hegemonic masculinity (continuously available, prioritizing of work, task focussed). Women are accordingly constrained in how their ambition can be articulated, not only by gender norms that require them to demonstrate less careerism than men but also because of caring responsibilities that compromise their ability to fit with the ideal.

Instead, as McRobbie (2009) and others have argued, women are required to work on themselves in bodily terms in order to become the ideal postfeminist subject. Supported by an emphasis on 'makeover' geared towards body enhancement, beauty practices are represented as offering women self-determined choices, centring on consumerist discourses of freedom, emancipation and pleasure (Lazar, 2011; Gill and Scharff, 2011). In this respect, commentators such as McRobbie (2009) and Gill (2008) have highlighted how socially constructed ideals of beauty or sexiness have been 'internalized', signifying a shift from objectification (captured in understandings of the 'male gaze' and the desire to please men) to subjectification where women gain pleasure from their bodies and please themselves. Here, Gill refers to media constructions of "a young, attractive, heterosexual woman who knowingly and deliberately plays with her sexual power" (Gill, 2008: 437). Rather than being presented as passive subjects of an assumed male gaze, women are increasingly presented as active, desiring, heterosexual subjects—"feisty, sassy and sexually agentic" (Gill, 2008: 438). As she argues, this is an attempt to redefine femininity and forms part of a postfeminist sensibility based on an intensification of scrutiny of women's bodies and an expectation that women should always 'look good'. However, as McRobbie contends and as argued by Lewis et al. (2017), by advancing individualism for women through technologies of self that are oriented towards notions of female beauty and the *spectacularly feminine* (McRobbie, 2009), women's freedom of movement both physically and symbolically within organizations is restricted whilst those constraints are constituted as freely chosen.

Individualization and the project of the self, key dimensions of both neoliberalism and postfeminism, therefore overlook the profoundly gendered context in which this project takes place. The regime and ethos of individualism and personal responsibility separate the gendered self from its gendered context where, with reference to the latter, the gender order remains intact. As Chen (2013) suggests, individualization and the autonomous ability to realize one's potential through effort and choice may not in fact be emancipatory, as both neoliberalism and postfeminism suggest, but lead to the reinforcement of the status quo—particularly when enhancement and self-realization are translated in gendered, bodily terms.

Postfeminism, 'Deservingness' and the Embodied Performance of Merit

As we argue in this section, one reason for this lack of emancipation and progression is the conflation of merit with *deservingness* whereby, to gain recognition and credit, merit must be appropriately performed and visibly displayed. As Pojman (1978) has claimed, whilst talent, skills and ability are the qualities that comprise merit, 'desert' captures effort, commitment and 'good will'—highlighting the significance of the appropriate performance of merit through displays of commitment and 'fitting in'. In other words, deservingness relies on (traditional masculine) displays of acceptability, work prioritization and occupational success thereby providing, as Sommerlad contends, a 'teleological argument for rewarding the embodied cultural practices of white male elites' (Sommerlad, 2015: 2325). The recognition of merit in the form of deservingness is accordingly predicated upon particular, gendered embodied practices and enactments, with profound implications for the new postfeminist subject.

Following the aforementioned, we have seen how a postfeminist sensibility is partly centred on assumptions of the success of equal opportunities which go hand in hand with understandings of femininity as a bodily property and a re-articulation of traditional gender norms (e.g. McRobbie, 2009; Gill, 2007). In a world of work still largely dominated by patriarchal values (Kerfoot and Knights, 1993, 1998), these embodied performances of femininity can serve to penalize women and undermine their organizational success. In this respect, some research has indicated how the tasks and skills of management and ideas of successful leadership (i.e. what counts as meritorious) are still inscribed onto the bodies of (white, middle class) men through shared notions of discipline, rationality, detachment, direction and control (Kerfoot and Knights, 1993). Women's bodies, however, are often seen as 'problematic signifiers' (Brewis and Sinclair, 2000: 195) and 'out of place' in a leadership role—carriers of 'nature, sexuality, emotions and hormones' (Swan, 2005: 319) and hence incongruent with the demands for rationality, authority and control.

Here, Ashcraft (2013) has referred to the importance of alignment and 'fit' through her construction of the 'glass slipper' effect. This encapsulates the need for an alignment between occupational identity (the nature and characteristics of the job) and embodied social identities (or embodied dispositions) of workers. Ashcraft identifies two main forms of body-work associations—one based on physical characteristics and *demographic alignment* so that occupational identity develops around the (gender, race) profile of those doing the work. The second is *symbolic alignment* whereby some groups may be 'discursively or emblematically' associated with some forms of work—i.e., how work is coded through social identities such as through the sex typing of particular tasks. Management and leadership are therefore demographically aligned with men given their numerical dominance and symbolically aligned with masculinity in that these roles are seen as more appropriate for the (detached, rational) bodies of men. This suggests a need to recognize that particular occupations may be deemed more 'suitable' or 'appropriate' for some groups than others. What might be seen as merit and as the 'meritorious' are not fixed, disembodied categories but depend in part on embodied performances and on the meaning attached to the bodies in which occupational merit is supposedly contained.

As example, we draw on media coverage of a controversial appointment—the recruitment of Professor Noreena Hertz in 2016 to the role of economic editor at Independent Television (ITV) in the UK, which we read through a postfeminist lens, paying particular attention to language and meanings conveyed through the text. The appointment of Professor Hertz provoked an outcry concerning her supposed lack of suitability for the role with attention drawn to her 'inexperience' as well as to her dress and appearance. The *Daily Mail* (Mail online, 2016) devoted two pages to the issue and included in the text no less than eight photographs of Professor Hertz in various sexually charged poses. In one of these photographs, she can be seen to exemplify a particular sexualized and excessive femininity in terms of posture and attire (long fair hair brushed to one side, broad smile directed at the camera, lipstick, revealing red dress tied at the waist, prominent breasts, bare arms) that conforms to an understanding of the postfeminist subject: groomed, feminine, aware of her sexual power. Another photograph sees her seated and speaking into a hand-held microphone. Her legs are crossed and she is wearing a very short dress, revealing an expanse of thigh, and high-heeled strappy sandals. Both images convey a particular postfeminist subject in terms of her display of feminine attractiveness as well as her evident career success—showing her to be ambitious and aspirational, having benefited from equal opportunities in her achievement of senior professorial and management roles.

Nevertheless, despite an impressive CV in terms of credentials and experience (professorships and visiting professorships in Economics at three top-ranking universities, directorships at several companies), and amidst assertions that journalists were "*horrified*" by her appointment, she was referred to in the *Daily Mail* article in strongly negative terms that queried her competence to do the job (*"no experience"*; *"no background in journalism"*), while her claim to be an economist was also dismissed (*"she's not an economist at all—just a self-publicist"*). In more tempered tones, a *Guardian* piece similarly headlined her lack of experience, quoting her as admitting *"I know I have a lot to learn"* (www.theguardian.com/media/2016) while The Times (Baxter, 2016) drew light-hearted attention to her appearance (*"the brainy lady with a glamorous updo"*) and referred to the advice Hertz gave to women to wear red. As Hertz is reported to have commented, *"Waitresses get more tips if they do"*, advice that contains implicit acknowledgment of the power of female sexuality which women, as postfeminist 'choosing' agentic subjects, can now use 'to their own ends' in whatever role they do. In short, the articles in different ways drew attention to her embodied femininity whilst raising doubts about her merit and her suitability for the job.

This highlights how some forms of embodied, feminine display may undermine claims to a meritorious self in particular contexts—in Ashcraft's (2013) terms, how a misalignment may occur between the embodied social identity of the worker (female, young, sexually attractive) and the occupational identity, in this context a senior editorial role. In support of this idea, Brink and Benschop (2012) refer to how appearance (e.g. a slight stature) can influence perceptions of abilities, particularly in leadership and management. Further, as Lewis (2014) points out in the context of entrepreneurship, excessive displays of femininity (as in the 'wrong' kind and/or the 'wrong' amount) can work against women being seen as a 'serious' or legitimate entrepreneurs. In other words,

> Those who are deemed as being excessively feminine without the counterweight of masculinity will be interpreted as violating the hegemonic norms that are valued in an entrepreneurial context.
>
> (Lewis, 2014: 1858)

By embodying in a traditional sense the feminine, non-rational, pleasure-giving characteristics of attractiveness as well as (through the smile) a care and concern for others, Professor Hertz can be seen to have undermined claims to masculinized traits of rationality, independence and autonomy—traits that are given value in a leadership role. While the uptake of a postfeminist subjectivity relies in part on a groomed and sexually 'savvy' agentic self, these work-based enactments and displays do not take place in a gender neutral context but are often performed and evaluated within a largely masculinist domain. However, as we have seen, these broader social and cultural factors are routinely overlooked in favour of individualized explanations for failure so that the influence of gender practices is denied. Thus, as Lewis contends,

> Women who display what are perceived to be extreme (traditional) feminine behaviours will be designated as not legitimate business people

and blamed for their own exclusion. . . . with little attention directed at
the structural and cultural constraints which act on them.

(Lewis, 2014: 1858)

As our earlier example suggests, merit is not just a set of skills and attributes that an individual possesses, as a form of physical capital anchored on
a gender neutral body, but also involves embodied performances whereby
merit, to have value, is given recognition and seen as deserved. Merit has to
be demonstrated appropriately through dress, language, comportment and
self-presentations in order to persuade others that merit not only is present but also has worth. The need for the effective communication of merit
was recognized by Sandberg (2013) as part of her incitement to women to
'lean in' through self-promotion. However, this is to not only overlook the
gendered nature of ambition (discussed earlier) where self-advocacy may
violate gender norms but also to fail to take into account the significance
of embodied displays. Thus, the extent to which merit is seen as deserved
will depend in part on the meanings attached to the bodies in which merit is
partly contained, with 'excessive' displays of femininity (Lewis, 2012) having potential to undermine merit-based claims to legitimacy.

The 'meritorious' worker, therefore, is viewed as someone who not only
possesses merit in the form of qualification and skill but also through their
embodied comportment and performance deserves to be recognized and
rewarded—a performance which, as Sommerlad (2015) suggests, often
favours white male elites. This emphasis on the need for merit to be effectively displayed therefore has a strong gendered dimension. Referring to the
gendered nature of 'fitness to practice' in law and accountancy firms, and
similar to Lewis's (2012) argument, Haynes (2012) describes how success
is predicated upon a masculine body and how women must distance themselves from negatively constructed aspects of their femininity (dress, voice
and self-presentation) and perform aspects of masculinity if they wish to be
taken seriously. Merit, embodied in 'fitness to practice', is not therefore a
neutral, objective and measurable construct but is contingent upon a particular embodied performance of gender.

Contradictions and Inconsistencies

We have highlighted in this chapter some of the tensions and contradictions
within postfeminism whereby 'gender neutral' choice and agency take place
in a context saturated with gendered power—signifying in McRobbie's
(2009) terms, the 'entanglement' of feminist and anti-feminist ideas. These
find parallels within some of the inconsistencies inherent within discourses
and practices of merit. Thus, firstly, rather than an objective measure of
worth that protects against discrimination, merit can be seen to support bias
through reliance on subjective judgments that then help define the so-called
objective criteria on which merit is based—reflecting as Brink and Benschop

(2012) argue, a masculine model of what is seen as deserving and successful. In other words, as we have seen, while merit is based on so-called objective measures, *deservingness* is socially and hierarchically inscribed. Merit is upheld as gender neutral while deservingness and the recognition of merit depend on particular gendered displays.

Secondly, and relatedly, while young women in particular believe in merit as a fair and just way of distributing rewards (underpinned by neoliberal assumptions of endless potential) and have faith, as postfeminist subjects, in its ability to deliver personal success, they are at the same time pathologized by its assumptions and exhortations—seen in individualistic terms as deficient should the project of the self become 'unstuck'. Lack of progress translates into making the 'wrong' choices or insufficient investment in career, signifying personal failure within a postfeminist cultural terrain that celebrates equality and female success and where structural constraints are denied. Women must write their own biographies, but within a gendered context which, as McRobbie (2009) suggests, has been more characterized by 'gender retrenchment' rather than the freeing up of gender based norms.

Thirdly, and following the aforementioned, we have seen how the entrepreneurial, choosing and aspiring female subject has been partly redefined through bodily properties of sexual attractiveness and sexual agency—a form of 'hyper-femininity' that relocates women into traditional gender hierarchies, concealed through a rhetoric of personal choosing. The requirement for women to practice and display feminine grooming and attractiveness (long hair, revealing clothes, high heels) may, as McRobbie suggests, be response to the threat to patriarchal power from women's workplace success while its voluntaristic structure serves to conceal that "patriarchy is still in place" (McRobbie, 2009: 69). Individualism and agency can lead, problematically, to objectification through the need for bodily displays of a particular femininity that appeals to men and which in the context of work, can undermine women's bid for masculine power and success. The performance of merit is accordingly highly gendered and must be seen as *appropriate* in order to be recognized—in Ashcraft's (2013) terms, in order to align with the social definition of the job. We can therefore see within the practices and discourse of merit an appeal to feminist ideas of equal opportunities, autonomy and achievement—ideas that have become insinuated into everyday thinking and accepted as mainstream—whilst drawing on masculine norms and enactments and concealing persistent and pervasive gendered power.

Conclusion

We have sought in this chapter to place merit, as an essential component of the claim to equality of opportunity, within a particular postfeminist context, drawing parallels between neoliberalism on which merit is based and a postfeminist sensibility. We have therefore sought to explore the postfeminist logic that supports and underpins practices and discourses of merit—how it is located within a specific socio-economic and cultural terrain. In so doing, we have drawn out the significance of the recognition of merit through gendered, embodied performance. Specifically, rather than being predicated upon objective measures and on assumptions of gender neutrality at both market and institutional levels, merit relies on traditional practices and displays of work-based masculinity that preclude postfeminist embodiments of femininity. The performance of merit is therefore gendered 'masculine' and while women are expected to participate in merit-based achievement at work, their ability to engage successfully with its taken-for-granted regime is undermined by the requirement to also enact an embodied femininity—preventing merit's recognition as being 'deserved'. We have shown how these discourses and practices of merit, as well some of its internal inconsistencies, are intricately bound up with the neoliberal emphasis on market relations and an enterprising self as well as, relatedly, on the postfeminist emphasis on individualism and agency grounded in claims that equality has been achieved. Therefore, whilst recruitment and reward practices based on merit are generally seen in disembodied terms as objective, just and fair, they rely on gendered, embodied performances and leave the traditional gender order undisturbed, forming part of a gender based, 'celebratory' postfeminist cultural regime.

References

Acker, J. (1990). Hierarchies, jobs, bodies: A theory of gendered organizations. *Gender and Society*, 4(2): 139–158.

Ashcraft, K. (2013). The glass slipper: "Incorporating" occupational identity in management studies. *Academy of Management Review*, 38(1): 6–31.

Baxter, S. (2016). Let it rip: Make Noreena's globaloney fight it out with some right-wing news. *The Times*, 22 May.

BBC news online. (2016). *Saatchi Boss Kevin Roberts Resigns*. Available at: www.bbc.co.uk/news/business-36963686/ Accessed 7 September 2016.

Benschop, Y., Brink, van den M., Doorewaard, H., and Leenders, J. (2013). Discourses of ambition, gender and part-time work. *Human Relations*, 66(5): 699–723.

Brewis, J., and Sinclair, A. (2000). Exploring embodiment: Women, biology and work. In J. Hassard, R. Holliday and H. Willmott (Eds.), *Body and Organization* (pp. 192–214). London: Sage.

Brink, van den M., and Benschop, Y. (2012). Gender practices in the construction of academic excellence: Sheep with five legs. *Organization*, 19(4): 507–524.

Chen, E. (2013). Neo-liberalism and popular women's culture. *European Journal of Cultural Studies*, 16(4): 440–412.

DeSario, N. (2003). Reconceptualizing meritocracy: The decline of disparate impact discrimination law. *Harvard Civil Rights- Civil Liberties Law Review*, 38: 479–510.

Gill, R. (2007). Postfeminist media culture: Elements of a sensibility. *European Journal of Cultural Studies*, 10(2): 147–66.

Gill, R. (2008). Culture and subjectivity. *Neoliberal Times*, 25: 432–445.

Gill, R., and Scharff, C. (2011). Introduction. In R. Gill and C. Scharff (Eds.), *New Femininities: Postfeminism, Neoliberalism and Subjectivity* (pp. 1–20). Basingstoke: Palgrave Macmillan.

Haynes, K. (2012). Body beautiful? Gender, identity and the body in professional services firms. *Gender, Work and Organization*, 19(5): 489–507.

Kauppinen, K. (2013). "Full power despite stress": A discourse analytical examination of the interconnectedness of postfeminism and neoliberalism in the domain of work in an international women's magazine. *Discourse and Communication*, 7(2): 133–151.

Kelan, E. (2010). Gender and the MBA. *Academy of Management (Learning and Education)*, 9: 29–43.

Kerfoot, D., and Knights, D. (1993). Management masculinity and manipulation: From paternalism to corporate strategy in financial services in Britain. *Journal of Management Studies*, 30: 659–677.

Kerfoot, D., and Knights, D. (1998). Managing masculinity in contemporary organizational life: A man(agerial) project. *Organization*, 5: 7–26.

Kumra, S. (2014). Gendered constructions of merit and impression management within professional service firms. In S. Kumra, R. Simpson, and R. Burke (Eds.), *The Oxford Handbook of Gender in Organizations* (pp. 269–290). Oxford: Oxford University Press.

Kumra, S., and Vinnicombe, S. (2008). A study of the promotion to partner process in a professional services firm: How women are disadvantaged. *British Journal of Management*, 19: 65–74.

Lazar, M.M. (2011). The right to be beautiful: Postfeminist identity and consumer beauty advertising. In R. Gill and C. Scharff (Eds.), *New Femininities: Postfeminism, Neoliberalism and Subjectivity* (pp. 37–51). Basingstoke: Palgrave Macmillan.

Lewis, P. (2012). Postfeminism and entrepreneurship: Interpreting disgust in a female entrepreneurial narrative. In R. Simpson, N. Slutskaya, P. Lewis, and H. Höpfl (Eds.), *Dirty Work: Concepts and Identities* (pp. 223–238). Basingstoke: Palgrave Macmillan.

Lewis, P. (2014). Postfeminism, femininities and organization studies: Exploring a new agenda. *Organization Studies*, 35(12): 1845–1866.

Lewis, P., Benschop, Y., and Simpson, R. (2017). Postfeminism, gender and organization. *Gender Work and Organization*, 24(3): 213–225.

Mail Online. (2016). *Backlash over ITV's New Economics Editor: Journalists Are "Horrified" by Decision to Appoint Leftie with No TV Experience and Whose Husband Is Politically Correct Former BBC Boss*. Available at: www.dailymail.co.uk/news/article-3599936/Backlash-Leftie-ITV-s-appointment-economics-editor-Noreena-Hertz.html#ixzz4JaTomz2R/ Accessed 7 September 2016.

McRobbie, A. (2009). *The Aftermath of Feminism: Gender, Culture and Social Change*. London: Sage.

McRobbie, A. (2011). Beyond postfeminism. *Public Policy Research*, 18(3): 171–184.

Pojman, L. (1978). Belief and will. *Religious Studies*, 14(1): 1–14.

Rose, N. (1990). *Governing the Soul: The Shaping of the Private Self*. London: Free Association Books.

Sandberg, S. (2013). *Lean in: Women, Work and the Will to Lead*. New York: Random House Inc.

Simpson, R., Ross-Smith, A., and Lewis, P. (2010). Merit, special contribution and choice: How women negotiate between sameness and difference in their organizational lives. *Gender in Management: An International Journal*, 25(3): 198–208.

Sommerlad, H. (2011). The commercialization of Law and the enterprising legal practitioner: Continuity and change. *International Journal of the Legal Profession*, 18(1-2): 73–108.

Sommerlad, H. (2012). Minorities, merit and misrecognition in the globalized profession. *Fordham Law Review*, 80: 2481–2512.

Sommerlad, H. (2015). The social magic of merit: Diversity, equity and inclusion in the English and Welsh Legal Profession. *Fordham Law Review*, 83(5): 2325–2347.

Swan, E. (2005). On bodies, rhinestones and pleasures: Women teaching managers. *Management Learning*, 36(3): 317–333.

Thornton, M. (2007) Otherness on the bench: How merit is gendered. *Sydney Law Review*, 29(3): 391.

Tincknell, E. (2011). Scourging the abject body: Ten years younger and fragmented femininity under neoliberalism. In R. Gill and C. Scharff (Eds.), *New Femininities: Postfeminism, Neoliberalism and Subjectivity* (pp. 83–98). Basingstoke: Palgrave Macmillan.

7 Analysing Entrepreneurial Activity Through a Postfeminist Perspective

A Brave New World or the Same Old Story?

Helene Ahl and Susan Marlow

Introduction

A critical component of the contemporary neoliberal turn has been the rise of entrepreneurship and entrepreneurial behaviours (Campbell and Pedersen, 2001). In developed nations, this era has been exemplified by a marked increase in entrepreneurship and new venture creation; entrepreneurial activity has also been integrated into the corporate environment encouraging individualised employee agency to generate innovative problem solving (Dannreuther and Perren, 2012) At a micro-level, we have seen the emergence of the 'enterprising self' and society where individuals assume responsibility for their own lives managing social welfare provisions previously provided by the state (du Gay, 1994; Down and Warren, 2008; Ahl and Nelson, 2015). These shifting expectations have been made possible by enabling legislative and institutional changes such as de-regulation, the decline of trade unions, privatisation of state services and liberalised markets (Perren and Dannreuther, 2012). Contemporaneously, the populist cultural promotion of entrepreneurship through various media has positioned it as a desirable career option with increasing status and social worth (Swail, Down, and Kautonen, 2013).

This discourse chimes with the analytical foundations of postfeminism which, despite various and contested iterations (Gill, 2007; McRobbie, 2009), suggests that social and employment liberalisation in a context of decreasing sexism and greater equalities have generated a meritocratic society and so, rendered feminist subordination critiques obsolete. As Gill (2007: 147) notes, meritocratic achievement is available to the postfeminist woman through, "self-surveillance, monitoring, self-discipline, a focus on individualization, choice and empowerment". Thus, entrepreneurial activity—centred upon the agentic exploitation of potential—accords with the sentiments underpinning postfeminist arguments where the individual can use agency and ability to fulfil potential through self-employment and new venture creation. Indeed, a distinctive gendered discourse has emerged within the field of entrepreneurship research and policy initiatives focusing specifically upon women's entrepreneurial activity. As such, women have become the cipher of the gendered subject being in this particular field. The underpinning theme of this debate being: the 'problem' of women's underrepresentation as business owners, their lack of entrepreneurial competencies and the alleged under-performance of their ventures. Addressing such issues is seen to be the responsibility of women who are encouraged to pursue entrepreneurial opportunities as a form of self-actualisation whilst at the same time, contributing to the socio-economic productivity of advanced economies (Carter and Shaw, 2006; Marlow and McAdam, 2013).

In this chapter, we critically explore the alleged complementarities of these debates. We suggest that rather than revealing new opportunities, the alleged postfeminist woman business owner, by virtue of gendered ascriptions and constraints, will find her entrepreneurial activities subject to contextualised discriminatory assumptions, biases and challenges. As such, we argue that melding entrepreneurship and postfeminism generates a fictive gender-neutral space where women are positioned as free agents able to fulfil their personal, social and economic potential. However, evidence suggests this space is fundamentally gendered (Henry, Foss, and Ahl, 2016) and so, compromised by the intrusion of discriminatory discourses. This generates a paradox; expectations of achievement are based upon notions of a postfeminist meritocracy, whereas experiential outcomes are subject to gendered constraints. Thus, any differences between men and women regarding entrepreneurial propensity and firm performance are ascribed to a blame discourse attributed to feminine lack and deficit (Marlow and McAdam, 2013). The false promise of entrepreneurship in the alleged postfeminist era not only deceives but also generates a blame narrative to disguise this deception.

To elaborate upon these arguments, we focus specifically upon governmental policy initiatives focused upon encouraging and supporting women's business ownership. In addition, we acknowledge the importance of context in shaping theory and practice (Zahra, Wright, and Abdelgawad, 2014). To that end, we draw upon two differing contexts to explore the nuanced influence of gendered ascriptions upon entrepreneurial activity—those of the United Kingdom and Sweden. In the former, there is a regulatory framework of equality which, it is assumed, offers meritocratic opportunity for women to pursue entrepreneurial activity whereas in Sweden, there is a focus upon the value attributed to specific womanly merits and opportunities which can be used as a resource for entrepreneurial activity. To critically evaluate these arguments, this chapter is structured as follows; we introduce our analytical framing by outlining dimensions of postfeminism; this is followed by an exploration of the Swedish and UK context. We then consider the implications of these arguments and finally, we conclude by questioning the capacity of entrepreneurship to fuel a postfeminist future whereby women can claim new pathways to personal emancipation.

Dimensions of Postfeminism

Cultural Postfeminism

Postfeminism suggests, in its most basic interpretation, that women are now finally emancipated such that they have equivalence with men in all facets of life and, therefore, feminism is a redundant project which has achieved its key objectives (Coppock, Haydon, and Richter, 2014). This raises the point of why should we continue to fight for something which is already achieved? Postfeminism has been a phenomenon of academic inquiry primarily in cultural and media studies (Banet-Weiser and Portwood-Stacer, 2006). Research has analysed the representation of women in popular films, novels, television and other media, as well as how contemporary female artists and those deemed 'celebrities' enact gender (McRobbie, 2011). Successful, sexually liberated and independent working women are portrayed in contemporary films and television as women who have used their agency and initiative to negotiate the complexities of modern society free from sex and gender bias (Tasker and Negra, 2007; McRobbie, 2004, 2009). Yet, the imagery is of youthful, heterosexual, attractive, white, educated women whose continued possession of youth and beauty is achieved through the consumption of luxury goods and a constant critical gaze on the self to ensure the subjective being reaches normative recognisable standards as a successful postfeminist woman. This woman not only has to exert surveillance of the self, regarding her personal appearance, she also has to be economically independent whilst pursuing the 'perfect' male partner. In effect, postfeminism reproduces an idealised feminine avatar of the desirable, independent heterosexual woman. Even in *Queer Eye for the Straight Guy*, a popular US television show in which five gay men undertake a complete makeover of a straight guy, they do so in order for him to become attractive to a female partner. As Cohan (2007: 177), dryly notes, "Some formulations of postfeminism have so readily absorbed the impact of queer theory but left out the queerness".

So, whilst postfeminism celebrates women's achievements in former male arenas, it also reinforces a traditional reproduction of femininity—but with a twist; women are portrayed as having all the choices in the world, and freely, willingly and proudly *choosing* to enact traditional femininity. McRobbie (2004) describes it as a double entanglement—neo-conservative gender, sexuality and family values coexist with processes of liberalisation regarding choice of the same. Lazar (2006: 510) notes a similar paradox: beauty advertisements speak to women's agency and power ("You make it happen", "Shape your destiny" "It's my body. I'll call the shots"), but the focus of agency is confined to one's own physical appearance and sex appeal and the means for this agency is consumption. The postfeminist role model presents an ideal to aspire for, attainable through material means and through consumption. Lifestyle television teaches us how to wine and dine, how to design our homes and gardens and where to travel. The shows are "about the self and about the achievement of social distinction through consumption" (Roberts, 2007: 228).

Besides beautiful and sexy, postfeminist role models are, with few exceptions, young, white, educated and middle class—one gets the impression that they can *choose* to work; it is not an inevitable life necessity. Working-class women, older women or women of colour are the invisible others. On the topic of representation of black women in US media, Springer (2007: 251) asserts that "postfeminism seeks to erase any progress toward racial inclusion that feminism has made since the 1980s. It does so by making racial difference, like feminism itself, merely another commodity for consumption". But postfeminism is a phenomenon with global circulation. Dosekun (2015) notes that it produces class differences all over the world, irrespective of skin colour, between women who find themselves "already empowered" in terms of material standards, level of consumption and self-determination, and those who do not.

Neoliberal and Entrepreneurial Postfeminism

It has been noted that postfeminism chimes with a neoliberal ideology, which privileges the market before the state, and which is characterised by deregulation, privatisation and state withdrawal from many areas of social provision (Harvey, 2005; Perren and Dannreuther, 2012). Privatisation is often argued in terms of providing citizens with a choice of provider for a variety of services previously managed by the state. The language of choice is central to the neoliberal ideology; it constructs a new, agentic citizen, assumed to be—and assumed to want to be—self-governing and self-regulating and keeping the state at a distance (Campbell and Pedersen, 2001). As Rose (1993) points out, this is a new form of governmentality, in which the citizen internalises government and governs by making the right choices on the market.

It is at this moment in time that postfeminism emerges as a contemporary gender ideology, which just as neoliberalism stresses personal agency, responsibility and freedom of choice (Chen, 2013). But it ignores that there is no level playing field, so old hierarchies of gender, sexuality, race and class are reinstated (Butler, 2013). As Gill (2008: 443) argues,

> It seems to me that this neoliberal postfeminist moment is importantly—perhaps pre-eminently—one in which power operates psychologically, by "governing the soul" . . . Indeed, it is not simply that subjects are governed, disciplined or regulated in ever more intimate ways, but even more fundamentally that notions of choice, agency and autonomy have become central to that regulatory power.

And somehow, people govern themselves in such a way that old hierarchies are reproduced.

The step from neoliberalism to entrepreneurship, or *entrepreneurialism*, (du Gay, 2004) is a short one. The new, self-regulating citizen is also the new, entrepreneurial citizen. The enterprising self extends to all spheres of life, not least work, where the new employee is morally obliged to maximise their own human capital, be flexible, and align personal fulfilment with the interest of the employer (Kauppinen, 2013), which in less upbeat words could be described as having to live with job insecurity and no boundary between work and leisure (Noon and Blyton, 2007). The exemplary entrepreneurial citizen starts their own venture thereby, achieving personal independence and individuality whilst creating new employment, generating economic growth and contributing tax returns to the state.

Feminist Postfeminism?

Postfeminism is an elusive label, difficult to pin down. Complicating the issue is that it used in different ways by different scholars (Gill, Kelan, and Scharff, 2016). To explicate the understanding of postfeminism used in this chapter, it might be best to start with what it is not. While some writers equate postfeminism with poststructuralism (or postmodernism or postcolonialism, see Gill et al., 2017), we do not. We perceive poststructuralist feminist theory as a distinct epistemological perspective that sees gender as socially constructed as opposed to biologically given, and which interrogates how gender is done, or performed, paying particular attention to resulting gender hierarchies (Ahl and Marlow, 2012; Butler, 1990; West and Zimmerman, 1987). Moreover, postfeminism is not intersectional theory either, which extends the interrogation of gender constructions to intersecting constructions of race, ethnicity, class and other social categories (Crenshaw, 1991).

Neither is it third-wave feminism, which Butler (2013) defines as a quasi-political movement which emerged as a response to perceived limitations of second-wave feminism. Third-wave feminism created a space for feminist action for women of colour, for young women, and for wider expressions of gender identities including "girlie" feminism which is a "can-do, sex-positive, all-access pass that allows women to be independent, strong, smart and sexy all at once", and which favours consumer-based "cultural" activism before overt political activism (Butler, 2013: 42). Third-wave feminism is still feminism, though, in the sense that it wants to improve women's situations, but, argues Butler (2013), it provides women with a fundamentally neoliberal space—inclusive, welcoming and without the negative connotations of old-school, political feminism.

If not a new feminist wave, is there anything feminist about it at all? Several scholars argue that it is *not* feminism, but rather a *response* to feminism. This response has been articulated in three ways according to Butler (2013). The popular interpretation is that it is the end of feminism, i.e. women's liberation has been achieved so feminism is no longer necessary. The critical interpretation, most clearly voiced by Faludi (2009) is that it is a backlash against feminism. The third version is postfeminism as an up-to-date, sex-positive version of feminism. But it is more complicated than so, argues McRobbie (2004). Postfeminism does not negate feminism; it rather co-opts it. According to Tasker and Negra (2007: 2), "Postfeminist culture works in part to incorporate, assume, or naturalize aspects of feminism;

crucially, it also works to commodify feminism via the figure of woman as empowered consumer".

The perceived victories of past feminist action are thus part of the post-feminist story, but incorporated and taken for granted and seldom mentioned explicitly. Because of this, it also renders 'old-fashioned' first- and second-wave feminism (in the sense of taking political, collective action for women's rights) dated and irrelevant. Even if one can easily demonstrate that feminism has not yet done its job quite yet, victories have been made; postfeminism does account for, even builds on, this, and postfeminist cultural expressions are pervasive, so one cannot just write it off from feminist discussions. Scott (2006) makes a persuasive case for the benefits to women of commodified female beauty; her empirical analysis of the development of the beauty and fashion industry in the United States, which is an achievement by women, as workers, sales people, editors or business owners suggests it has indeed provided women opportunities for financial and personal freedom and independence. Being against commodification of female beauty is not a feminist position argues Scott (2006); rather, it is a prudish position. Postfeminism is paradoxical in that it holds feminist as well as anti-feminist discourses. Gill (2007: 163) writes that postfeminism holds a patterned nature of contradictions in which "notions of autonomy, choice and self-improvement sit side by side with surveillance, discipline and the vilification of these who make the 'wrong' choices".

Pinning Down Postfeminism

The academic literature on postfeminism seems in agreement that a clear definition of postfeminism is beyond reach. Current scholarship, converging around foundational work of authors such as Gill (2007) or McRobbie (2004, 2009), conceives of postfeminism as a 'discursive entity' (Lewis and Simpson, 2016), a 'discursive formation' (Butler, 2013), a 'postfeminist gender regime' (McRobbie, 2004) or a 'distinct sensibility' made up of a number of interrelated themes (Gill, 2007). Building on Gill (2007), Butler (2013:44) compiles a list of postfeminist themes cited below. We added the final point from Lewis and Simpson (2016). An analytical object may be identified as postfeminist if it incorporates one, or more, of the following themes:

- sees femininity as a bodily property and revives notions of natural sexual difference;
- implies that gender equality has been achieved and feminist activism is thus, no longer necessary;
- marks a shift from sexual objectification to sexual subjectification;
- encourages self-surveillance, self-discipline and a makeover paradigm;
- sees individualism, choice and empowerment as the primary routes to women's independence and freedom;
- promotes consumerism and the commodification of difference; and
- perceives of the retreat to home as a matter of choice, not obligation.

Gill et al. (2016) explain further that postfeminism is *the analytical object*, not a theoretical stance or position. They perceive themselves as "analysts of postfeminist culture rather than postfeminist analysts", pointing to a problematic slippage common in writing about postfeminism.

Analysts of postfeminism usually employ analytical strategies that build on poststructuralist feminist theory. As mentioned earlier, poststructuralist feminist theory is a distinct epistemological perspective that sees gender as socially constructed as opposed to biologically given and which interrogates how gender is done, or performed, paying particular attention to resulting gender hierarchies (Ahl and Marlow, 2012; Butler, 1990; West and Zimmerman, 1987). Analytical techniques used by poststructuralist analysts are often versions of discourse analysis, or deconstruction.

Postfeminism as a Lens in Entrepreneurship Research

Since the 1980s, entrepreneurship research has matured into an established field with a number of well-respected specialty journals. As a specific strand of research activity, analyses of the influence of gender upon women's entrepreneurial activity has emerged somewhat more slowly and has progressed through several iterations. Over time, this debate has demonstrated progressive development and increasing coherence (McAdam, 2013) whereby the focus has shifted from relatively blunt positivist, objectivist analyses using founder sex as a variable through which a male norm was utilised as a comparator for women's entrepreneurial activities (Carter and Cannon, 1992; Mukhtar, 1998) to contemporary feminist critiques (Ahl and Marlow, 2012; Henry et al., 2016). The former stance invariably found women wanting in terms of entrepreneurial competencies and achievements *even* though when analysed as populations, there are few performance differences between male and female-led firms (Ahl, 2006; Robb and Watson, 2012). Feminist poststructuralist scholarship, however, has demonstrated that the construction of the woman entrepreneur as secondary is the result of a number of unquestioned assumptions prevalent in mainstream entrepreneurship research (and elsewhere)—namely, the assumptions that the primary purpose of entrepreneurship is profit (on the business level) and economic growth (on the societal level), that entrepreneurship is something male, that it is an individual undertaking, that men and women are different and that work and family are separate spheres where women prioritise (or ought to prioritise) family (Ahl, 2004, 2006). Other scholars have also fruitfully employed a poststructuralist perspective in order to reveal the gendering of entrepreneurship in different contexts (Bruni, Gherardi, and Poggio, 2004; Calás, Smircich, and Bourne, 2007), but explicit feminist perspectives are, nevertheless, still rare in entrepreneurship research (Jennings and Brush, 2013) and a postfeminist perspective is most definitely a novelty.

In terms of utilising the list of postfeminist themes noted earlier and comparing it to the assumptions in published mainstream research on women's entrepreneurship (see Ahl, 2006), one might conclude that this body of research is in itself a postfeminist expression—most of the points may be identified.

Lewis (2014) analyses how feminine subjectivities (or "entrepreneurial femininities") are constructed in the gender and entrepreneurship literature. Lewis (2014) adopts a doing-gender approach as an analytical strategy, and looks explicitly for postfeminist elements in the construction of the female entrepreneur. She finds four different entrepreneurial femininities: First, the 'entrepreneur' who is supposedly gender neutral, meritocratic and where individual men and women have an equal chance of success if they commit energy and enthusiasm. Postfeminist elements stress individual choice and the lack of gender specific barriers. Perhaps not so postfeminist is that this entrepreneur distances herself from traditional femininity and from the private sphere. Second, the 'mumpreneur' who has a home-based business offering products or services associated with motherhood. Postfeminist elements would be individualisation (actually running a business), the retreat to the home, and the commercial valuing of traditional femininity. Third, the 'female entrepreneur' who performs traditional, relational femininity—she is a transformative leader, shares power, promotes trust and pursues collective goals. Family and home are valued, since this is the place where such skills were developed in the first place. Postfeminist elements are the stress on essential sex difference, and the valuing of the feminine in a professional or commercial context as complementary to masculine values. Fourth, 'non-preneur' is a person who performs 'excessive' femininity—vulnerability, dependence, etc.—without compensating this with contemporary, postfeminist assertiveness, confidence and self-determination.

Following the example of Lewis (2014), we now turn to an analysis of postfeminist elements in policy for women's entrepreneurship, using material that we are familiar with from our own countries, Sweden and the United Kingdom.

Government Support for Women's Entrepreneurship in Sweden

The term postfeminism does not have a wide circulation in Sweden. A Google search on Swedish language pages reveals that before 2010, it could be counted in two-digit numbers and since that time has mostly been found in academic student papers utilising the theme of cultural postfeminism. This rather more limited engagement with the notion of postfeminism may reflect the notion that old-fashioned feminism is alive and well in Sweden. Sweden has, in 2016, a purportedly feminist government, a feminist foreign policy, even a feminist party trying to make inroads into parliament, as well as a uniquely "women friendly" welfare system and family policies (Hernes, 1987; Sainsbury, 1999). Today's 19-year-olds in Sweden are happy to identify themselves as feminists according to a marketing study among potential new students by Jönköping University.

This does not mean that the phenomenon of postfeminism is absent. Sweden, like most western European states, went through a period of neoliberal changes after the financial crisis in the early 1990s with downsizing of the public sector and privatisation of former publicly owned operations in education, care, health care, transportation and infrastructure that continue to this day (Ahl et al., 2016). Parallel to this is the rise of the entrepreneurship discourse. It is private entrepreneurship which is to step in where the State steps out and since the State used to employ many women, there is a special call for women to fill the void. The Swedish government has had policies and programmes to support women's business ownership since the early 1990s (see Ahl and Nelson, 2015, for a full description). In this section, we look for postfeminist elements in the arguments for such programmes, paying particular attention to changes over time. The quotes that follow are from Swedish government publications such as decisions, investigations, transcribed parliament debates or program evaluations. The quotes were translated by the authors. The first programme in 1994, Resource Centres for Women, was argued as follows:

> The goal could be to promote women's independence so that women, irrespective of where in the country they reside, can live a dignified life measured by women's standards. This means equal conditions for women and men regarding education, income and influence in society. It means that society's resources—ownership, right of disposition—are equally divided between the sexes. It means freedom from patronizing, abuse and other violations from men.
>
> (Friberg, 1993)

This quote is firmly anchored in old-school feminist thought, both liberal (stress on equal chances) and socialist (stress on equal outcome). The propositions and motions that follow, though, stress that men and women are indeed different and need different measures. The second quote that follows contains a postfeminist, upbeat version of women's difference—they are the ones that will secure long-term financial stability:

> Problem descriptions and analyses must take into account that women and men have different needs and conditions and measures must be designed so that they further both women and men. Special measures for women are also needed.
>
> (Proposition, 1993/94: 140)

> There is reason to believe that female entrepreneurship is an industry of the future . . . studies have shown that women's businesses are more long-lived, stable and grow less dramatically. The effect is that women have been able to expand in a business cycle when men are forced to lay off people.
>
> (Motion 1993/94:A460, 1994)

The new broader programme from 2007–2014 focused on women as an under-utilised resource for economic growth. The gender equality argument is gone.

> More women business owners would mean that more business ideas are taken advantage of and that Sweden's opportunities for increased employment and economic growth is strengthened . . . The program shall contribute to more new women owned businesses and that more businesses owned by women grow. The program shall thus make more women consider starting a business, chose to run a business full time and choose to employ others.
>
> (Regeringsbeslut, 2011)

The programme has provided training and advisory services for women, a number of development projects, organised activities for prospective female entrepreneurs at colleges and universities, mapped existing networks for women and trained support staff in gender awareness. There was an ambassador programme in which 880 female entrepreneurs inspired school pupils with the female entrepreneurship message (unpaid), a "Beautiful Business Award" competition and exhibitions of women's innovations.

This discourse could easily be characterised as postfeminist. Apart from the first quote, there is no mention of feminist activism. Women are assumed to be different from men; they possess unique womanly skills that can be drawn upon for commercial success. Women need to use the available business support and start their own companies, as well as inspire other to do the same. Postfeminist elements of individualism, choice and empowerment are clearly present; references to changing discriminatory structures are absent.

Regarding the outcomes of such programmes, it emerges that women's self-employment did indeed increase, from a historic figure of around 25%–30% to 36% in 2012 (Statistics Sweden, 2014). But almost all of the increase in the formerly publicly owned sectors was in child care, a feminine gendered business with very low earnings and profit potential (Sköld and Tillmar, 2015). The other formerly publicly owned sectors such as health care used outsourcing procedures that favoured male-owned, large oligopolies (Sköld, 2015; Sundin and Tillmar, 2010). There is little evidence that the postfeminist discourse of women's entrepreneurship in Sweden is matched with corresponding results, i.e., gender equality is not achieved—existing gender hierarchies are recreated. But there *is* evidence, we claim, that the postfeminist discourse tends to conceal this fact.

UK Government Initiatives to Promote Women's Business Ownership

Reflecting the Swedish context, postfeminist critiques of government policy to support women's entrepreneurial activity do not feature within this debate. However, unlike Sweden, affiliation to feminist principles within

UK policy initiatives is not evident (Fawcett Society, 2015). The focus has been more upon an individual 'enabling' approach which reflects the United Kingdom's engagement with the neoliberal agenda dating back to the close relationship between Thatcher and Reagan in the 1980s (King and Wood, 1999). As such, it was not deemed to be the role of the state to promote or protect specific disadvantaged populations. Rather, the emphasis was upon creating an environment where market forces enabled the most talented individuals to employ their agency to achieve on the basis that markets do not recognise sex, colour, class, etc. The absurdity of such arguments has since emerged. Free market liberalism as a pathway to greater equality has not been effective; rather inequality has become more entrenched particularly since the recession in 2008 and related policies of austerity (Tyler, 2013). Yet, successive governments of differing persuasions have maintained allegiance to the neoliberal project; this has been evident in terms of the continued privatisation of services and in recent years, a significantly reduced public sector (McKay et al., 2013). A cornerstone of such political dialogue has been a continued and enthusiastic support of entrepreneurship (Dannreuther and Perren, 2012) as a desirable representation of the self-sufficient individual. It is also a useful vehicle to transform unemployment into self-employment in an era of public sector redundancies.

Regarding the emergence of government policy initiatives for women's enterprise since the late 1990s, focus and provision has been volatile and fragmented. Successive Labour governments (1997–2010) developed numerous initiatives to encourage and support more women to enter self-employment. So for example, they sponsored umbrella organisations such as Prowess (Promoting Women's Enterprise Success and Support) and produced a number of policy documents outlining a pathway to increase women's entrepreneurially activity (Small Business Service, 20013; 2010) with action embedded in Regional Development Agencies (Huggins and Williams, 2009). Since the election of the Coalition Government in 2010 and successive Conservative governments in 2015 and 2017, the discrete focus upon women's entrepreneurial activity has diminished becoming subsumed into a broader stance upon equality and opportunity (Fawcett Society, 2015). In response to such diminishing interest, a Women's Enterprise Policy Group (WEPG) was formed in 2012 which reported,

> From a policy perspective, there has been a very limited focus on women in business from the Coalition government. Though, interestingly, the 'women on boards' agenda, following the publication of the Davies report, has been widely debated and has received many more column inches within the media than women's business ownership. This has served to deflect discussion on, arguably, the more important issue of creating a pipeline of growth-oriented female-led businesses which will provide the FTSE board directors of the future.
>
> (www.womensenterprisepolicygroup.com/index.htm)

Thus, focused support for women's enterprise in the United Kingdom has had a somewhat chequered history; prior to 1997, there were virtually no discrete policy initiatives. This changed significantly during the early 2000s with a distinct strand of government support invested in promoting women's enterprise. Since 2010, whilst governments still make reference to the importance of women's enterprise there have been very limited direct policy or funding focused upon this issue (WEPG, 2012).

In terms of the impact of government policy, Carter et al. (2015) note that recent estimates by the Office for National Statistics (ONS) indicate that women comprise about 29% of the United Kingdom's self-employed population and 22% of incorporated businesses are women-led (BIS, 2013; Causer and Park, 2009). Women-owned businesses contribute about £75billion to Gross Value Added (GVA) productivity, about 16% of the approximate GVA of all UK SMEs (BIS, 2013). Despite the recent decline in focused support for women's entrepreneurial activity, rates of self-employment and firm ownership have actually notably increased in the last few years (ONS, 2015). This may suggest that a combination of previous policies, the cultural embedding of an entrepreneurial mindset and higher rates of entrepreneurship education are fuelling an increasing propensity for women to create new ventures. McKay et al. (2013) however, note the impact of recession and austerity policies since 2010 such that the sharp contraction of the public sector in the United Kingdom has had a devastating impact on women who dominate such employment. This would suggest that much of the increase in self-employment has been fuelled by public sector redundancies; moreover, the ONS suggests that reduced employment opportunities are preventing normal levels of churn such that those women who might normally wish to self-select back into employment given dissatisfaction with self-employment are unable to do so (ONS, 2015). Moreover, as in the case of Sweden, distinct gendered occupational segregation persists within self-employment and small firm ownership (Marlow, 2014) whilst women are still far more likely to start home-based part-time firms in an effort to combine domestic labour and economic participation (Jayawarna, Rouse, and Kitching, 2013).

Regardless, however, of which government has been in power, their willingness to invest in women's enterprise policy initiatives or the impact of such, there is a consistent underpinning theme to the discourse which informs this debate. The emphasis is upon the responsibility of the individual woman to exploit her entrepreneurial potential with policy initiatives aimed at assisting her to overcome her feminised entrepreneurial deficit. This differs from the Swedish discourse where the distinct value of feminine attributes is more to the fore. Within UK policy documents, there is a sense of longing and regret that women are not more entrepreneurial, this is tinged with a moral judgement upon their failure to make a greater contribution to the wealth of the nation. So unpicking the themes within a comprehensive briefing paper of 2003, 'A Strategic Framework for Women's

Enterprise', a consistent plea is for more women to enter self-employment to reflect levels in the United States:

> The overall objective is to increase significantly the numbers of women starting and growing businesses in the UK, to proportionately match or exceed the level achieved in the USA.

As Marlow, Carter, and Shaw (2008) pointed out, this is a completely specious ambition given the differences in markets, welfare systems and crucially, how business ownership is defined. Thus, the pressure for women in the United Kingdom to step up and reflect the contribution of their transatlantic cousins is positioned as a moral responsibility. To achieve this expansion, women are urged to overcome their feminised deficits such as risk aversion, fear of finance, reluctance to develop innovative ideas and make the move from benefits to enterprise. Whilst these are certainly issues which do affect most people considering new venture creation, they have been packaged as peculiarly feminine such that women require special help to overcome such deficits. As Marlow and Swail (2014: 80) noted, the generic sentiment being "if only women could be more like men". Bringing this more up to date, the Federation of Small Business in their recent report on support for women business owners noted,

> Key challenges included balancing work and family life (40%), achieving credibility for the business (37%) and a lack of confidence (22%). All of these are limiting women's ability to start, run and grow their businesses.
>
> (Women in Enterprise: Untapped Potential: 2016:4)

With the exception of the first issue, the other challenges would appear to be generic to all who seek to create a new venture but are transposed into particular feminised issues when articulated through a gendered lens and applied to women.

Thus, adopting a postfeminist analysis, the assumption informing successive government policy initiatives is of the individual woman as the unit of analysis—it is she who must change and adapt in order to realise her entrepreneurial potential and in so doing, engage in self-development and contribute to the wealth of the nation in so doing. As such, it is women who require dedicated support to develop entrepreneurial attitudes and competencies to overcome feminised deficits and so enjoy the promise of entrepreneurship. There are no feminist reflections regarding the impact of persistent discrimination, the continuing disparity in terms of domestic/economic labour divisions and generic structural challenges women experience as a category and how this may impact upon their entrepreneurial activity. In addition, there is certainly no reflection that given such socio-economic constraints, entrepreneurship is a poor choice for many women as they are very unlikely to be able to utilise agency to overcome such barriers. In fact, secure public sector employment is a much better option for most women to achieve flexible, secure pathways to income generation; however, this is contradictory to the current fetishal reverence afforded to entrepreneurship as open and meritocratic, reaping benefits for the individual and society.

Conclusion

This chapter has reviewed the concept of postfeminism as used in academic research, primarily in cultural studies, and applied it to the field of entrepreneurship, using the discourse on women's entrepreneurship in two different countries as illustrative examples. In Sweden, we reviewed government policy for women's entrepreneurship comparing it to the approach within the United Kingdom. In both instances, we found that the discourse might be characterised as postfeminist. It celebrates individual agency, empowerment and choice. It is built on the notion that a woman can build her own bright future by starting a business. It assumes that all structural barriers have been removed and that women are now free to actualise themselves and to make money through entrepreneurship, while simultaneously contributing to the common good by contributing to economic growth. The discourse has developed alongside neoliberal economic policy and transformation, and is decidedly part of the neoliberal discourse. Our critical evaluation of the promise of entrepreneurship in liberal societies suggests this is fragile promise which rests upon aspirational arguments. Entrepreneurship does not challenge existing gender inequalities; it just recreates them in a new form.

We draw three main conclusions from this analysis: First, this might be the time for postfeminist discourse, but these are not postfeminist times. Rather, women's subordination appears to be recreated, and not only that, *the postfeminist discourse renders feminist (collective) action—which could potentially change this state of affairs—obsolete.* There is reason to speak of postfeminism as an especially insidious governmentality (Dean, 1999) which makes women *conduct themselves* in such a way as to recreate their own subordination. This is illustrated within the debate on entrepreneurship as the subtext in the policy discourse assumes the need for a postfeminist 'fixing' of women. Given the opportunities made available to women within the postfeminist era of equality and choice, those who fail to achieve or exploit available opportunities must, on the basis of such rational arguments, only have themselves to blame. Thus, the moral underpinning of such arguments suggest women who refute the promise of entrepreneurship, or whose ventures do not realise expected returns, are failing themselves and also, wider society as clearly, their own shortcomings are to blame.

Second, the analysis demonstrates how postfeminism, as described earlier in this chapter, as a certain discursive formation made up of a number of interrelated themes is very useful as a way to describe, or characterise, the results of an analysis of contemporary discourse around gender and femininity. It is particularly promising in the field of entrepreneurship studies since this field is imbued with neoliberal assumptions that are taken for granted, but have consequences for the gender/power order. Analysing these through the postfeminist lens can make the assumptions, as well as the consequences visible and thereby possible to critique or amend.

Third, we argue that an analysis of postfeminist expression in organisations or in entrepreneurship should not stop at the discursive level. It should be accompanied by old-fashioned analysis of the gender order, which in organisation studies is best and most persuasively undertaking by reviewing the evidence. Are there now more women leaders, senior managers or entrepreneurs? Critically, do they make more money and/or have more power and influence? Do organisations or governments have policies in place that make it possible to combine work and family and divide house chores evenly between men and women? Empirical evidence in the form of numbers can have a sobering effect given that whilst there certainly has been change, this has been slow. Moreover, it may be argued that such change has been detrimental to some women as it has not been a case of social change eroding gendered challenges making it easier to be successful leaders, managers and entrepreneurs but rather, greater efforts have been exhorted from individual women to fuel such achievements. The current focus upon entrepreneurship is an exemplary case in point; the postfeminist context suggests it presents new opportunities to recognise and celebrate individual achievements without ever acknowledging the persistence of gendered barriers which obstruct progress. Nor does it question or challenge the desirability of entrepreneurship as a 'good choice' for women in terms of their health, welfare or wealth.

The gender/power implications of the postfeminist condition must be recognised. Using a poststructuralist analysis to deconstruct the lived meanings of women business owners and critically evaluating these in light of policy assumptions is essential to reveal the fragile foundations of the promise of postfeminist rhetoric. Given this, we propose that an analysis of postfeminism or the 'postfeminist condition' within the field of organisation science is necessary. It offers a conceptual tool that may help us to describe how power is operating in organisations and society.

References

Ahl, H. (2004). *The Scientific Reproduction of Gender Inequality: A Discourse Analysis of Research Texts on Women's Entrepreneurship*. Copenhagen: CBS Press.

Ahl, H. (2006). Why research on women entrepreneurs needs new directions. *Entrepreneurship Theory and Practice*, 30: 595–621.

Ahl, H., Berglund, K., Pettersson, K., and Tillmar, M. (2016). From feminism to FemInc. ism: On the uneasy relationship between feminism, entrepreneurship and the Nordic welfare state. *International Entrepreneurship and Management Journal*, 12: 369–392.

Ahl, H., and Marlow, S. (2012). Exploring the dynamics of gender, feminism and entrepreneurship: Advancing debate to escape a dead end? *Organization*, 19: 543–562.

Ahl, H., and Nelson, T. (2015). How policy positions women entrepreneurs: A comparative analysis of state discourse in Sweden and the United States. *Journal of Business Venturing*, 30: 273–291.

Banet-Weiser, S., and Portwood-Stacer, L. (2006). "I just want to be me again!" Beauty pageants, reality television and post-feminism. *Feminist Theory*, 7(2): 255–272.

BIS. (2013). *Business Population Estimates for the UK and Regions 2013*. London: Department for Business, Innovation and Skills.

Bruni, A., Gherardi, S., and Poggio, B. (2004). Doing gender, doing entrepreneurship: An ethnographic account of intertwined practices. *Gender, Work and Organization*, 11: 406–429.

Butler, J. (1990). *Gender Trouble: Feminism and the Subversion of Identity*. London and New York: Routledge.

Butler, J. (2013). For white girls only? Postfeminism and the politics of inclusion. *Feminist Formations*, 25: 35–58.

Calás, M.B., Smircich, L., and Bourne, K.A. (2007). Knowing Lisa? Feminist analyses of "gender and entrepreneurship". In D. Bilimoria and S.K. Piderit (Eds.), *Handbook on Women in Business and Management* (pp. 78–105). Cheltenham, UK: Edward Elgar Publishing Ltd.

Campbell, J.L., Pedersen, O.K. (2001) *The Rise of Neoliberalism and Institutional Analysis*. Princeton, NJ: Princeton University Press.

Carter, S., and Cannon, T. (1992). *Women as Entrepreneurs: A Study of Female Business Owners, Their Motivations, Experiences and Strategies for Success*. London: Academic Press.

Carter, S., Mwaura, S., Ram, M., Trehan, K., and Jones, T. (2015). Barriers to ethnic minority and women's enterprise: Existing evidence, policy tensions and unsettled questions. *International Small Business Journal*, 33(1): 49–69.

Carter, S.L., and Shaw, E. (2006). *Women's Business Ownership: Recent Research and Policy Developments*. Report to the UK Small Business Service. Available at: http://strathprints.strath.ac.uk/8962/1/SBS_2006_Report_for_BIS.pdf/

Causer, P., and Park, N. (2009). Women in business. *Regional Trends*, 41: 31–51.

Chen, E. (2013). Neoliberalism and popular women's culture: Rethinking choice, freedom and agency. *European Journal of Cultural Studies*, 16(4) (August 1): 440–452.

Cohan, S. (2007). Queer eye for the straight guise: Camp, postfeminism, and the fab five's makeovers of masculinity. In Y. Tasker and D. Negra (Eds.), *Interrogating Postfeminism* (pp. 176–200). Durham and London: Duke University Press.

Coppock, V., Haydon, D., and Richter, I. (2014). *The Illusions of Post-feminism: New Women, Old Myths*. London: Routledge.

Crenshaw, K. (1991). Mapping the margins: Intersectionality, identity politics, and violence against women of color. *Stanford Law Review*, 43(6): 1241–1299.

Dannreuther, C., and Perren, L. (2012). *The Political Economy of the Small Firm*. London: Routledge.

Dean, M. (1999). *Governmentality*. London: Sage.

Dosekun, S. (2015). For western girls only? Post-feminism as transnational culture. *Feminist Media Studies*, 15: 960–975.

Down, S., and Warren, L. (2008). Constructing narratives of enterprise: Clichés and entrepreneurial self-identity. *International Journal of Entrepreneurial Behavior & Research*, 14(1): 4–23.

du Gay, P. (1994) Making up managers: bureaucracy, enterprise and the liberal art of separation. *British Journal of Sociology*, 45(4): 655–674.

du Gay, P. (2004). Against enterprise but not against "enterprise" for that would be silly. *Organization*, 11: 37–57.

Faludi, S. (2009). *Backlash: The Undeclared War Against American Women*. New York: Broadway Books.

Fawcett Society: Election. (2015). *Take Action*. Available at: www.fawcettsociety. org.uk/our-work/campaigns/general-election-2015-fawcetts-plans/

Friberg, T. (1993). *Den andra sidan av myntet—om regionalpolitikens enögdhet: en idéskrift ur kvinnligt perspektiv från Glesbygdsmyndigheten*. Östersund: Glesbygdsmyndigheten.

Gill, R. (2007). Postfeminist media culture elements of a sensibility. *European Journal of Cultural Studies*, 10: 147–166.

Gill, R. (2008). Culture and subjectivity in neoliberal and postfeminist times. *Subjectivity*, 25: 432–445.

Gill, R., Kelan, E. K. and Scharff, C. M. (2017) A postfeminist sensibility at work. *Gender, Work and Organization*, 24(3): 226–244.

Harvey, D. (2005). *A Brief History of Neoliberalism*. Oxford: Oxford University Press.

Henry, C., Foss, L., and Ahl, H. (2016). Gender and entrepreneurship research: A review of methodological approaches. *International Small Business Journal*, 34: 217–241.

Hernes, H. (1987). *Welfare State and Women Power: Essays in State Feminism*. Oslo: Norwegian University Press.

Huggins, R., and Williams, N. (2009). Enterprise and public policy: A review of Labour government intervention in the United Kingdom. *Environment and Planning C: Government and Policy*, 27(1) (February 1): 19–41.

Jayawarna, D., Rouse, J., and Kitching, J. (2013). Entrepreneur motivations and life course. *International Small Business Journal*, 31(1): 34–56.

Jennings, J.E., and Brush, C.G. (2013). Research on women entrepreneurs: Challenges to (and from) the broader entrepreneurship literature? *The Academy of Management Annals*, 7: 663–715.

Kauppinen, K. (2013). "Full power despite stress": A discourse analytical examination of the interconnectedness of postfeminism and neoliberalism in the domain of work in an international women's magazine. *Discourse & Communication*, 7: 133–151.

King, D., and Wood, S. (1999). The political economy of neoliberalism: Britain and the United States in the 1980s. *Continuity and Change in Contemporary Capitalism*, 13(January): 371–397.

Lazar, M.M. (2006). "Discover the power of femininity!" Analyzing global "power femininity" in local advertising. *Feminist Media Studies*, 6: 505–517.

Lewis, P. (2014). Postfeminism, femininities and organization studies: Exploring a new agenda. *Organization Studies*, 35: 1845–1866.

Lewis, P., and Simpson, R. (2017). Hakim revisited: Preference, choice and the postfeminist gender regime. *Gender, Work & Organization*, 24(2): 115–133.

Marlow, S. (2014). Exploring future research agendas in the field of gender and entrepreneurship. *International Journal of Gender and Entrepreneurship*, 6(2): 102–120.

Marlow, S., Carter, S., and Shaw, E. (2008). Constructing female entrepreneurship policy in the UK: Is the US a relevant benchmark? *Environment and Planning C: Government and Policy*, 26: 335–351.

Marlow, S., and McAdam, M. (2013). Advancing debate and challenging myths-exploring the alleged case of the under-performing female entrepreneur. *International Journal of Entrepreneurial Behaviour and Research*, 19(1): 114–124.

Marlow, S., and Swail, J. (2014). Gender, risk and finance: Why can't a woman be more like a man? *Entrepreneurship and Regional Development*, 26: 80–96.

McAdam, M. (2013). *Female Entrepreneurship*. London: Routledge.

McKay, A., Campbell, J., Thomson, E., and Ross, S. (2013). Economic recession and recovery in the UK: What's gender got to do with it? *Feminist Economics*, 19: 108–123.

McRobbie, A. (2004). Post-feminism and popular culture. *Feminist Media Studies*, 4: 255–264.

McRobbie, A. (2009). *The Aftermath of Feminism: Gender, Culture and Social Change*. London: Sage.

McRobbie, A. (2011). Beyond post-feminism. *Public Policy Research*, 18(3): 179–184.

Motion 1993/94:A460. (1994). *Motion 1993/94:A460: Kvinnoperspektiv på regionalpolitiken*.

Mukhtar, S.M. (1998). Business characteristics of male and female small and medium enterprises in the UK: Implications for gender-based entrepreneurialism and business competence development. *British Journal of Management*, 9(1): 41–51.

Noon, M., and Blyton, P. (2007). *The Realities of Work*. London: Palgrave.

ONS: Statistical bulletin: UK Labour Market: August. (2015). *Estimates of Employment, Unemployment, Economic Inactivity and Other Employment-Related Statistics for the UK*. Available at: www.ons.gov.uk/employmentandlabourmarket/people inwork/employmentandemployeetypes/bulletins/uklabourmarket/2015-08-12/

Perren, L., and Dannreuther, C. (2012). Political signification of the entrepreneur: Temporal analysis of constructs, agency and reification. *International Small Business Journal*, 32(2): 231–245.

Proposition. (1993/94:140). *Bygder och regioner i utveckling*. Stockholm: Riksdagstryck.

Regeringsbeslut. (2011). *Regeringsbeslut 2011: N2011/1250/ENT*. (Vol. 2012). Stockholm: Regeringen.

Robb, A.M., and Watson, J. (2012). Gender differences in firm performance: Evidence from new ventures in the United States. *Journal of Business Venturing*, 27: 544–558.

Roberts, M. (2007). The fashion police: Governing the self in what not to wear. In Y. Tasker and D. Negra (Eds.), *Interrogating Postfeminism* (pp. 227–248). Durham and London: Duke University Press.

Rose, N. (1993). Government, authority and expertise in advanced liberalism. *Economy and society*, 22: 283–299.

Sainsbury, D. (1999). Gender and social-democratic welfare states. In D. Sainsbury (Ed.), *Gender and Welfare State Regimes* (pp. 75–115). Oxford: Oxford University Press.

Scott, L.M. (2006). *Fresh Lipstick: Redressing Fashion and Feminism*. New York: Palgrave Macmillan.

Sköld, B. (2015). *Vad hände? Kvinnors företagande och de strukturella villkoren—en studie i spåren av den offentliga sektorns omvandling*. Linköping: Linköping University.

Sköld, B., and Tillmar, M. (2015). Resilient gender order in entrepreneurship: The case of Swedish welfare industries. *International Journal of Gender and Entrepreneurship*, 7: 2–26.

Springer, K. (2007). Divas, evil black bitches, and bitter black women: African American women in postfeminist and post-civil-rights popular culture. In Y. Tasker and D. Negra (Eds.), *Interrogating Postfeminism* (pp. 249–276). Durham and London: Duke University Press.

Statistics Sweden. (2014). *Women and Men in Sweden: Facts and Figures 2014*. Örebro: Statistics Sweden.

Sundin, E., and Tillmar, M. (2010). The masculinization of the elderly care sector: Local-level studies of public sector outsourcing. *International Journal of Gender and Entrepreneurship*, 2: 49–67.

Swail, J., Down, S., and Kautonen, T. (2013). Examining the effect of "entretainment" as a cultural influence on entrepreneurial intentions. *International Small Business Journal*, 33(5): 425–446.

Tasker, Y., and Negra, D. (2007). Introduction: Feminist politica and postfeminist culture. In Y. Tasker and D. Negra (Eds.), *Interrogating Postfeminism* (pp. 1–26). Durham and London: Duke University Press.

Tyler, I. (2013). *Revolting Subjects: Social Abjection and Resistance in Neoliberal Britain*. London: Zed Books, 11 January.

West, C., and Zimmerman, D.H. (1987). Doing gender. *Gender & Society*, 1: 125–151.

Women in Enterprise: Untapped Potential. (2016). Available at: www.fsb.org.uk/docs/default-source/fsb-org-uk/fsb-women-in-enterprise-the-untapped-potential

Zahra, S.A., Wright, M., and Abdelgawad, S.G. (2014). Contextualization and the advancement of entrepreneurship research. *International Small Business Journal*, 32(4): 479–500.

8 How Postfeminism Plays Out for Women Elite Leaders

Sharon Mavin and Gina Grandy

Introduction

In this chapter, we explore the experiences of women elite leaders through a postfeminist lens by revisiting our recent empirical studies. We illustrate postfeminism as a 'property' that surfaces issues of surveillance, makeover, transformation and choice. In our work we view postfeminism as a key feature of the feminist lexicon, one which reflects the dominance of choice and agency, "an emphasis on individualism, the retreat from structural accounts of inequality and the repudiation of sexism and feminism" (Gill, Kelan, and Scharff, 2017: 227). Postfeminism is now under debate in gender and organisation studies (see Gill et al., 2017; Lewis, 2014; Lewis and Simpson, 2016) and our aim here is to draw upon a postfeminist lens to explore our recent theorising of women elite leaders' experiences. We do not identify as postfeminist researchers, rather we follow Gill et al. (2017) and engage with postfeminism as a "gender regime" or "sensibility" (Gill et al., 2017: 226) in order to critically revisit our recent studies and extend understandings of women elite leaders' gender relations. Specifically, we explore the question, how does postfeminism play out for women at the top of UK organisational hierarchies?

We are aware of how our work on women elite leaders may appear awkwardly situated as critiques of postfeminism can view women elite leaders as part of the postfeminist problem. As such, we tread carefully. However, our key assumption is that to include postfeminism into understandings of work and organisation, there is immense value in understanding the experiences of women elite leaders and in recognising that not all women elite leaders share the same experiences. The persistent rarity of women who hold such senior positions in organisations illustrates why the experiences of women elites are imperative in feminist futures.

We first provide an overview of postfeminism to ground our postfeminist reading. We then introduce women elite leaders who can be perceived as postfeminists who (directly and indirectly) undermine 'true' feminist theory and practice. With this critique as a backdrop, we provide an overview of the empirical research that informs our published studies and progress to critically re-read the work through a postfeminist analysis. We focus upon three themes informed by existing postfeminism theory—namely, double entanglements, choice and body-care. We discuss our contribution and offer insights into the possibilities for feminist research that provides space to hear and learn from women elite leaders.

Postfeminism

Seen by many as an active process through which feminist gains of the past are undermined, postfeminism can reflect "an array of machinations, elements of contemporary culture which are effective in an undoing of feminism, while simultaneously appearing to be engaging in a well-informed and even well-intended response to feminism" (McRobbie, 2004: 255). Postfeminism can be viewed as taking feminism into account while "installing a whole repertoire of new meanings which emphasise that it is no longer needed, it is a spent force" (McRobbie, 2004: 255). It refers to discourses that constitute part of a backlash against feminist achievements or aims; "the 'post' signalling a reaction against feminism (Faludi, 1991)" (Gill et al., 2017: 229). Postfeminism is also conceptualised as a 'girly', 'sexy' brand of feminism (Lewis, 2014) which has a "generational ethos" (Gill et al., 2017: 228) used synonymously with third-wave feminism or as a new kind of feminism for a new context for debate (Hollows, 2000). Critical work connects postfeminism with neoliberalism (Adamson, 2017; Gill and Scharff, 2011; McRobbie, 2008) so that it is "safe and unchallenging for corporate culture" (Gill et al., 2017: 226). This changing face of femininity is reflected through a newly empowered subject that holds postfeminist agency and is distanced from outmoded notions of female disadvantage—"a discourse of a highly individuated new femininity which leaves little room to raise questions of gender inequality or to articulate the experience of difficulty and disadvantage" (Baker, 2010: 186).

Rottenberg's (2014) thesis of postfeminism highlights how women's liberation is now framed in extremely individualistic terms in a way which erases issues of social and collective justice and incorporates neoliberal governmentality. This feminism does not systematically critique male dominance in business and is individuated in the extreme, where "the subject is feminist in the sense that she is distinctly aware of current inequalities between men and women . . . she disavows the social, cultural and economic forces producing this inequality" and "accepts full responsibility for her own well-being and self-care" (Rottenberg, 2014: 420). In this way, the postfeminist subject converts "continued gender inequality from a structural problem into an individual affair" (Rottenberg, 2014: 420). As a feminist entrepreneurial subject she directs her efforts and resources towards intense calculation and personal initiative (Rottenberg, 2014).

Our aim here is to re-examine our studies of women elite leaders' experiences from a "common sense of postfeminism" (Gill et al., 2017: 8). We follow Lewis (2014) and Dean (2010a) and understand postfeminism as a critical concept "best understood in terms of 'an ambivalent set of hegemonic discourses around gender, feminism and femininity (Dean, 2010b, p. 19), which shape manifestations of contemporary femininity" (Lewis, 2014: 1846). Gill et al. (2017) suggests that postfeminism can be understood as discursive moves serving as a sensibility or gender regime (Acker, 2006). This 'sensibility' simultaneously recognises that gender and inequalities matter and dismisses sexism and feminism as 'yesterday's' concern, no longer relevant. From this perspective, "inequalities are presented as 'just how it is', in ways that do not require social transformation" (Gill et al., 2017: 226), and success is the result of harder work and entrepreneurialism from individual women. The work of McRobbie (2004) also helps to frame our re-reading of the experiences of women elite leaders. McRobbie (2004) offers a series of possible conceptual frames that reflect postfeminism. First, she talks about *double entanglement* (p. 255) as the co-existence of feminism alongside renouncing feminism. Double entanglement involves feminism dismantling itself, where feminism is taken into account but also distanced. Feminism changes focus "from challenging centralised blocks of power to dispersed sites e.g. talk, discourse and the concept of subjectivity" (McRobbie, 2004: 256). McRobbie (2004) also highlights the notion of *female success* where "ideal subjects are subjects of excellence" (p. 257) attached to privilege and there is a displacement of feminism as a political movement. Third, postfeminism is manifested through the premise *unpopular feminism*, where feminism is routinely disparaged by media while communicating female individualism and success; an undoing of feminism (McRobbie, 2004: 258). Finally, *choice* as part of individualisation is at the heart of this postfeminism, where "women's freedom and choice airbrush out inequities that still mark relations between men and women" (McRobbie, 2004: 260). Postfeminism demarcates between those who succeed through this personal responsibility and those who fail and there is a lack of consideration of the structures in which this personal responsibility is enacted (McRobbie, 2004). It is against this background of postfeminism that we introduce women elite leaders in organisations.

Postfeminism and Women Elite Leaders

In an effort to incorporate postfeminism and neoliberal analysis into gender and organisation studies, Adamson (2017) analysed the biographies of four celebrity women CEOs. She suggests, "the CEO autobiography genre may be contributing to the emerging 'balanced femininity' discourse" (p. 325) and that more research is needed in this area. Women on boards and women who have reached the top of organisational hierarchies are a risky site to offer a postfeminist analysis. Rottenberg (2014) notes a trend of high-powered women in the United States publicly espousing feminism; however, this feminism "is predicated on the erasure of issues that concern the overwhelming majority of women in the USA and across the globe" (p. 419). Women such as Sheryl Sandberg and Anne-Marie Slaughter are those perceived by postfeminist scholars to have "delivered self-declared feminist manifestos" which are "symptomatic of a larger cultural phenomenon" of neoliberal feminism (Rottenberg, 2014: 419). Gill et al. (2017) see the highly publicised topic, 'Women on Boards', as over emphasised while other feminist issues are ignored. Sandberg's *Lean In* is critiqued as not confronting or challenging structural, political, economic and social inequalities but focussing on what women can change themselves—the individualised project—which "require constant self-monitoring" (Rottenberg, 2014: 424). This is seen to fail feminism, "rendering it hollow" (Rottenberg, 2014: 424). The feminist subject is decoupled from social inequalities and the "structures of male dominance, power or privilege" (Rottenberg, 2014: 425) remain intact and unchallenged. In Rottenberg's (2014) critique Sandberg's 'true equality' is grounded in an agenda where individuals progress *"one woman at a time"* (p. 426, emphasis in original). This creates an isolated feminist consciousness which internalises the revolution. In other words, the revolution has already taken place and radicalism is rejected, all women need to do is "rouse themselves by absorbing and acting on this reality" (Rottenberg, 2014: 426). This is positioned as an inward turn to produce an individuated feminist agent, who alone is accountable for her own revolutionary energy. This individualised, entrepreneurial and highly privileged subject is directed away from solidarity and common goals, towards her personal initiative in order to improve her career prospects in the corporate world.

Reflecting on scholars' approaches to postfeminism and having embedded ourselves in accounts of experiences from 80+ women elite leaders, we feel torn. We recognise the privileging of certain voices—that is, women elites and middle-class women (women scholars—of course fall under this 'label'), may render others voiceless. Yet, we want to unearth a more nuanced postfeminist analysis, one that recognises our felt discomfort with postfeminism, while providing space for our feminist aim of reflecting the women leaders' voices. Is there more to learn from women elite leaders beyond Sheryl Sandberg and Anne-Marie Slaughter if we bring a postfeminist lens to our theorisations of women elite leaders' accounts?

Studies of Women Elite Leaders

Our Empirical Context

In order to re-examine our previous theorisations of women elite leaders' experiences from a postfeminist perspective we introduce the research participants whose voices we analysed. The accounts from women leaders re-read through a postfeminism sensibility for this chapter are based on research with 81 women from UK-based organisations, interviewed for a wider study: 36 executive directors/non-executive directors in Financial

Times Stock Exchange (FTSE) 100/250 companies and 45 elite leaders identified in an annual regional newspaper supplement of the top 250/500 influential leaders. The women were aged between 33 and 67 years: 73 self-declared as white British/Irish/other white backgrounds, two black/mixed backgrounds, with six non-declared; 62 women worked full time; 14 part time with five non-declared. Thirty-five women had at least one other non-executive director/chair of board role and eight had at least one other governor/trustee role in education, charities or legal organisations. These women leaders are primarily white and have significant power and status at the top of organisational hierarchies, holding substantial economic and social power.

As outlined in Mavin, Grandy and Williams (2014: 6), the women engaged in a research project exploring women leaders' social relations with other women at work. Constructionism grounded our original work whereby we were interested in how meanings were re-constructed over time as these women came to understand their (and others) experiences and identities in particular contexts (Denzin and Lincoln, 2000; Fletcher, 2006). Following Grandy (forthcoming) we viewed ourselves as co-constructors of the 'realities' discussed and we engaged with the retrospective accounts through lenses interwoven with our own lived experiences (Alvesson and Deetz, 2000; Dick and Cassell, 2004). Semi-structured interviews lasting on average 90 minutes were undertaken by three research assistants utilising an interview guide and were recorded, transcribed, anonymised and coded. Within a context of women's intra-gender relations, the questions focused on women's progress to elite leader positions, ambition, friendship, cooperation, competition and key issues for other women.

Our Original Theorisation

For this chapter, we re-read our theorisation and empirical data through a postfeminism sensibility from three published studies which analyse the women elite leaders' accounts: 'Experiences of Women Elite Leaders Doing Gender: Intra-gender Micro-Violence between Women' published in *British Journal of Management* (Mavin et al., 2014); 'A Theory of Abject Appearance: Women Elite Leaders' Intra-gender "Management" of Bodies and Appearance', published in *Human Relations* (Mavin and Grandy, 2016a); and 'Women Elite Leaders Doing Respectable Business Femininity: How Privilege Is Conferred, Contested and Defended Through the Body', published in *Gender, Work and Organization* (Mavin and Grandy, 2016b). Our re-reading here offers insights into how postfeminism plays out for women elite leaders.

In Mavin et al. (2014) we theorised 'intra-gender micro-violence' to illustrate how a masculine symbolic order shapes and constrains women elite leaders' social relations with other women. We fused the literatures on gendered contexts, doing gender well and differently (Mavin and Grandy,

2012, 2013), intra-gender competition and female misogyny. We interpreted three themes (disassociating, suppression of opportunity, abject appearance) from the empirical accounts illustrating the complexities which underpin and explain negative intra-gender social relations of women.

In Mavin and Grandy (2016a) we developed a theory of Abject Appearance to explain women elite leaders' embodied identity work as a possible material effect or consequence of women's abjection in organisations. Building on the work of Kristeva (1982); Hopfl (2004); Rizq (2013); Fotaki (2013); Gatrell (2014) and Jones (2007), we suggest that women's maternal bodies (and just the threat of pregnancy), render women abject in organisation—a site of both intrigue and disgust. As such, despite achieving 'success' in organisations and afforded privilege through formal authority, women elite leaders are both One *and the Other*, always at the margins in organisations. We describe abject appearance in this way:

> Abject Appearance explains the dynamic ways in which women elite leaders can be reminded of their abjection through their feminine bodies. The process is dialectical in that it reflects tensions. It explains women elite leaders' active efforts to navigate a *fascination* (simultaneous *attraction* and *repulsion*) with their *own* and *other* women's bodies and appearance and the relational efforts to monitor boundaries and risks through embodied identity work . . . As power envelopes women's co-constructions within a paradox of One and the Other, Abject Appearance explains how women elite leaders as embodied speaking subjects can engage in agentic praxis (Mumby and Ashcraft, 2006: 75).
>
> (Mavin and Grandy, 2016a: 1101)

In this published work, we presented three analytical themes to illustrate Abject Appearance as interpreted through the women leaders' accounts—namely, *Fascination with Appearance; Refocusing from the Body and Appearance* and *Achieving a Professional Balance*.

In the third piece, Mavin and Grandy (2016b), we developed a theory of Respectable Business Femininity to explain the contested nature of women elite leaders' privilege as manifested through a disciplining of the body and appearance in the elite leader role (Mavin and Grandy, 2016b). To do this, we built upon research on privilege as unstable (Atewologun and Sealy, 2014), women's body work (Gatrell, 2013; Gimlin, 2007; Sinclair, 2005; Wolkowitz, 2011) and their "troubling bodies" (Brunner and Dever, 2014: 463) (but not men's) and respectable femininity (Fernando and Cohen, 2014; Fischer, 2014; Radhakrishnan, 2009). We theorise how historical notions of respectable femininity, where particular forms of femininity are constructed and constrained within class-based and heterosexual structures (Krane et al., 2004), persist in organisations and play out in contemporary (Western) organisations for women elite leaders. Historically, respectable femininity is marked by rules of 'appropriate' body and appearance (e.g., dress neatly and modestly, well mannered, self-restrained). It is understood as a form of social control and identity policing, through which women can achieve respect, dignity, self-worth and value. We advanced historical notions to theorise *Respectable Business Femininity* as a discursive and relational process. It explains the tensions and contradictions that women elite leaders experience (Mavin and Grandy, 2016b), as "sometimes privileged" (Atewologun and Sealy, 2014). Privilege is conferred, contested and/or defended through the body and appearance. These struggles, we theorised, involve acceptance and/or rejection of practices of self-care and self-monitoring in performing the elite leader role. On revisiting the work through a postfeminist lens, we suggest that the study and our theorising surface how postfeminism is reflected through women's bodies and appearance. In what follows, we explore this further.

The Complexity of Double Entanglements in Women Elite Leaders' Accounts

As a 'property' of postfeminist discourses, double entanglements (McRobbie, 2004) refer to the recognition of a need for a feminist agenda while simultaneously distancing from such an agenda. In this way, there is a "selective take-up of feminist principles" (Lewis et al., 2017: 215) alongside a rejection of such principles. We suggest that through a postfeminist sensibility of the women elite leaders' accounts this complexity is vividly apparent in discussions of board appointments. Specifically, there is a call to action for increasing women's representation on boards but this political movement is almost muted by a cautionary 'tread carefully' undertone. Through our re-reading we interpret that it is espoused as a feminist cause worthy of pursuit for the 'right' women but not for all women. In effect, it implies that equality must be reserved for special women and thus equality is attached to privilege (McRobbie, 2004). We offer two accounts from our re-readings to illuminate these double engagements. Specifically, on revisiting the women leaders' accounts included in our published article on intra-gender micro-violence, we can see a postfeminist discourse of recognising inequality while simultaneously reflecting a backlash against feminist achievements or goals (Gill et al., 2017). For example, when talking about the drive to increase numbers of women on company boards, Wendy says,

> A lot of this comes out of all this gender diversity on boards women need to think really, really hard, just as men do, when they take on a senior position. They are difficult jobs with lots of responsibility and hard work. I really worry in terms of the discussions around [name of senior role] diversity that it all, it all seems to be conversations about the appointment. We need to appoint more women to the boards. There's

little acknowledgement of what a serious job that is and what it entails. I do slightly worry that some of the consequences of what we're seeing at the moment is women—at its best women will be encouraged to, to progress through those sorts of things. At the worst, women will feel entitled to get some of those positions . . . we shouldn't have a sense of entitlement any more than anybody else [man]. These are big jobs.

(Wendy in Mavin et al., 2014: 446)

Wendy acknowledges the need for more women on company boards but we interpret that she sustains inequality by arguing that women should not feel entitled to a board position. Her talk indicates that these are 'serious jobs' appropriate for hard-working individuals (read men). We might even go as far to suggest that her account implies that men take these jobs more seriously (than women) and that only special women are fit for such privilege. Similarly, Martha acknowledges the 'appoint more women to boards cause' but expresses concern that such appointments should be reserved for *certain* women (not younger women). She somewhat mutes what might be interpreted as disdain for women "who are not exactly up for the job" by couching her discussion under a solidarity umbrella intended to protect such women from being in a position where they will "end up being . . . unhappy".

Especially now where there is a real desire socially and in society to appoint women, the real risk is that women are appointed who are not exactly up to the job and then to confirm implicit feelings that women can't really do it or can't be as good as men which is not the case, it's only a case of having chosen the wrong woman but because these younger women are not corrected anymore and perhaps the pressures are a little bit less there's more positive discrimination. The real risk is that they actually end up being quite unhappy in a position where they shouldn't have been in the first place and that's a real problem.

(Martha in Mavin et al., 2014: 449)

Our intent here is not to judge the women elite leaders; rather, we wish to illuminate the complexities faced by women elite leaders' as they navigate through a web of power dynamics. A postfeminist sensibility re-reading offers an opportunity to surface and discuss such complexities. For example, in the discussion section of Mavin et al. (2014), we recognise that

women can only be liberated from patriarchy through a struggle to change the system as system (Cockburn, 1991: 8). Yet it is impossible to confront a common condition before we have recognised it; we cannot begin to find our own power until we consciously recognise our non-power (Rowbothan, 1973).

(p. 14)

We argue in the article that in 'naming' intra-gender micro-violence and raising consciousness to destructive relational processes between women that take place in gendered contexts and constrain solidarity behaviours this is our attempt at recognising a common condition and disrupting the system. Some of the women's accounts reflect neoliberal postfeminist discourses, yet others do not. Further, our own voices are again a combination of challenge to patriarchal systems and hierarchies of masculinities alongside empowering women at the individual and the collective, as we struggle for an alternative path to postfeminist discourses.

Governmentality and Illusion of Choice?

In our re-readings we also were intrigued by the explicit and subtle references to choice. It has been argued elsewhere that choice serves to sustain inequalities and pervasive systems of power that continue to advantage men and some privileged women. Lewis et al. (2017) suggest that postfeminism discourses are often marked by a "shift from objectification to 'voluntary' subjectification" (p. 214). Choice is entangled "alongside the re-articulation of traditional expectations and traditional gender stereotypes around motherhood, beauty and female sexuality" (Lewis et al., 2017: 214). The neoliberal subject has choice (Gill et al., 2017); this subjectification neither recognises nor challenges the patriarchal systems that constitute and sustain what many feminists would view as a dangerous illusion of choice. Ruth and Clare's accounts offer illustrative examples of governmentality and the seductive nature of the entrepreneurial individual subject who is *free* to choose her own path to success.

> I will have conversations with women who are in their early to mid-thirties who've had one child, possibly going to have the second one, want to work part time yet equally are sort of saying to me "but this may jeopardise my career opportunities and positions. I don't want to lose pace". And I have to say I think that's the shadow (issue), the interesting test, because I sit here with very mixed emotions. Clearly as a supporter of these women I don't want to see them lose pace, but equally one has to be pragmatic and you make choices and if you've got three four five years out the workplace and you're part time, it is tough to say, unless you're a particular specialist functions, you're going to keep track with other colleagues and other peers.
>
> (Ruth, from Mavin et al., 2014: 446)

> I feel very strongly that women should not put themselves into a position where they reject leadership . . . There may be career choices which actually mean that you have to make that sacrifice. You can't expect the framework of the career will entirely bend . . . because of what you demand . . . Some of the areas where I have worked have been about

the absolute pinnacle of quality of something and that doesn't fit with taking half your time off or going home when you need to look after the children.

(Clare, from Mavin et al., 2014: 447)

Ruth's talk about women's caring responsibilities, working part time and the effects on career, highlights the discourse of an individuated subject at the heart of postfeminism. It illustrates her struggle between supporting other women yet realising they will "lose pace" with men (and other women without caring responsibilities) by working part time to care for children. At the same time, she does not fully acknowledge or challenge the inequalities at play which facilitate these struggles. Rather she sees choice, as Rottenberg (2014) points out, within a discourse of neoliberal postfeminism, as within an individual woman's control. Similarly, Clare expresses a rejection of a feminist political agenda and the need to challenge and change the systems and structures, rather women have choices within that system and "can't expect the framework of the career will entirely bend". It implies an acceptance that it is their "responsibility for their own well-being and self-care" based on "crafting a felicitous work-family balance based on a cost-benefit calculus" (p. 420). Here, again we see inequalities as 'just how it is' without critical challenge (Gill et al., 2017).

Both Ruth and Clare's accounts reflect a discourse which Rottenberg (2014) critiques in Sheryl Sandberg's *Lean In*. Rottenberg (2014) contends that elite leaders as Sandberg are so individuated they are unable to see social inequalities and do not consider or challenge male dominance, power or privilege (Rottenberg, 2014). The postfeminist issue of choice is surfaced in the accounts in relation to the women's choice to take on board roles; to work part time or not; and other women elite leaders' judgement of these choices. What might be seen as Ruth's judgement of women with children can be interpreted as ambivalence: supportive in that she wants women to succeed but also as reflecting neoliberalist feminism, reinforcing the ideal worker as masculine and adapting her preferences to an unequal and discriminatory context (e.g., Hirschmann, 2010). Rottenberg's (2014: 432) suggests the impact is dangerous: "As more and more white middle-class women enter and remain in the public sphere, even after they have children—by choice and by necessity"—neoliberal postfeminism "helps to neutralize the potential critique from other strands of feminism". Rottenberg (2014) goes as far as to comment that she is "no longer concerned with issues such as gendered wage gap, sexual harassment, rape or domestic violence, ambitious individual *middle class women* (emphasis in original) themselves become both the problem and the solution in the neoliberal feminist age" (p. 432). Lewis et al. (2017) propose what we feel is a more constructive way forward to unpack the complexities of said women's experiences: "instead of presenting 'choice' as the answer as to why there is still a minority of women in senior management positions . . . we can approach the notion of 'choice' as a question, such as what are women seeking to achieve when they cite 'choice' as the reason" (Lewis et al., 2017: 216) to opt-out of (or into) motherhood or leadership.

Postfeminism as a Bodily Property: Body-Care

"The enactment of femininity within the world of business must be 'measured' and not perceived as disruptive . . . women must be 'properly' feminine . . . but not engage in unnecessary or unwarranted feminine displays (Lewis, 2012)" (Lewis, 2014: 1858). Some of these women elite leaders come to view the enactment of their femininity as crucial to the entrepreneurial subject; the leveraging of their feminine body and appearance is "a form of governance of everyday life in which individuals practice their freedom" (Lewis et al., 2017: 215). Their entrepreneurial spirit and commitment (Gill et al., 2017) manifests through their body-care. In the accounts of Alice and Amanda we interpret that there is an acceptance that body-care and leveraging the right kind of femininity (Mavin and Grandy, 2016b) is simply part of "playing the game" (Anita, from Mavin and Grandy, 2016b), without much questioning of the pervasive power dynamics at play.

> I would say I've also noticed that being a woman that I often have the ability to—I can get the attention of men more easily than other men might be able to because, I don't know if it's because of my accent or because I wear dresses not suits, I find that I can get meetings perhaps a little bit more easily or get time in if I need it or get the attention of people if I'm speaking. Yeah I think it's because there aren't very many women often in the meetings I'm in that I do feel that I command respect and attention when I'm saying something.
>
> (Alice, from Mavin et al., 2014: 446)

> Sometimes they've [women] known how to play men very cleverly. You do have to learn how to do that. This whole argument about how you use your looks or your sexuality at work which would have to me been completely anathema as a concept. More and more I recognize we are all sexual beings and I've seen women who are very attractive do very well. I don't mean that they slept around or that they've been nasty to other women but they use their inherent female attractiveness and obviously you also need the power of intellect.
>
> (Amanda from Mavin et al., 2014: 446)

Reflecting on these accounts through a postfeminism sensibility, we suggest that the postfeminist subject is feminine. But it is expressed as an individual calculated femininity, one which serves to obscure the self-monitoring and surveillance which constitutes it. Postfeminism plays out through the body and demands choice, empowerment, and surveillance for success. So those who succeed take responsibility for their own success, "*one woman at a time*" (Rottenberg, 2014: 426) and *choose* to engage and play the game. Those who succeed experience "feelings of autonomy and dignity. . . [and] privilege is stabilized" (Mavin and Grandy, 2016b: 385), reflecting postfeminism as a bodily property.

This isn't to say that the earlier accounts reflect the experiences of all women elite leaders with whom we engaged. Many did challenge the patriarchal systems in which they were placed and that which restrained them and other women. For example, many talked about how they refused to concede to the pressures to display oneself as the measured professional, while others challenged the systems within which they were celebrated (e.g., refusing to permit—and in some cases calling them out—the media to write about their body and appearance and their status as mother). Nevertheless, they were very aware of the body-care expectations under which success typically was fostered in this context.

How Postfeminism Plays Out for Women Elite Leaders

In the discussion that follows, we do not personally subscribe to an individuation discourse of postfeminism which ignores the challenge of women's oppression within patriarchal systems and masculine hierarchies. Yet, we are also adamant that women elite leaders' voices do count in organisational theorisations and in conversations about feminism.

Returning to our research question of how postfeminism plays out for women at the top of UK organisational hierarchies, our re-examination of our published studies of women elite leaders' accounts could be seen to have highlighted postfeminism at work: the individualised, entrepreneurial and highly privileged subject who is focussed on her own "personal initiative in order to improve her career prospects, particularly in the corporate world" (Rottenberg, 2014: 432). Significantly, our studies illustrate how postfeminism is surfaced where women engage in choice and struggle around their understandings of disadvantage and privilege, surveillance, makeover, self-reinvention and transformation in order to perform as credible successful elite leaders. The women are not victims; they are confident and powerful, distanced from outmoded notions of female disadvantage and draw upon femininity and feminism while deflecting any alienation from men leaders. Change for the women elite leaders comes through an entrepreneurial spirit and commitment (Gill et al., 2017). Indeed, it could be argued from a critical postfeminism reading that in assuming individual responsibility for successful navigation within the system, these elite woman leaders neglect the complexity of the structures and systems that sustain a gendered order and which persist to disadvantage women.

For us, the double entanglements and expressions of choice mark out the felt complexity and ambivalence that women elite leaders face. We suggest it is not that they don't care about a feminist agenda, but that the governmentality in which the entrepreneurial subject is constituted is sometimes so pervasive that it is becomes impossible to recognise its power effects. Indeed, sustaining such enactments of postfeminism without any challenge threatens a feminist agenda. We propose, however, that attacking and harshly criticising women elite leaders' enactment of postfeminism creates a boundary around feminism which keeps women leaders out. These women challenge the gendered status quo simply by holding their organisational positions. Yet in this system they remain One and the Other, struggling to defend and/or protect their credibility (Mavin and Grandy, 2016a). As feminist scholars who also hold positions of privilege, we identify with their struggles. While we do challenge patriarchy and a gendered order in our own work (and in the three published studies), as women leaders, we too struggle to find paths through which we can 'get ahead' in our careers by enacting choice, empowerment and body-care. We return to the question posed by Lewis et al. (2017), what do women seek to achieve when they cite choice as a rationale for the decisions they make and impose upon other women? We didn't explore this specifically with the women leaders, so we can only speculate here. As we reflect on our experiences, we are left wondering if sometimes this is simply a function of trying to make a difference in the only space we feel we can—ourselves. We suggest future research starts to more fully unpack how and why choice frames and guides the experiences of women elite leaders. We propose, perhaps naively, that through a postfeminism sensibility we might create space to engage in constructive debates, spark curiosity and trigger an unsettling of the neoliberal subject (for ourselves and others).

In addition, in all three studies the women's accounts reflect postfeminism with the following features: body-care as a means of stabilising their privilege and enabling their empowerment, as well as distancing from critiques of gendered inequalities and alienating men; how they look and present themselves is their own individual responsibility; their success as elite leaders in this regard is dependent on their personal initiative and entrepreneurialism; the need for individual self-care and self-monitoring, as well as the surveillance of other women through their bodies and appearance; demonstration of choice, pleasure and success; and a coming together of women leaders with opportunities for challenge. Within this space "women draw on discourses of individualism, choice, merit as much as their male colleagues, having an impact on masculine power" (Lewis and Simpson, 2016: 6).

As such this postfeminism outlines a discursive space where "feminism is boldly affirmed at the same time that a distance from radicalism is secured"—as such a "more moderate [acceptable], less excessive feminism" located in the present (Dean, 2010: 395/393). This feminism is marked by care provided by individual women to their own bodies and appearance, 'by you, for you'. Women identify their own body work needs and take steps to meet them; they take time to prioritise their body and appearance and to know where they 'stand' on their own body and appearance as elite leaders, as well as towards other women's body and appearance. This post-feminism illustrates a way of encouraging "assimilation into the corporate mainstream" which does not reject feminism but yet is less radical than "a complete deconstruction (or at least re-thinking) of the system as a whole" (Cooley, 2016: 1).

Reflecting on our work here, we are cognisant of a feminist backlash towards women elite leaders, who are sometimes viewed as distasteful for perpetuating postfeminism, perceived to restrict other feminisms and constrain collective action against oppression. Women who have reached the top of organisational hierarchies and engaged in postfeminism are criticised for ignoring gender inequalities, discrimination and male dominance in corporate cultures. Such women leaders can be viewed as the conduit of postfeminisms in that they can be seen to dilute feminism. However, within our studies, there remains substantial evidence from the women's accounts and our theorisations, of external challenge to women's oppression and patriarchal contexts and opportunities for solidarity and common goals. In this way, we suggest that women elite leaders' experiences become a site for both postfeminist discourse and a feminist agenda for recognising and challenging embedded gender orders.

Conclusion

In this chapter, we have re-examined our studies of women elite leaders through a postfeminist lens and reflected on our understandings of experiences of work-based gender relations. We hope we have provoked critical thinking about postfeminism in organisations by revisiting women elite leaders' accounts and exploring how postfeminism plays out in our studies. As we end the chapter, we are focussed on Hirschmann's (2010) point that a critical challenge for feminism is the "right to choose" (p. 271) and respecting that the choices made will not always be the ones we want. For some feminists, the choices some women elite leaders have made and continue to make will not be the ones hoped for. For us, as we reflect on our research approaches, we have become conscious that we are frustrated by a lack of collective action (see also Mavin and Grandy, 2012, 2013). We have studied why this collective action is constrained but have not yet found a way to overcome the processes of fragmentation between women elite leaders. It is this frustration and our struggle for alternative paths that will shape our future studies.

References

Acker, J. (2006). Inequality regimes: Gender, class, and race in organizations. *Gender & Society*, 20(4): 441–464.
Adamson, M. (2017). Postfeminism, neoliberalism and a "successfully" balanced femininity in celebrity CEO autobiographies. *Gender, Work and Organization*, 24(3): 314–327.

Alvesson, M., and Deetz, S. (2000). *Doing Critical Management Research*. London: Sage.

Atewologun, D., and Sealy, R. (2014). Experiencing privilege at ethnic, gender and senior intersections. *Journal of Managerial Psychology*, 29(4): 423–439.

Baker, J. (2010). Claiming volition and evading victimhood: Postfeminist obligations for young women. *Feminism and Psychology*, 20(2): 186–204.

Brunner, L.K., and Dever, M. (2014). Work, bodies and boundaries: Talking sexual harassment in the new economy. *Gender, Work & Organization*, 21(5): 459–471.

Cooley, O. (2016). *Women's Studies Major 10 May Quora*. Available at: www.quora.com/What-is-corporate-feminism/ Accessed 3 January 2017.

Dean, J. (2010a). Feminism in the papers: Contested feminisms in the British quality press. *Feminist Media Studies*, 10(4): 391–407.

Dean, J. (2010b) *Rethinking Contemporary Feminist Politics*. Basingstoke, UK: Palgrave Macmillan.

Denzin, N., and Lincoln, Y. (2000). Introduction: The discipline and practice of qualitative research. In N. Denzin and Y. Lincoln (Eds.), *The Handbook of Qualitative Research* (pp. 1–28). Thousand Oaks, CA: Sage.

Dick, P., and Cassell, C. (2004). The position of policewomen: A discourse analytic study. *Work, Employment and Society*, 18: 51–72.

Faludi, S. (1991). *Backlash: The Undeclared War Against Women*. London: Chatto and Windus.

Fernando, W., and Cohen, L. (2014). Respectable femininity and career agency: Exploring paradoxical imperatives. *Gender, Work & Organization*, 21(2): 149–164.

Fischer, G. (2014). Tanzanian women's move into wage labour: Conceptualizing deference, sexuality and respectability as criteria for workplace suitability. *Gender, Work and Organization*, 21(2). Online first. DOI: 10.1111/gwao.12026

Fletcher, D. (2006). Entrepreneurial processes and the social construction of opportunity. *Entrepreneurship and Regional Development: An International Journal*, 18: 421–440.

Fotaki, M. (2013). No woman is like a man (in academia): The masculine symbolic order and the unwanted female body. *Organization Studies*, 24(9): 1251–1275.

Gatrell, C.J. (2013). Maternal body work: How women managers and professionals negotiate pregnancy and new motherhood at work. *Human Relations*, 66(5): 621–644.

Gatrell, C.J. (2014). Monstrous motherhood versus magical maternity? An exploration of conflicting attitudes to maternity within health discourses and organizational settings. *Equality, Diversity and Inclusion: An International Journal*, 33(7): 633–647.

Gill, R., Kelan, E., and Scharff, C.M. (2017). A postfeminist sensibility at work. *Gender, Work and Organization*, 24(3): 226–244.

Gill, R., and Scharff, C. (2011). *New Femininities: Postfeminism, Neoliberalism, and Subjectivity*. London: Palgrave Macmillan.

Gimlin, D. (2007). What is "body work"? A review of the literature. *Sociology Compass*, 1(1): 353–370.

Grandy, G. (forthcoming). An introduction to constructionism for qualitative researchers in business and management. In C. Cassell, A. Cunliffe, and G. Grandy (Eds.), *Handbook of Qualitative Research in Business and Management* (2 vol.). London: Sage Publications Inc.

Hirschmann, N.J. (2010). Choosing betrayal. *Perspectives on Politics*, 8(1): 271–278.

Hollows, J. (2000). *Feminism, Femininity, and Popular Culture*. New York: Manchester University Press.

Höpfl, H. (2004). Julia Kristeva. In S. Linstead (Ed.), *Organization Theory and Postmodern Thought* (pp. 88–104). London: Sage.

Jones, L. (2007). Women and abjection: Margins of difference bodies of art. *Visual Culture & Gender*, 2(1): 62–71.

Krane, V., Choi, P.Y.L., Baird, S.M., Aimar, C.M., and Kauer, K.J. (2004). Living the paradox: Female athletes negotiate femininity and muscularity. *Sex Roles*, 50(5-6): 315–329.

Kristeva, J. (1982). *Powers of Horror: An Essay on Abjection*. New York: Columbia University Press.

Lewis, P. (2012). Postfeminism and entrepreneurship: Interpreting Disgust in a female entrepreneurial narrative. In R. Simpson, N. Slutskaya, P. Lewis, and H. Hopfl (Eds.), *Dirty Work: Concepts and Identities* (pp. 223–238). Basingstoke, UK: Palgrave Macmillan.

Lewis, P. (2014). Postfeminism, femininities and organization studies: Exploring a new agenda. *Organization Studies*, 35(12): 1845–1866.

Lewis, P., Benschop, Y. and Simpson, R. (2017) Postfeminism, gender and organization. *Gender, Work and Organization*, 24(3): 213–225.

Lewis, P., and Simpson, R. (2016). Hakim revisited: Preference, choice and the postfeminist gender regime. *Gender, Work and Organization*. Online First. DOI: 10.1111/gwao.12150

Mavin, S., and Grandy, G. (2012). Doing gender well and differently in management. *Gender in Management: An International Journal*, 27: 218–231.

Mavin, S., and Grandy, G. (2013). Doing gender well and differently in dirty work: The case of exotic dancing. *Gender, Work and Organization*, 20: 232–251.

Mavin, S., and Grandy, G. (2016a). A theory of abject appearance: Women elite leaders' intra-gender "management" of bodies and appearance. *Human Relations*, 69(5): 1095–1120.

Mavin, S., and Grandy, G. (2016b). Women elite leaders doing respectable business femininity: How privilege is conferred, contested and defended through the body. *Gender, Work and Organization*. Online First. DOI: 10.1111/gwao.12130

Mavin, S., Grandy, G., and Williams, J. (2014). Experiences of women elite leaders doing gender: Intra-gender micro-violence between women. *British Journal of Management* 25(3): 439–455.

McRobbie, A. (2004). Post feminism and popular culture. *Feminist Media Studies*, 4(3): 255–264.

McRobbie, A. (2008). *The Aftermath of Feminism: Gender, Culture and Social Change*. London: Sage.

Mumby, D.K., and Ashcraft, K.L. (2006). Organizational communication studies and gendered organization: A response to Martin and Collinson. *Gender, Work and Organization*, 13(1): 68–90.

Radhakrishnan, S. (2009). Professional women, good families: Respectable femininity and the cultural politics of a "new" India. *Qualitative Sociology*, 32(2): 195–212.

Rizq, R. (2013). States of abjection. *Organization Studies*, 34(9): 1277–1297.

Rottenberg, C. (2014). The rise of neoliberal feminism. *Cultural Studies*, 28(3): 418–437.

Rowbothan, S. (1973). *Woman's Consciousness, Man's World*. Harmondsworth: Penguin.

Sinclair, A. (2005). Body and management pedagogy. *Gender, Work & Organization*, 12(1): 89–104.

Wolkowitz, C. (2011). The organisational contours of "body work". In E. Jeaner, D. Knights, and P.Y. Martin (Eds.), *Handbook of Gender, Work and Organization* (pp. 177–190). Hoboken, NJ: Wiley.

Part III

Future Directions in Postfeminism and Organization

9 *Make Do and Mend?* Working Postfeminism and Vintage

Philip Hancock and Melissa Tyler

Introduction

Growing interest in postfeminism within organization studies has reinvigorated debate about who feminism is seeking to emancipate, from what or whom, and on what basis. The charge that feminism is no longer concerned with gender emancipation but rather with placing restrictions on women's choices, both at home and in the workplace, has even led certain public figures to state publicly that they are 'not feminists'. For some, feminism has become 'the other f word'. Others, however, are continuing to speak out in the name of feminism, through, for example, the United Nations' 'He for She' campaign, and the international women's marches on the first full day of Donald Trump's presidency. Yet, postfeminism is arguably only one possible response to these circumstances, one that largely reflects the neoliberal emphasis on individual choice alongside which it has evolved (Gill, 2007, 2016). Interestingly, however, another cultural phenomenon that is also enjoying increasing popularity, and which has emerged in parallel if not in dialogue with debates about feminism's past, present and future is 'vintage', the focus of our discussion here.

While associated in many people's minds with clothing, vintage represents a constellation of ideals and practices revolving around the re-appropriation, re-introduction and, we argue, re-organization of not only past styles of dressing, but ways of living, working and consuming.[1] While often considered to embrace many of the principles associated with postfeminism—most notably individuality, the pursuit of glamour and the valorization of traditional feminine practices such as cooking and baking we develop an alternative argument below. Namely, that by considering not only the production, distribution and consumption of vintage goods, but also the social relations, values and beliefs underpinning them, vintage can also be thought of as an organizational phenomenon, one that, we suggest, might point to a more collaborative ethos of connection with the struggles and achievements of feminism's past than does postfeminism.

While there has long been a market for 'retro' clothing and artefacts, the current popularity of vintage can be traced back to the first decade of the twenty-first century when it began to move 'from sub culture to mass culture' (Palmer, 2005: 197). Whether or not this increasing popularity can be attributed to cultural, economic, ecological or perhaps ontological factors, for us it raises interesting and important questions for the study of gender relations within work and organization studies and beyond. We ask, if vintage is about 'looking forward through the window of the past' (Walsh, 2010, cited in Cassidy and Bennett, 2012: 242), what does this mean for feminism, and organization studies? And how does vintage relate to the also popular and seemingly all-pervasive phenomenon of postfeminism, and the inroads that the latter is beginning to make into the study of work and organizational life?

With these questions in mind, this chapter critically evaluates vintage, particularly what has been termed 'vintage femininity' (Ferreday, 2008), considering whether or not it might offer the basis for a possible alternative to that proffered by postfeminism and its links to neoliberalism within work and organization studies. In doing so, we do not ignore the more problematic ideas and troubling imagery associated with vintage, but seek to consider its latent progressive content, based on a dialectical reading of the immanent possibilities present within its professed organizational values of community, connection and collaboration. For while on the one hand, vintage is often associated with the conspicuous consumption of a nostalgic, sugar-coated past that repositions women's role as primarily that of homemaker and stylized accessory (associated for instance, with Cath Kidston), we argue that vintage might also potentially remind us of our connection to a past that recognizes the value and significance of women's histories, skills and everyday working lives, offering an alternative to postfeminism that emphasizes connection and continuity rather than denial and disavowal.

The chapter begins by considering postfeminism as a largely socio-cultural movement, including the limited but growing engagement with postfeminism within work and organization studies. The aesthetics and ethics of vintage and vintage femininity are then critically examined, focusing in particular on two organizational phenomena through which the dynamics of vintage are played out: so-called 'new burlesque' and 'Make Do and Mend'. We explore these two examples in order to connect our discussion of vintage femininity specifically to work and organization and to evaluate the extent to which a discernible form of 'vintage feminism' might be identified. Finally, the possibilities of vintage feminism as a critical alternative to postfeminism with which scholars of work and organization might be able to engage is considered. While sounding an appropriate note of caution, the chapter ends with an optimistic emphasis on vintage's potential to move feminism forward not by severing connections with its heritage, but by reclaiming those aspects of it that continue to speak to values of dignity, solidarity and generosity.

Postfeminist Themes and Discourses

Postfeminism has been discussed variously as an historical period or movement '*after* feminism' (see Hall and Rodriguez, 2003), as a political backlash *against* feminism (Faludi, 1992; Whelehan, 2000), as a theoretical development *within* feminism (Brooks, 1997; Yeatman, 1994) and as a socio-cultural phenomenon somehow *distinct* from feminism. Until recently, however, it has been the subject of fairly limited discussion amongst scholars of work and organization. One exception to this is Lewis (2014: 1848), who has drawn on insights from postfeminism in her account of female entrepreneurs, arguing that for analytical purposes, postfeminism is best understood as a cultural entity 'made up of interrelated themes connected to a complex set of discourses'. Of particular interest to Lewis (2014), and developed here, is the connection between postfeminism as a cultural phenomenon and gender subjectivity; for Lewis, postfeminism implies the emergence of a particular kind of entrepreneurial gendered subject. Also in recent work, Adamson (2016) has emphasized how postfeminism intersects with neoliberal logics in her critique of gender subjectivity in CEO autobiographies, exploring choice narratives and discourses of work-life balance. But aside from these notable exceptions, postfeminism has made relatively limited inroads into work and organization studies thus far.

By comparison, however, a burgeoning body of literature on postfeminist subjectivity has emerged in media and cultural studies (Butler, 2013; Gill, 2007, 2016; McRobbie, 2004; Tasker and Negra, 2005). Within this field, Gill (2007) in particular has discussed how, despite postfeminism becoming a widely cited reference point in contemporary cultural analysis, there is very little agreement about what it actually is. In her most recent writing on the subject, Gill (2016: 613) emphasizes how

> As a 'sensibility' deeply enmeshed with neoliberalism, . . . postfeminism is a critical analytical term that refers to empirical regularities or patterns in contemporary cultural life, which include the emphasis on individualism, choice and agency.

In earlier work, however, Gill (2007) defined postfeminism with reference to a number of interrelated themes and motifs that, as both Lewis (2014) and Adamson (2016) note, are particularly relevant to work and organization studies. These include an 'obsessive preoccupation with the body' as women's source of power, identity and value (Gill, 2007: 149), a cultural sexualization marked by a symbolic vocabulary of youthful, unselfconscious pleasure seeking (see also Kim, 2001), an 'emblematic blurring of the boundaries between pornography and other genres' (Gill, 2007: 151; see also Walter, 2010) and a shift from sexual objectification to subjectification through which

> women are not straight-forwardly objectified but are portrayed as active, desiring sexual subjects who *choose to present themselves in a seemingly objectified manner because it suits their liberated interests* to do so.
>
> (Gill, 2007: 151, *emphasis added*)

With regard to this last point, Gill's concern with postfeminism is primarily its unreflexive emphasis on individual choice and empowerment; both of which, we would argue, have significant implications for workplace and organizational practice. In particular, its association with being and pleasing oneself means that, for Gill, postfeminism misleadingly presents women as individualized, autonomous agents no longer constrained or compelled by structural inequalities or power imbalances, especially those associated with work. As Tasker and Negra (2005: 107) observe in this respect, this 'choice biography' packages freedom as a highly commodifiable entity, 'effectively harnessed to individualism and consumerism', seemingly reconciling feminist claims to subjectivity and autonomy with the organizational demands of a capitalist society and a neoliberal political economy (see also Genz, 2006). This analytical theme has been developed further by (Jess) Butler (2013: 35), who argues that postfeminism is best understood not with reference to an overly simplistic linear trajectory culminating in 'the death of feminism',[2] but rather 'as a neoliberal discursive formation' propped up by an ever expanding ideological celebration of autonomy, individualism and consumer choice.

For McRobbie (2009) postfeminism signifies, in this sense, simply an instrumental deployment of feminist ideals by media culture and the state as 'evidence' of women's progress and relative freedom, with a ubiquitous choice narrative working to conceal emerging and persistent modes of gender regulation at home, in everyday life, and at work. As (Jess) Butler (2013: 43) reflects, the tenor of much of this celebratory discourse, and its evidential basis, is highly unreflexive and ethnocentric, not to mention class-biased in its assumptions; as she puts it, 'the idealized postfeminist subject is a white, Western, heterosexual woman' (Butler, 2013: 47). Yet it is against this cultural backdrop, and its neoliberal basis, that feminism is being framed as a thing of the past. In particular, postfeminism implies a celebration of neoliberal values of individual autonomy and self-sufficiency and, in particular, a corrolary rejection of solidarity and interconnection (McRobbie, 2004; Stephens, 2011).

Vintage Lifestyles and Values

While postfeminism continues to make headlines in popular culture and limited inroads into work and organization studies, another phenomenon that (much like postfeminism) has been of considerable interest within media culture of late, but which has received even less attention than postfeminism from work and organizational scholars, is the increasing presence of 'vintage'. Despite this apparent lack of academic recognition, however, as a popular and increasingly global phenomenon there can be little doubt that vintage, from a commercial perspective in particular, is now 'in' (Fischer, 2015: 46) featuring as it does in everything from the retro marketing of cleaning products, to corporate heritage branding (Balmer and Burghausen,

2015). While much of the emerging research on vintage has focused on production and consumption, particularly of fashion (De Long, Heinemann, and Reiley, 2005; Duffy et al., 2012), as Dirix (2014: 89, emphasis added) stresses, vintage culture has also become 'a growing influence on the way we decorate, accessorize, and *effectively curate our lives*'. Arguing that this represents an attempt to recapture a lost authenticity, Veenstra and Kuipers (2013) suggest that vintage is informed largely by a sense of nostalgia brought about as a reaction to the organizational values of mass, disposable consumer culture. While this is not to suggest that vintage consumers are intrinsically radical or subversive in and of themselves, as such lifestyle choices often appropriate many of the tropes of consumer culture such as performative identities and acts of distinction (Bourdieu, 2009); nonetheless, they frequently seek to distinguish themselves by virtue of a distancing from mainstream 'style' and lifestyle expectations, particularly those associated with mass consumption (Fischer, 2015)[3] and the 'makeover' paradigm that Gill (2007) refers to.

What connects all of the practices and motifs associated with vintage is arguably what Samuel (1994) calls 'the aura of pastness', emphasizing as it does the potential contained within the past to provide connection and continuity. Sarial-Abi et al. (2016: 182) attribute this not simply to individual life circumstances but rather to a broader social condition they describe as the need for a 'sense of intertemporal interconnection', which vintage is deemed to provide. As they suggest,

> Major economic uncertainty creates existential unease and presents a global threat to meaning. In our view this might well have led consumers to seek vintage items—tangible, consoling products—in order to assuage the meaning threat caused by economic malaise.

This is an argument that has been developed by other researchers who similarly equate the growing popularity and cultural ubiquity of vintage to 'a yearning for familiarity in a society that is constantly changing' (Palmer, 2005: 201) and 'as a form of stability against a rapidly changing environment, which helps consumers reconnect with a time gone by' (Cassidy and Bennett, 2012: 242).

Yet vintage goods, services and experiences are valued not only because of what they represent or signify culturally but also because of what is perceived to be their continuing use value; in other words, they are still deemed to be 'in good working order'. Sarial-Abi et al. (2016) identify two distinctive characteristics of vintage in this respect. Firstly, vintage goods are valued specifically because they have been made and used in the past; they have a history that precedes acquisition by the contemporary consumer. Secondly, vintage items are appealing because they represent an opportunity to 'give new life' to something that might otherwise be overlooked or disposed of (see Campbell, 1987). Bardley and Cogliantry (2002: 22) develop this last point further by emphasizing the 'mixing' of old and new, original/genuine vintage and so-called repro (new but 'old styled') as a way of highlighting this re-valuing of the past, and connecting it to the present and future, with vintage being attributed value largely because it has 'stood the test of time, and represents the continuity of existence'.

This emphasis on social connectedness weaving these two themes together links distinct but interrelated dimensions of vintage that constitute its social ontology—namely, the *materiality of vintage* goods, services and experiences, and the *meaning of vintage*. The latter is discernible in the ideas, values and practices associated with past eras, or with particular periods in our history, including in the form of what might be thought of as a vintage sociality. In combination these two dimensions are, of course, shaped by the 'particular' and like any other retrospective movement, vintage runs the risk of invoking a cultural sensibility based on selective memory, and what is arguably a nostalgic sanitizing or 'sugar coating' of past ways of life and lived experiences—an issue to which we return below.

Developing the idea of vintage as a lifestyle choice, as it has begun to extend its influence beyond consumption and fashion, the conviction that one can more fully adopt a vintage approach to aspects of one's life has also become increasingly prevalent. A notable example of this is the aforementioned association of vintage with opposition to the organization of mass-produced, so-called 'fast fashion' (Cassidy and Bennett, 2012), with vintage being equated with an 'ecological ethics and historicity' (Fischer, 2015: 59). In particular, Cassidy and Bennett (2012: 243) elaborate on this connection between vintage and an ethos of eco-sustainability, emphasizing their view that vintage signals a post-war mentality, as vintage consumers adopt the ' "repair, reuse, recycle" attitude', one that 'challenges the "throwaway fashion" idea as people hold on to garments longer and choose to repair rather than discard them'. This is not to suggest that those who subscribe to this wider definition of vintage necessarily seek to 'live in the past', but rather that the ideas, practices and values of bygone eras might be drawn on as cultural and organizational resources informing aspects of how we live today.

Indicative of this, is the fact that not only have a number of vintage style guides emerged in recent years (cf. Hemingway and Hemingway, 2015), so too have what amount to 'manifestos' for pursuing a vintage-inspired life. As a notable example, *Her Vintage Life* magazine describes its 'vintage values' as follows:

1   Preserve heritage and tradition
2   Uphold past wisdom and skills
3   Promote community
4   Protect nature and the environment

It is this retrospective understanding of lifestyle, values and of relating to each other, that perhaps raises some of the more interesting, and possibly challenging questions for contemporary feminism, particularly in relation to the forms of femininity within vintage culture. These questions include for instance, how might feminism relate to, or even draw sustenance from, vintage as a social-cultural phenomenon, and in this sense, how might 'vintage' be mobilized, in turn, against the more discomforting excesses of postfeminism?

From Vintage Femininity to Vintage Feminism?

One doesn't have to look too far into the pages of lifestyle magazines such as *Her Vintage Life*, into book series such as Cath Kidston's *Make! Patch! Stitch! Sew!*, or glance through the promotional materials produced by the organizers of vintage fairs and festivals, to see that femininity features as a recurring theme. Indeed, vintage fashion and style can be observed to directly address itself to a mode of female subjectivity that, at first sight at least, appears to be far more passive and deferential than contemporary feminism might countenance. Feminists such as Dirix (2014: 89) have been notably critical of what she calls the 'new domesticity' associated with vintage, arguing that while the sexualization of women in contemporary visual culture has been the subject of increasing critique, this regressive, domestic femininity has escaped critical interrogation on a similar scale. As she puts it, what has emerged is 'something very pretty and seductive . . . that apparently celebrates a less sexualized and more wholesome femininity, but one which in fact has more problematic roots and consequences' (Dirix, 2014: 91). Her main concerns with the increasing ubiquity and popularity of vintage, particularly for women are, first, that it presents us with a 'hermetically sealed' past, one that is not necessarily historically accurate ('a copy without an original') and which rejects questioning, undermining the possibility of critical reflection or subversion. Second, vintage is primarily a style within consumer culture, its products and their promotion; vintage is thus 'a hollow term . . . loaded with sentimental and emotive nostalgia'. Yet what Dirix is particularly critical of is arguably a limited version of vintage, one that is signified by a class and race privileged retrospective domesticity that is particularly retrogressiveo in its origins and implications. While we share certain aspects of her critique in this respect, below, we also consider the possibility that alongside this co-opted, retrospective vintage femininity, there can be discerned a more reflexive version on which contemporary feminism, including in work and organization studies, might begin to draw—a theme to which we return in due course.

In addition to this largely passive, ostensibly de-sexualized model of domestic femininity, there is also, however, a more obviously sexualized and indeed strikingly postfeminist side to vintage. Alongside the cupcakes and 'pinnies', images of female glamour from the 1920s flapper through to the 1950s 'pin ups' depict idealized forms of female sexuality that are ubiquitous in vintage culture. Combine these with everything from make-up routines to full-page advertisements for vintage lingerie and the resonances that exist between postfeminism with its stress on sexual playfulness and self-invention, and a vintage femininity that idealizes the attainment of movie star glamour, is almost self-evident. And perhaps nowhere is this more apparent than in the working environment of what has come to be referred to as 'new burlesque' (Ferreday, 2008).

Often presented as an updated pastiche of mid-century 'girlie entertainment', as Walsh (2010) observes, burlesque has become a major part of vintage business. On both sides of the Atlantic, artists such as *Immodesty Blaze* and *Dita von Teese* have attracted a huge, diverse following, with many of their fans identifying with the vintage aesthetic of their performances as well as the spectacle itself. Such new burlesque performers enact largely parodic shows, involving highly sexualized routines that appear legitimated by virtue of their professed self-knowing irony and a purported exercise of sexual power over their audience. That burlesque can rightly claim such legitimacy for itself is, however, once again challenged by writers such as Dirix (2014), Siebler (2015) and Penny (2009) who view such claims as little more than a convenient forgetting of the continuing power relations underpinning burlesque that reduce bodies to objects of a disciplinary, consuming gaze that is often mocking, if not overtly hostile. This is seen at best to represent 'the most irritating of all bastardizations of vintage culture' (Dirix, 2014: 93) and at worst little more than a 'sexed-up culture of consolation' for those who perform it (Penny, 2009: 1).

Despite the evident force of these criticisms, the idea that vintage femininities, as exemplified in both mainstream vintage and burlesque, may yet be able to contribute to our aforementioned revivification of feminism is not beyond credibility, however. In the case of burlesque, for example, there are those who remain eager to defend the industry for a number of reasons. Ferreday (2008), for instance, argues that new burlesque represents both a queer challenge to heteronormative models of feminine sexual passivity, and at the same time, a problematization of an assumed distinction between feminist politics and femininity, associating the latter with the pleasurable experience of a sexualized performativity. In a similar vein, unlike more passive forms of say striptease, burlesque is often promoted as representing female sexual agency (see, for example, Weldon, 2010) as well as championing an openness to a range of body types and physical abilities. Perhaps more interesting in the context of this chapter, however, are observations such as Ferreday's (2008) that the preoccupation with vintage aesthetics in much of the discussion and reception of burlesque overlooks the significance of co-operation and resourcefulness that characterizes burlesque as a working environment. In particular, she highlights the importance of burlesque performers' capacity for bricolage and 'DIY' when she notes how 'burlesque is aligned with recycling, thrift shopping and the revival of traditional crafts such as knitting and weaving' (Ferreday, 2008: 57).

This emphasis on the skills, capacity and resourcefulness of burlesque performers returns us, perhaps somewhat paradoxically, to our earlier critique of what appears to be a re-domestication agenda at the heart of dominant representations of vintage femininity. While there is no doubt that the purported joys of domestic organization and its aesthetic stylization are endemic throughout vintage culture, in many instances representations of domestic labour are grounded in an ethos of creativity, gendered agency and values of solidarity and cooperation not unlike those associated with the more progressive elements of burlesque culture championed particularly by Ferreday (2008). To borrow from Gill (2007, 2016), the vintage adoption of the cultural sensibility associated with the 1943 Board of Trade pamphlet, 'Make Do and Mend' (Cassidy and Bennett, 2012) is a particularly striking example of this. In our view, this example provides further insight into the dynamic relationship between feminism, postfeminism and vintage culture. This is because it has the capacity to illustrate how vintage femininity might potentially open up space for a more critical reflection on the characteristics of postfeminism (Gill, 2007, 2016) and, in doing so, offers scope for the emergence of a form of vintage feminism both within, and beyond, the sphere of the work organization

'Make Do and Mend' was a home-front campaign, launched in the midst of the Second World War,[4] and was part of a broader initiative to provide housewives with useful advice on how to organize both frugally and stylishly during a period of rationing, when access to ready-made clothes and materials to make one's own clothing, along with other household items, was severely limited. In his foreword to the pamphlet, Hugh Dalton, the then Chancellor of the Exchequer, began by thanking its assumed readers for accepting clothes rationing, and thereby assisting the war effort through saving 'much-needed shipping space, manpower and materials', the presumption being that the labour ('manpower') referred to had been taken up by women. Indeed, there is even a tacit, albeit somewhat qualified, acknowledgement of this when Dalton explains that the advice proffered had been prepared, tested and approved by the Board of Trade's Make Do and Mend Advisory Panel, 'a body of practical people, mostly women' (Dalton, 1943: 1). Its female readers were given advice on how to make clothes last longer by storing and repairing them, on how to wash and iron to avoid unnecessary wear, on how to 'turn out and renovate', and on how to unpick and creatively re-knit or re-sew garments to prolong the life of the materials used. They were also encouraged to join sewing classes, or to teach others to sew or knit, including through local Women's Organizations, to pool ideas and equipment as well as skills and 'know how', and to share outgrown garments through clothing and shoe exchanges. In particular, however, they were encouraged to work collectively by organizing groups to share repair and renovation skills and, through the personnel departments of local factories, to repair the clothing of local war workers.

Today, these work and organizational experiences are frequently presented within vintage lifestyle magazines as a positive template for contemporary women. Often illustrated by Miller's (1943) poster, 'We Can Do It', this cultural emphasis on women's mutual recognition and self-reliance during this period seeks to reclaim feminist ideals and practices that might otherwise be marginalized or forgotten. Thus the role of women who not only led far more independent lives but who were also active in industry and the armed forces usually in co-operation with other women, is presented as inspirational and as offering a very contemporary model for female agency. As such, the inference of 'make do and mend' as an incitement to a woman to 'put up' with her lot and accept her circumstances as a form of 'making do', has the potential to become transformed into a far more active and co-productive notion of female organization. Making and doing and mending, framed in this way, can be thought of, therefore, as a possible alternative way of enacting gender subjectivity to that of postfeminism, one that contrasts with the individualism and consumerism associated with the latter, and shares something in common with the 'DIY' ethos and radical performativity ascribed to new burlesque as a working practice.

Mountfield (2014) hints at this by reminding us that women from previous generations who now inspire a contemporary vintage style were pioneers who brought about positive changes in the role and status of women in the workplace and beyond, so that vintage effectively acts as an important cultural reminder of their work and struggles. Similarly, Jenss (2005: 179) suggests that vintage in this sense provides an important connection to women's everyday lives and work in the past emphasizing how vintage clothing, in particular, helps us to engage with this in a very tactile, material way. To elaborate, and returning to the social ontology of vintage referred to earlier, while most everyday clothing, whether home-sewn or factory-made, is produced by individuals (usually women) sitting at sewing machines, or working by hand, older techniques were much more labour intensive. This resulted not only in the production of better quality items, designed to last and withstand multiple alterations and repairs but also (for contemporary consumers) in a tactile connection to the work undertaken, apparent, for instance, in hand-sewn stitching or evidence of so-called invisible repairs or meticulous alterations. The connections engendered involve not simply an appreciation of the time, labour and skill invested in the production of the garments or objects in question (Fischer, 2015), giving them a certain 'authentic integrity' resembling that attributed to handcrafted or artisanal products. They also invite a more reflexive interest in the contexts of their production (Franklin, 2002; Pickering and Keightley, 2006) and an appreciation of our connections (and even indebtedness) to these contexts, potentially leading us to think critically and reflexively about 'which and whose pasts' endure, and are recognized, and on what basis (Macdonald, 2013: 120).

Postfeminism and Vintage Femininity

In our discussion so far we have explored, albeit somewhat briefly, what appear to be both the convergences, and critical differences, between post-feminism and the values and activities associated with what has been termed 'vintage femininity' (Ferreday, 2008). In this penultimate section, we reflect on these overlaps and differences in order to explore our interest in the question of whether it is possible to think about not only a vintage femininity but also a 'vintage feminism'. In particular, we consider the extent to which the latter might, in some way, offer an alternative sensibility to that discernible within contemporary postfeminism, and the inroads that the latter is beginning to make into work and organization studies.

As intimated earlier, postfeminism and vintage femininity appear, at first sight at least, to share many similarities. As we observed at the beginning of the chapter, vintage echoes a number of important postfeminist motifs, not least its enthusiasm for glamour, a playful emphasis on feminine aesthetics and a championing of women's right to a freedom of (albeit a heavily stylized) expression. Further, both appear to represent a critical reaction to what are perceived to be the restrictions that feminism has placed, somewhat ironically, on a woman's right to choose. Be it the choice to act like a man in the workplace, perform in a burlesque show or stay at home and make cupcakes, both postfeminism and vintage seem to reclaim the right 'to feel like a woman'. Yet while the idea of choice and the sanctity of the individual are, as we well know, often difficult to contest, the neoliberal core of such ideas—as evident here—serves to undermine the very conditions of feminism's possibility. For while feminism has always concerned itself with the individual woman, it has also emphasized that gender emancipation is a collective and social act. By undermining, if not ridiculing this principle, postfeminism merely serves up a caricature of feminism—even in its more liberal forms—within which collective emancipation is seen either to have been achieved, or is framed as simply no longer relevant to women's everyday working lives and lived experiences.

Nonetheless, even if this is the case, must the idea of a vintage feminism be condemned along with what appears to be its postfeminist sibling? As we have already suggested, immanent to a range of vintage portrayals of femininity there also exists a clear and strong counter-narrative to all of this—one that continues to extol the virtues of solidarity, cooperation and the location of women in society as a collective force for change. Furthermore, and again as we have observed, where this narrative is at its strongest is in accounts and representations within vintage culture of the working and organizational lives of women, alongside the struggles they faced, which in fact served to bring about the conditions under which feminism, in all its forms, was able to flourish.

Höpfl (2010) explores many of these motifs in her discussion of the 'death of the heroine', an account that reminds us of the themes we have considered in relation to *Make Do and Mend* and vintage culture more generally. Weaving together personal biography and theoretical reflection, Höpfl explores how the stories of past heroines are tales of more than heroic virtue; they are stories of opposition. For Höpfl, when we are led to believe that such stories are tales of female oppression that has now been 'overcome', we are effectively deceived on two counts if we are also taken in by more contemporary postfeminist narratives of liberation that, she argues, misrepresent women's lives in both the past and the present. In contrast to what she regards as the misleading claims of postfeminism about women now and in the past, and referring to her own copy of Arthur Groom's (1952) *The Girls' Book of Heroines* (given to her as a school prize), Höpfl (2010: 395) reflects how

> what is striking about all these short accounts is the way in which women are represented as strong, determined, self-sacrificing and able to cope with hardship in order to achieve their goals. In one sense, this is not perhaps surprising given the period in which the book was published and when I read them again now after some fifty years I can see not only how these stories influenced me but how they influenced a generation of women.

As Höpfl notes, virtues such as dignity, honesty, integrity and courage have been widely condemned as outmoded Victorian ideals and replaced by the rights culture of neoliberalism, and within work and organizational life particularly, by a dominant discourse of strong, strategic leadership. As such, virtue, she argues, has come to be perceived by postfeminists as 'restrictive and contrary to individual freedom' (ibid: 398). And so, while we acknowledge Dirix's (2014) critique of, for example, the new domesticity associated with vintage, as Gill (2016) argues, the multi-dimensional nature of contemporary feminism, and of gender relations, is far too complex for a simple, linear critique such as this, postulating that earlier forms of feminism, or ways of doing gender, as now redundant or outmoded.

As such, what we are suggesting here is that while vintage femininity might indeed constitute one element in the constellation of ideas and practices that compose postfeminism, it is not in itself necessarily reducible to or synonymous with it. Like Höpfl's (2010) heroines, vintage femininity might also remind us that honesty and integrity, combined with solidarity, generosity and the agency to be found in an act of making, doing and, where necessary mending, remain powerful ideals for feminism, especially in the context of women as working subjects. In not only recognizing the power and agency of women but also their contemporary and historical interdependencies, a vintage feminism brings back into view an intellectual and cultural basis for those forms of workplace organization and structures of mutual support that postfeminism appears to so casually eschew.

What, therefore, might such a vintage feminism look like, if not necessarily in practice, then in the form of a series of emerging propositions? Well, four starting points might be as follows in so far as a vintage feminism:

1 Embraces gender as a continuing process of negotiation and citation at work and beyond, emphasizing that feminist activism now, in the past and in the future must be recognized as shaping this process.
2 Promotes 'make, do and mend', rather than a makeover paradigm, in order to favour an organizational/organizing ethos premised upon solidarity, integrity and connection.
3 Criticizes an empty promise of individuality, free choice and empowerment as the primary *routes* to women's independence and freedom, in favour of organizational/organizing practices of community, interdependence and collective freedom as sustainable and desirable ways forward.
4 Rejects limitless consumption in favour of the organizational principles of re-using, recycling and recirculating as ethically and socially responsible.

How these principles may actually be enacted in the workplace remains open to speculation of course. Perhaps it might be that all a vintage feminism could offer, as we have suggested elsewhere, is a reminder of other ways of being that impact on how work is both envisaged and organized—one that remains critical of, but resonant with, aspects of postfeminist thought.

Concluding Thoughts

If, as (Jess) Butler (2013: 45) has emphasized, postfeminism might most usefully be thought of as a 'historically specific discursive formation', we have sought to suggest here that vintage might provide the basis for an alternative constellation of ideals and practices. Attached to this are certain risks of course, not least that vintage and postfeminism alike may work to conceal emerging and intensifying modes of gender regulation, relating for instance to the sexual commodification of women's bodies and the domestication of the female subject. Equally, the re-gendering of social relations implied by mobilizing cultural reference points from the past might, for many, involve an abandonment of critique and an associated relinquishing of feminism as a political identity. Just as McRobbie (2009: 57, cited in Butler, 2013: 45) warns us of the risks associated with postfeminism as a set of practices that are 'both progressive but also consummately and reassuringly feminine', so vintage might imply a future for women that involves a regressive 'slipping back' into a domesticated neo-essentialism or an 'ironic' sexualization and a resigned acceptance of a relatively narrow range of ways of being a woman. As noted earlier, alongside the risks associated with this retrogressive slippage, and a de-politicized stylization of feminism, vintage also carries with it the potential problem of sanitizing, through a selective re-appropriation, a very particular version of the past, including of feminist politics and gender relations. The danger, in this sense, is that we simply replace the fetishization of 'the new' that Gill (2016) and others associate with postfeminism, with an equally problematic fetishization of the past, 'the ultimate Marxist joke' as Dirix (2014: 97) puts it.

Yet despite all of these notes of caution, we would argue that vintage has the potential to also challenge the postfeminist privileging of neoliberalism's individualism and consumerism, in part as a way to redress the disconnections that are its perceived outcomes. Vintage feminism, as we have presented it here, suggests that this particular version of the past might not only be experienced but also articulated in resistance to these values by embracing a politics, aesthetics and ethics of community and continuity with feminism's past. Be it a connection with Höpfl's heroic women of bygone days, or a sense of continuity with women whose past struggles both at work [and to work] have inspired collective movements and solidarities, vintage feminism, while by no means some universal panacea to the ills of a postfeminist world, suggests at least a different and seemingly popular way of thinking about feminism.

We also sense that vintage is about more than this, however, and its growing presence as somehow beyond just another consumer experience suggests so. This is not least because it appears to offer scope for an alternative to the individualism and intensification that seems to characterize organizational and social life in its current forms. Perhaps in claiming this we are guilty of overly romanticizing vintage, but we (and others) find in it an inter-corporeal sociality largely absent from contemporary adult life as the latter has become so caught up in a mass mediated, overwork culture. As an organizational process or phenomenon, vintage arguably opens up an enactment of community and connection, values that signal, to borrow from (Judith) Butler, 'a defense of our collective . . . persistence in the making of equality and the many-voiced and unvoiced ways of refusing to become disposable' (Butler, 2014: 197). And it in is this vein, that vintage may offer something of an alternative to the many estrangements of contemporary organizational life, taking the latter not beyond, but back to, feminist values, ideals and practices.

Notes

1 The popular use of the term, particularly in relation to the consumption of goods and services is largely thought to derive from wine making, characterizing the year and location in which a particular wine was made (Fischer, 2015; Sarial-Abi et al., 2016)
2 On the cover of its 29 June 1998 issue, *Time* magazine asked, 'Is Feminism Dead?' As Butler (2013) notes, the cover also featured the faces of Betty Friedan, Gloria Steinem and postfeminist fictional television character, Ally McBeal, suggesting (she argues) that the answer was, of course, 'yes'. As Butler (2013: 38) goes on to emphasize, 'this *Time* cover story was only one of many news stories and magazine articles that began to emerge in the 1980s, all anxiously speculating about the status of feminism in contemporary society'.

3 As Fischer (2015: 63) notes the 'uniqueness', value and distinction bestowed on vintage goods may simply be because the object's copies are no longer in existence.
4 www.bl.uk/learning/timeline/item106365.html, belonging to the British Library. The 'Make Do and Mend' pamphlet was authored by the Ministry of Information for the Board of Trade in Britain and issued during the Second World War.

References

Adamson, M. (2016). *Successfully "Balanced" Femininity in CEO Autobiographies: The Intersection of Postfeminist and Neoliberal Logic.* Paper presented at ESRC seminar series on Gendered Inclusion, Canterbury, 9th March.

Balmer, J.M.T., and Burghausen, M. (2015). Explicating corporate heritage, corporate heritage brands, and organisational heritage. *Journal of Brand Management*, 22(5): 364–384.

Bardley, C., and Cogliantry, M. (2002). *Wearing Vintage.* New York: Black Dog Publications.

Bourdieu, P. (2009). *Distinction: A Social Critique of the Judgement of Taste.* London: Routledge.

Brooks, A. (1997). *Postfeminisms: Feminism, Cultural Theory and Cultural Forms.* London: Routledge.

Butler, J. (2013). For white girls only? Postfeminism and the politics of inclusion. *Feminist Formations*, 25(1): 35–58.

Butler, J. (2014). *Notes Towards a Performative Theory of Assembly.* Harvard, MA: Harvard University Press.

Campbell, C. (1987). *The Romantic Ethic and the Spirit of Modern Consumerism.* London: Sage.

Cassidy, T.D., and Bennett, H.R. (2012). The rise of vintage fashion and the vintage consumer. *Fashion Practice*, 4(2): 239–262.

Dalton, H. (1943). Foreword. In *Make Do and Mend* (p. 1). London: His Majesty's Stationery Office. Available at: www.bl.uk/learning/timeline/item106365.html

DeLong, M., Heinemann, B., and Reiley, K. (2005). Hooked on vintage! *Fashion Theory*, 9(1): 23–42.

Dirix, E. (2014). Stitched up: Representations of contemporary vintage style mania and the dark side of the popular knitting revival. *Textile: The Journal of Cloth and Culture*, 12(1): 86–99.

Duffy, K., Hewer, P., and Wilson, J. (2012). "Granny would be proud": On the labours of doing vintage, practices and emergent socialities. *Advances in Consumer Research*, 40: 519–525.

Faludi, S. (1992). *Backlash.* New York: Three Rivers Press.

Ferreday, D. (2008). "Showing the girl": The new burlesque. *Feminist Theory*, 9(1): 47–65.

Fischer, N. (2015). Vintage, the first 40 years: The emergence and persistence of vintage style in the United States. *Culture Unbound: Journal of Current Cultural Research*, 7: 45–66.

Franklin, A. (2002). Consuming design, consuming retro. In S. Miles, A. Anderson, and K. Meethan (Eds.), *The Changing Consumer: Markets and Meanings* (pp. 90–103). London: Routledge.

Genz, S. (2006). Third way/ve. *Feminist Theory*, 7(3): 333–353.

Gill, R. (2007). Postfeminist media culture: Elements of a sensibility. *European Journal of Cultural Studies*, 10(2): 147–166.

Gill, R. (2016). Post-postfeminism? New feminist visibilities in postfeminist times. *Feminist Media Studies*, 16(4): 610–630.

Groom, A. (1952) *The Girls' Book of Heroines*. London: Birn Brothers.

Hall, E., and Rodriguez, M.S. (2003). The myth of post-feminism. *Gender and Society*, 17(6): 878–902.

Hemingway, W., and Hemingway, G. (2015). *The Vintage Fashion Bible*. Newton Abbot: David and Charles.

Höpfl, H. (2010). The death of the heroine. *Management and Organizational History*, 5(3–4): 395–407.

Jenss, H. (2005). Sixties dress only! The consumption of the past in a retro scene. In A. Palmer and H. Clark (Eds.), *Old Clothes, New Looks* (pp. 177–195). New York: Berg.

Kim, L.S. (2001). Sex and the single girl in post-feminism. *Television and New Media*, 2(4): 319–334.

Lewis, P. (2014). Postfeminism, femininities and organization studies: Exploring a new agenda. *Organizaton Studies*, 35(12): 1845–1866.

Macdonald, S. (2013). *Memorylands*. London: Routledge.

McRobbie, A. (2004). Postfeminism and popular culture. *Feminist Media Studies*, 4(3): 255–264.

McRobbie, A. (2009). *The Aftermath of Feminism*. London: Sage.

Miller, J.H. (1943) *We Can Do It*. Available at: www.americanhistory.si.edu/collections/search/object/nmah_538122

Mountfield, R. (2014). Feminism vs. vintage: Are feminism and a love of vintage mutually exclusive? *In Retrospect*, 1(1): 10–13.

Palmer, A. (2005). Vintage whores and vintage virgins. In A. Palmer and H. Clark (Eds.), *Old Clothes, New Looks* (pp. 197–213). Oxford: Berg.

Penny, L. (2009). Burlesque laid bare. *The Guardian Online*, 15 May.

Pickering, M., and Keightley, E. (2006). The modalities of nostalgia. *Current Sociology*, 54(6): 919–941.

Samuel, R. (1994). *Theatres of Memory*. London: Verso.

Sarial-Abi, G., Vohs, K.D., Hamilton,R. and Ulqinaku, A. (2017). Stitching time: Vintage consumption connects the past, present and future. *Journal of Consumer Psychology*, 27(2): 182–194.

Siebler, K. (2015). What's so feminist about garters and bustiers? Neo-burlesque as post-feminist sexual liberation. *Journal of Gender Studies*, 24(5): 1–13.

Stephens, J. (2011). *Confronting Postmaternal Thinking*. New York: Columbia University Press.

Tasker, Y., and Negra, D. (Eds.). (2005). *Interrogating Postfeminism*. London: Duke University Press.

Veenstra, A., and Kuipers, G. (2013). It is not old-fashioned, it is vintage, vintage fashion and the complexities of 21st century consumption practices. *Sociology Compass*, 7(5): 355–365.

Walsh, J. (2010). A retro revolution: Why do we love all things vintage? *The Independent*, Friday 27 August.

Walter, N. (2010). *Living Dolls*. London: Virago.

Weldon, J. (2010). *The Burlesque Handbook*. London: Harper.

Whelehan, I. (2000). *Overloaded: Feminism and Popular Culture*. London: Women's Press.

Yeatman, A. (1994). *Postmodern Revisions of the Political*. New York: Routledge.

10 Postfeminism as New Materialisms

A Future Unlike the Present?

Marta B. Calás, Linda Smircich
and Seray Ergene

Introduction

The wider context of this chapter is the now prominent conversations on the Anthropocene—a new geological epoch the world may be entering due to what is arguably the accelerating pace of human-caused (anthropogenic) ecological harms and the possibility of mass extinction (see Braje (2015) for a recent review on debates; also Zalasiewicz, Williams, and Waters (2014)). No longer solely a matter of science fiction, this possibility is both the object of scientific research and a space for enriching the contemporary critical imaginary. How and what to think if/when humans would no longer be (thought of to be) the center of the universe while also being responsible for contributing to the path of extinction for their and other species?

Writing about postfeminism in this context may seem at best trivial, or even irrelevant. In the face of catastrophe, wouldn't it be frivolous to be caring about the contours of postfeminism? However, we argue that humanist postfeminism—as we will identify it in the rest of the chapter—is important for understanding these issues; not as a last (human) gasp for keeping intact the world we have now but as a parody of its old self—liberal feminism—needed for survival when extinction is the other alternative. Specifically, closely examining humanist postfeminism is a necessary move in the process of becoming posthuman, a way to reiterate the possibility of "a-human-we-can-no-longer-be" and open space for the possibility of "a-posthuman-we-can-become". Thus, re-thinking humanist postfeminism is an important element in the process of "becoming other" in the Anthropocene, whose advent is often claimed as part of an emerging historical moment.

There are growing literatures intersecting (post)feminisms, posthumanisms and ecological concerns, interdisciplinary in character—including the social sciences, the humanities and the natural and techno sciences (e.g., Åsberg et al., 2016; Deckha, 2016; Grusin, 2017; Kara, 2016; Sarkar, 2016). For instance, Kara, in an article we will revisit several times here, writes about the nascent genre of Anthropocenema, cinema in the age of mass extinctions, noting that films in this genre show "a rising interest in the tropes of extinction, primordiality, and epochal temporalities that have their own ecologies" (2016: 16) and a shift to female characters' point of view. At first look, most of these characters display an essentialized and pathologized femininity, associating women with motherhood, nurturing and caretaking roles, depression and even hysteria, *but notably these women are also the humans who at the end survive.*

In a second look at these characters, Kara suggests that their portrayals as vulnerable beings allow for subversive rather than stereotypical postfeminist gender interpretations. In particular, these characters move away from macho heroism "providing the opportunity to focus on affect rather than the masculinist techno-capitalism's ability to save the day in times of societal, economic, and ecological crises" (17) while embodying a minimal ethics, an "ethic of vulnerability" (17; citing Hird, 2013) recognizing the uncertainty of things they cannot control, and thus also recognizing the agencies of nature and nonhumans; a form of embodiment of humans intermeshed with a more-than-human world. Important for our argument, Kara articulates relationships between these cinematic representations as possible responses to contemporary global neoliberal capitalism, and the destructive capabilities it might accelerate (e.g., an economy of waste, including, literally, space waste). Isn't it possible that some of the humanist postfeminisms we are observing today are also plausible *responses* to contemporary global neoliberal capitalism by those who might be able to survive? What might come next?

These arguments and questions serve as our point of departure for a potential positive destination before extinction is the only other alternative to talk about. We move slowly in what follows toward this potential destination, with a disclaimer that ours is not a grandiose but a modest reading for *prefiguring* new theoretical possibilities in/for feminist analyses in organization studies.

First, we examine briefly contemporary contours of humanist postfeminism, in particular in relation to work and organization, noting what might have been highlighted in this literature while also addressing other contemporary humanist postfeminisms current literature might have overlooked. In so doing we underscore the co-existence of *a plurality of humanist postfeminisms* while also addressing flux and transformation as the always already processual nature of postfeminisms. That is, we see the ontological status of postfeminism as a process of transformation itself, as immanent and producing always already different conditions for the emergence of feminisms.

Next, we emphasize that for as much as neoliberalism has been highlighted as underscoring postfeminism, the actual historical *co-production* of the neoliberal and the humanist postfeminist subject has been left insufficiently examined. Moreover, as organizational scholars, we argue that examining this co-production is important for gender-related aspects of work and organization, whose theorizing and research may have had much to do with it. We carry out one such examination but also ask further, what would happen to contemporary humanist postfeminisms when/if neoliberalism is no longer viable? Or, more consistent with our arguments, what kind of (post) feminism(s) might be thus emerging? These 'knowledge-production' practices may be untenable at a time—the Anthropocene—when new figurations in our research and theorizing may be needed. What can be done instead?

The final section is poised to address this question. We ask explicitly for expanding our imaginary at this historical moment, including ontological framings and our posture as researchers. Can we still keep a posture of observers and commentators of the (humanist postfeminist) present? We think not. Yet, a posthuman (post)feminist subject might help in getting us out of this impasse to "partake in the creation of a future unlike the present" (Grosz, 2010: 154). Our conclusion emphasizes these points.

Contours of the Present: Humanist Postfeminisms in Organizations

Recent literature in organization studies followed Gill's (2007) formulation of postfeminism as a *cultural sensibility* as something to be read and analyzed as phenomena in contemporary culture *and*, more recently, in organizations (e.g., Adamson, 2017; Gill, Kelan and Scharff's, 2017; Lewis, 2014; Lewis and Simpson, 2017). We do not object to this analytical approach; to the contrary, we see it as a truly important positioning which we have also fostered in our work (Calás, Ou, and Smircich (2013: 714–715); Calás and Smircich (2014: 636–637). Here we follow specifically Gill, Kelan and Scharff's (2017) recent article to highlight briefly the contours of this postfeminist sensibility in the context of work and organization studies. This article becomes a clarification device along the route we are tracing, aiming to show eventually *how* this approach to analysis of postfeminism reiterates a humanist postfeminist subject—something to be made explicit before we can *re-think* the conditions of possibility for a posthumanist postfeminist sensibility. This is not a critique but a reflection on the difficulties of escaping from our contemporary modes of analysis and part, as well, of the chapter's trajectory.

Gill et al. (2017) address postfeminism as an analytical object, identifying the patterning of a postfeminist sensibility: a prominent discourse of "choice" and "agency", with an "emphasis on individualism, retreat from structural accounts of inequality, repudiation of sexism and of the need for feminism" (2). This approach to analysis connects postfeminism with the wider neoliberalization of contemporary culture, brings attention to language and discourse, and focuses on dynamics of power and inequality. It is also explicit in refusing the "post" of postfeminism as a historical understanding (i.e., as what comes after feminism, or as another feminist "wave") which may lead to teleological explanations. Rather, they highlight that "to speak of postfeminism as a sensibility is to speak of a constellation of beliefs, ideas and practices that are dynamic; that travel, and that change" (5). This observation, further articulated in the conclusion of their article, is also germane for our own arguments.

Further, their examples from work and organizational contexts show explicit relationships between postfeminism and neoliberalism. Both discursive practices seem structured "by a current of individualism" (6) dislodging the subject from its social and political moorings and therefore impervious "to pressures, constraints or influence from outside themselves in wider society". The individualist stance of postfeminism is particularly obvious in the notion of *choice* as "watchword of the sensibility" seemingly "unconstrained by any lasting power differences or inequalities" (6). As well, the subject of neoliberalism, "enterprising, autonomous, self-regulating [. . .] bears a strong resemblance to the active, freely choosing, self-reinventing subject of postfeminism". Finally, there is a tendency in these discourses to expect women "to work on and transform their selves" for instance encouraging working women to become more confident and resilient in the workplace, as promoted by several recent books on *corporate feminism* (e.g., Kay and Shipman, 2014; Sandberg, 2013).

Such firm belief in "choice" and the autonomy of the subject is of course the necessary ontological condition (free, disconnected, unrestrained) for the liberal humanist subject that underlies both contemporary neoliberalism and postfeminisms, our starting point in the next section. But before we move on we will first bring into the conversation other humanist postfeminist subjects in organizations that may have been left unattended in postfeminism literatures, including Gill et al.'s (2017).

Recent literature on the neoliberalization of feminism at a global scale exhibits similarities with analysis of postfeminism as a cultural sensibility; each of these literatures addresses gender within the wider neoliberalization of contemporary culture, brings attention to language and discourse and focuses on dynamics of power and inequality, but the neoliberalization literature also addresses structural arguments at a transnational scale absent in most postfeminist literature. Thus including the neoliberalization literature here illustrates postfeminism as constellation of belief, ideas, and practices that are dynamic and travel, reiterating as well that the travels start from "the west", which most humanist postfeminist literature represents but seldom reflects upon, and goes "to the rest". How and how much do they change in these travels; for whom and for what? These issues still call for investigation (e.g., Calás, Ou, and Smircich, 2013, on mobile subjectivities), but, more generally, how does the literature on the neoliberalization of feminism work as a humanist postfeminist literature?

Humanist Postfeminism at a Global Scale

Joan Acker (2004) argued we were at the time when "gendering globalization" had become necessary. Doing so would expose discontinuities between the realities of women's and men's lives in local arenas, and the discontinuities of those realities with mainstream scholarly work about global processes. Addressing these concerns, Acker's gendering analyses examine subjectivities, subject positions and institutions over time and space, observing them as relational products and producers of transnational and global processes. These processes are activated by decision makers under premises of neoliberal market capitalism.

Global decision making, Acker insisted, is coded "masculine" in specific ways, and the men and the few women who make decisions under this code are immediate beneficiaries of most of the wealth and power produced. At the same time, these decisions produce cultural and economic dislocations affecting gender/race/class relations in particular local arenas and at global levels among most other actual women and men in the world. Thus, "gendering globalization" makes visible the local and the global in relational patterns of everyday life, where decisions made by the few affect the many. Who makes decisions producing transnational and global processes, in theory and in practice? Acker's arguments bring to the fore a postfeminism-neoliberalism nexus through work and organizations at a global scale, articulating more humanist postfeminist formations.

The Transnational/Global: Shaping Women Decision Makers

Elias (2013) observes that there is now a distinctly postfeminist reading of gender resting on the production of neoliberal-compatible female subjectivities—"rational economic woman" or "Davos woman"—granting certain groups of women, such as those participating in the *World Economic Forum*, a privileged status in the current global order. Concurrently, other works examine the emergence of female-embodied privileged decision makers in corporate arenas usually having a global reach, such as through *Facebook*. For example, Gill (2016) and Rottenberg (2014) analyze the rise of corporate feminism or neoliberal feminism by focusing on specific texts such as Sandberg's (2013) and highlighting aspects of the genre contributing to the formation of the subject of neoliberalism: individualistic, entrepreneurial and complicit with capitalism. Importantly, both of these articles show—among other things—how corporate feminism—another humanist postfeminism—works in preventing the appearance of progressive social movements countering corporate interests and, as we argue, may do so at a global scale.

The Local: Women (and Girls) as Agents of Cultural and Economic Dislocations

A different literature, but with similar sensibilities to women in the context of the corporate-neoliberalism nexus, focuses on projects advancing global corporate interests at the most local of levels: poor women and girls in the Global South. These are often invisible subjects in the postfeminist literature which, we argue, become visible *as postfeminist subjects* by articulating them also as relational products and producers of transnational and global processes. Several of these works illustrate projects where corporations have used feminist notions such as "women's empowerment" to claim assumed gains for both women and companies.

For instance, Calkin (2015) and Roberts (2015) examine *Nike*'s project the "Girl Effect", started around 2005. This project promoted investing in adolescent girls in poor countries under premises that doing so would have the greatest impact on poverty alleviation. However, in practice women and girls become the focus of social policies aiming to shape "human capital" with market rationality according to corporate interests. In their simplification and privatization of social problems such projects serve to reproduce the same neoliberal macroeconomic conditions tending to create highly precarious labor markets at a global scale, which affect disproportionately women's employment—a very contradictory aim when it comes to poverty alleviation.

Further, "entrepreneurial subjectivities", often addressed in the post-feminism literature, have been consistently associated with the subject of neoliberalism and its global dispersion. The older and best-known projects fostering these subjectivities are microcredit/microenterprises activities, oriented towards creation of microfirms by very poor women. The original formulation, promoted by the World Bank in the 1970s and institutionalized in 1983 as women's projects by Grameen Bank in Bangladesh, promoted social solidarity among participants, encouraging improvement of their communities and reducing their dependence on usury loans (e.g. Rahman, 2001). However, critiques of these projects now abound. Transnational micro-lending has become big business, and the poor women involved ultimately function as necessary conduits for the circulation of global capital and its transnational viability (e.g., Calás, Smircich, and Bourne, 2009; Keating, Rasmussen, and Rishi, 2010; Rankin, 2001; Shetty, 2010; Yunus, 2011).

Yet, the reach and promises of entrepreneurship with women at the center have been extended beyond microenterprises, with some corporate projects claiming to empower poor women by developing their entrepreneurial capabilities. For instance, in *Unilever*'s Shakti project in India (Prügl, 2015), women in the rural countryside compete with each other in selling soap, among other things, through claims of enhancing community health (hygiene). Projects such as these, Prügl notes, destroy social solidarities in the communities by setting women against each other to compete in a limited market, "redefining the health needs of women and families to fit corporate agendas" (624). As we discuss later, these projects reproduce the likes of *Mary Kay* and other direct-marketing schemes for women deployed originally during the 1970s in the United States. Meanwhile, a Coca-Cola global campaign, "5by20", aims to "empower" five million women as small-scale entrepreneurs by 2020 (Tornhill, 2016). This campaign is one of many based on premises of corporate solutions to women's inequality in the Global South, encouraging and training them to become entrepreneurs. Importantly, "5by20" makes no promises of employment once training is completed. Training is focused explicitly on causes for success or failure as personal, often psychological issues, leaving no space for structural explanations such as lack of resources, which women participants often noted. Tornhill argues that projects such as this are typical in uneven neoliberal contexts, where transnational economic institutions, corporations and local governments support individual solutions to poverty while concealing needed structural changes for strong labor markets.

Following Acker, our examples here underscore global and local processes in relational patterns of everyday life, where decisions made by the few affect the many at a global scale. These relational patterns articulate (mostly liberal) feminism as justifications in the production of humanist postfeminist neoliberal subjects (Eisenstein, 2005, 2009; Fraser, 2009, 2013). Consistent with our arguments, what other kinds of humanist postfeminisms may have emerged en route to this point in time? Isn't it possible that gender and organization scholarship has been, perhaps unwittingly, complicit in these processes all along?

The Path of Humanist Postfeminisms in Organizations— Co-productions of Gender, Management and Neoliberalism

The growing literatures on postfeminisms as relevant cultural phenomenon in association with work and organization, including those illustrated earlier, would be hard to ignore. However, while the recent popularity of these arguments in diverse disciplines and publications outside of management may be newer, what these literatures are observing is not really a new phenomenon. The labeling may be somewhat different (pace Gill, 2016) but it's been there all along under the guise of a different name: women-in-management discourse, appearing in academic literature, in popular press, and in actual practice over the years. Thus, much of what is understood as postfeminism at present is mainly recent expressions—re-citations in Butler's (1990) sense—of the women-in-management discourse.

The women-in-management literature emerged in the 1970s in the USA, and its emergence was coterminous with the advent of neoliberal market capitalism in this country. They shared a political economy discourse representing the market as "the institutionalized solution to practically every human problem" (Centeno and Cohen, 2012: 331) and a liberal humanist sensibility required to activate this discourse, including gendered sensibilities as represented by liberal feminism and its postfeminist (masked) doppelganger. As co-productions of liberal humanism at a particular time and place, women-in-management and neoliberalism discourses and practices hinged on the promises of creating a better society, and increasingly have come to share a common vocabulary and logic. What has this co-production of women in management and neoliberalism meant for today's postfeminism sensibilities in organizations (and beyond)? What has become normalized? Gill et al.'s (2017) empirical examples show that gender inequalities are routinely allocated to the past or to other countries or contexts, that women are seen as the advantaged sex and that the status quo is accepted as just how workplaces are. How did we get here?

Not a Detour but a Brief Pause to Remember the Road

Liberal feminism and neoliberalism have their roots in the Western liberal political tradition developed in the seventeenth and eighteenth centuries, as feudalistic, church-dominated rule transitioned to capitalist civil society, and when aspirations for equality, liberty and fraternity were supplanting the monarchical order (Cockburn, 1991). Concurrently, a new vision of persons and society—i.e., liberal humanism—was emerging, supported by two key philosophical assumptions about human nature: *normative dualism* (mind/body dualism), where rationality is conceived as mental capacity separated from embodiment, and *abstract individualism*, where individual's actions are conceived as autonomous from social circumstances (Jaggar, 1983). A "good" or "just" society allowed individuals to exercise autonomy and fulfillment through a system of rights while in competition with other equally autonomous subjects of rights. Under these premises individuals—at that point only white, male, free and propertied—were assumed to inhabit a world of scarcity, and to be motivated to secure an as large as possible individual share of available resources.

In general, liberal feminism adheres to an ideal, ahistorical, universal humanity toward which both men and women should aspire—i.e., liberal humanism (Parvikko, 1990). However, liberal political thought and liberal humanism have a long history of debates regarding the inclusion of women and others—e.g., slaves, non-whites—as also subjects under these ideals. The civil rights and the feminist social movements of the 1960s in the United States are representations of these debates, and it is here where our observations in this section start. During the 1960s and 1970s what is now known as the "second-wave" women's movement—philosophically tied to liberal feminism—aimed to obtain women's equal access and equal representation in public life. Liberal feminism made a transition from themes of women's equality (equal rights), in the 1960s and 1970s, to themes of difference in the 1980s and 1990s (legal rights equality *and* gender/race/sexuality recognition). From this transition liberal feminism's overriding goal became sexual equity or "gender justice" (Evans, 1995; Tong, 1998). See also Calás and Smircich (1996, 2006).

Meanwhile, market neoliberalism, developing in the United States from the 1970s was a revision of eighteenth century classical economic liberalism promoting minimal state involvement in regulating everyday affairs and economic choices of citizens, corporations and other institutions. Neoliberalism would come to replace modern liberalism; the latter emerged in Western economies with the "Great Depression" and continued after WWII as states became active participants in economic life, facilitating essential goods and services (e.g., utilities; health care) and as instruments (through taxation) for redistributing wealth and achieving more equitable societies. Contemporary neoliberalism is thus a return to the premises of classical liberalism by reinterpreting the welfare state and other forms of state economic interventions as a temporary "wrong turn" and by focusing (again) on reducing state interventions, this time as a worldwide requirement addressing the competitive climate of globalization (e.g., Clarke, 2005; Gershon, 2011; Gray, 1995; Harvey, 2005; Kotz, 2002; Thorsen, 2010).

With this brief background, the rest of this section examines the emergence and development of humanist postfeminisms and their entanglements with neoliberalism as seen at present. These entanglements had their genesis during the 1970s in business schools in the United States with the appearance of women-in-management discourses, defining since then the contours of humanist postfeminism in/through management and organizations. Women-in-management discourses reiterate neoliberalism and liberal humanism as key premises for belonging to a privileged public sphere— white, male and affluent—*by assuming the gains of liberal feminism as a social movement while concurrently distancing from it*. In this context, Gill et al.'s (2017) observations represent contemporary aspects of these processes, but their conditions of possibility have a longer history.

The Psychology of Difference: Individualizing Women in Management

A novel legal and regulatory environment emerged in the United States in the 1970s as a result of 1960s social movements. A revised Civil Rights Act gave way to the Equal Employment Opportunity Act and to affirmative action programs. In that period, many women already labored in lower organization levels including staff and supervisory positions, but only a small number were at higher levels. While newer regulations would provide support for claims of sex discrimination in high positions, liberal humanism also furnished disclaimers. Insofar as promotion systems were based on the merit principles of liberal humanism (upheld by abstract individualism) those reaching high organization levels would have attained them due to individual accomplishments. With meritocracy as dominant logic, women not reaching higher positions needed explanations other than discrimination.

Consistent with liberal humanism's individualizing premises, explanations emerged very early in at least two areas of psychological research: gender socialization, gender roles and stereotypes (e.g., Hennig and Jardim, 1977; Schein, 1973, 1975; Terborg, 1977); and attributes differentiating women's and men's managerial capabilities of (e.g., Bem and Lenney, 1976; Chapman, 1975). These explanations inaugurated the field of women-in-management academic research. Sex inequality as a structural problem— e.g., sex discrimination—was seldom articulated; rather, "women's difference" was "the problem". A few structural explanations did appear at this time examining how organizations were gender systems (Kanter, 1977; Bartol, 1978) and some 1980s studies considered possible manifestations of sex discrimination in the workplace (e.g., Heilman and Martell, 1986; Taylor and Ilgen, 1981), yet "women's differences" continued as justification even when addressing known social issues affecting women's careers in management—e.g., work/family concerns; sexual harassment (Beutell and Greenhaus, 1983; Konrad and Gutek, 1986).[1]

Postfeminisms by Any Other Name: Women Managers and Entrepreneurs

Psychological explanations for gender disparity in managerial positions have continued to this day, with "difference" rather than "inequality" as conventional discourse for explaining gendered hierarchies in positions and rewards (e.g., Calás, Smircich, and Holvino, 2014). However, the structural hiatus from the late 1970s did leave behind a lasting image: "The glass ceiling"—a synonym still standing for women's difficulties in attaining fair access to high level managerial positions despite successes at lower levels (Hymowitz and Schellhardt, 1986).

In a *Wall Street Journal* article, these authors noted that women in management had made extraordinary progress in numbers, but despite all this, "a caste system of men at the top and women lower down still prevails in corporate America". Their more general point would call into question psychological explanations about women's limitations causing an otherwise structural oddity: the main obstacle women faced, and the most intangible, was that men at the top "feel uncomfortable with women beside them."

The "glass ceiling" notion produced significant and persistent overlaps between academic discourses on women-in-management and gender issues of interest in the larger society (Powell and Butterfield, 2015), remaining a point of reference for the progress, or not, of managerial women reaching the executive suite. However, while the article kept an eye on the prize of that ultimate and most valuable reward, it also observed that if women wanted to attain "that pinnacle" it may be easier to climb off the corporate ladder first and grow their own companies, eventually demonstrating as well their executive capabilities. Thus, the entrepreneurship avenue represented a temporary detour while reinforcing an ethos of individualism, scarcity and competition. That is, the "glass ceiling" narrative contributed to reducing the women-in-management literature more generally to that of the life history possibilities of only an elite few—a continuing blind spot in both the academic and the popular literature on these topics; it did not provide other possible understandings of working women's success.

These paths for working women, either trying to climb the corporate hierarchy to executive levels or taking an entrepreneurial route, also became cultural discourses in the 1980s. Journalists, cultural analysts and researchers addressing social issues used the terms "corporate feminism" and "market feminism", calling attention to how each of these alternatives involved appropriations of feminist ideals *with the purpose of advancing corporate interests* For instance, observing the myriad self-help books and women's conferences proliferating then, Gordon (1983) articulated "the new corporate feminism", critiquing ways the feminist movement's ideals, political impulses, and the power of collective action were redirected to facilitating tactics in support of individual effort and achievement. In her words, "what has happened to reformist feminism in the past decade is perhaps the most dramatic example of American capitalism's genius at defusing protest by winning the protesters over to the very values and institutions they once attacked" (1).

Gordon's trenchant observations addressed further contradictions. By becoming members of a system of masculinist capitalism, despite its ills having been amply criticized by feminist and other social movements, both women and men in the business world couldn't do it differently

> because no one in corporate America has the freedom to live by values other than those of corporate America (5). Everyone entering this business world "must shed" their politics, emotions, ideals while also standardizing their attitudes, behaviors, and skills—i.e., dressing for success; as such, "[w]omen must become company women because there is nothing left to be".
>
> (1983: 5)

These words also reflected the early institutionalization of supply-side economics under President Reagan, fragmenting social movements, weakening progressive politics, and abandoning collective ideals. As part of "trickle down" economics along the lines of neoliberalism—claiming that eventually everyone would benefit—these policies redirected large amounts of capital into the private sector while affecting the power of labor unions and women's and minorities' movements, whose demands for adequate standards of living couldn't be supported by an increasingly privatized social system and a weak welfare state (Abramovitz and Hopkins, 1983; Frank, 1981; Petr, 1982).

During this time, "corporate feminism" also assumed an apparently entrepreneurial form with the rise of the Mary Kay Cosmetics direct-marketing company in the 1970s (Banks and Zimmerman, 1987). Mary Kay "entrepreneurs" attained social independence by selling products from home rather than working from company locations. Yet, by operating under a corporate umbrella, they lacked control of their own enterprise. Mary Kay's discourses and practices, also emulated by other companies, deployed concepts from the '60s feminist movement (individualism, autonomy and earning power)—i.e., "market feminism"[2]—while redressing contradictions between conventional ideologies of the stay-at-home wife and mother and the increasingly real economic necessity of middle and working-class families, now requiring two incomes just to maintain their living standards.

In fact, entrepreneurship was already understood in the United States as secondary employment for housewives with children (Hisrich and Brush, 1984) and for poverty alleviation in the "Third World" through microcredit schemes for poor women. No surprise direct-marketing entrepreneurial schemes have re-appeared in the likes of *Unilever*'s Shakti project in India (Prügl, 2015).

While Gordon (1983) and Banks and Zimmerman (1987) illustrated the limited options women in the United States were facing when joining the labor force in the '70 and '80s, feminist sociologists Blum and Smith (1988) explored how women-in-management discourses and practices reproduced these conditions while losing the focus on gender equality. In an extended analysis of representative academic literature and practical— e.g., consultants—applications, they noted the narrowing explanations for women's disadvantages to psychological or corporate structure options, even when claiming feminist sensibilities. For instance, reflecting on consultants' use of prevalent psychological explanations for women limitations in organizations, they noted that despite tendency to

> blame the female victim [. . .] the implication that women need only change themselves to succeed, that what seems to be a problem within the structure of the corporation is in fact under the individual's control, has proved to be enormously appealing.
>
> (1988: 531)

As this quote makes apparent, the discourse of "individual choice" was already operating as a normal(izing) practice for women in organizations at that time.

Blum and Smith also noted limitations in women-in-management academic literature taking a structural approach (e.g., Kanter; "glass ceiling" literature) because of its primary focus on the upward mobility of women. This literature was partial to high status fields and positions, representing the interests of already privileged women while overlooking the different bases of employed women's social stratification both outside and inside organizations. Further, the literature did not pay sufficient attention to the capitalism-corporate structure nexus, relying excessively on changing organizations from the top through a notion of "empowerment" which "individualizes the responsibility for change, directing attention away from larger questions of ownership and control" (1988: 544). As we have already noted, this notion of "empowerment" together with the other neoliberal favorite, "choice," has become standard lexicon constituting the subject of contemporary "neoliberal feminisms" in corporate global projects (Calkin (2015); Roberts (2015); Tornhill (2016) and has an immediate resonance with contemporary postfeminisms.

In short, the 1980s were a significant period in the co-optation of liberal feminist ideals for advancing corporate interests, and very much located in the advent of "trickle down" economics signaling the taking off of global market neoliberalization. Contemporary "corporate feminism" (a humanist postfeminism) is the heir of these events (e.g., Gill, 2016; Rottenberg, 2014).

Neoliberalism: Changing the Subject

We decoupled the discussion of neoliberalism from the aforementioned to maintain continuity in the women-in-management narrative, but also underscored at certain points the traffic between these two narratives as coterminous and co-producing discourses in the process of emergence, in particular during the Reagan-Thatcher era. Here we further advance this argument, reiterating that the women-in-management discourse was, and still is, part of articulations normalizing neoliberalism as political economy by providing the necessary contours for the subject of neoliberalism.

Finer-grained details of these arguments and critiques of neoliberalism abound (e.g., Saad-Filho and Johnston, 2005), but, generally, neoliberal political economy practices and policies include an emphasis on deregulation, privatization, employers' quest for labor flexibility, and reduction of social safety nets (e.g., Harvey, 2005; Kalleberg, 2009). This would facilitate market capitalism to do its work, but for such policies and practices to be acceptable and valued more broadly it would need broader philosophical underpinnings. In Harvey's definition,

> Neoliberalism is in the first instance a theory of political economic *practices* that proposes that human well-being can best be advanced by liberating individual entrepreneurial freedoms and skills within an institutional framework characterized by strong private property rights, free markets and free trade.
>
> (2005: 2; our emphasis)

The repetition of these ideas as almost a mantra has created an air of inevitability but for these practices to function accordingly a newer type of human stance is required. Constructing a political or economic theory on top of assumptions about human nature is not unique to neoliberalism. As we discussed, liberal political and economic thought is premised on conception of self-interested and abstract individuals. Under these premises, all humans are equal at their core and share a common capacity to reason—i.e., liberal humanism—*with a moral compass pointed towards attaining, in typical utilitarian fashion, the greatest good for the greatest number.*

Neoliberalism, by contrast, works towards dislodging several features of the individual of classical liberalism and constructing a new kind of subject in its place. No longer merely a philosophical assumption, this subject can be developed concretely—i.e., it is not argued that it exists in nature—as 'human nature'—but that it can become so if it is brought into being. This shift from the liberal to the neoliberal subject is described by Gershon (2011) as a move from a vision of individuals owning themselves as proprietors of their *labor* (the liberal subject) to a vision of individuals owning themselves *as if they are a business* (the neoliberal subject). This shift has important consequences: the subjects of liberalism sell their property as labor in the market (e.g., as employees) while the subjects of neoliberalism are "businesses" (i.e, entrepreneurs) whose assets—skills and traits—must be invested in and managed continually in the market. Everyone "a business" and also a market entity, would aim to enter into relationships with other market entities, creating partnerships to distribute their responsibilities and risks.

Gershon, further notes that neoliberalism "depends on transforming liberalism's possessive individualism [. . .] into *corporate individualism*, viewing all agents as commensurate corporate entities so that social organization or differences in scale can be ignored" (2011: 543—our emphasis). Has this worked? As Kalleberg (2009) observes, in practice neoliberalism as political economy has produced untenable workers' insecurity and the advent of precarious work. These conditions have been in the making at least since the 1970s, connected to globalization and the spreading logic of market capitalism, involving greater capital mobility, as well as the reduction of social safety nets, which led to social responsibilities becoming individual responsibilities. Why has this become acceptable (i.e., hegemonic)?

Neoliberalism also includes perspectives on morality and notions of the virtuous person (Thorsen, 2010). Virtuous individuals are competent in accessing markets and functioning in them by willingly accepting risks and adapting to rapid change. These moral agents would make decisions freely and thus be responsible for their choices and their consequences: *individual rights moralism* (Ahlers and Zwarteveen, 2009). No longer bound by the utilitarianism premises of liberal humanism, here *inequality and social injustice would be morally acceptable when they are considered as outcomes of long chains of individuals' freely made decisions*. Therefore,

> demands that the state should regulate the market or make reparations to the unfortunate, who have been caught at the losing end of a freely initiated market transaction [. . .] is viewed as an indication that the person in question is morally depraved and underdeveloped.
> (Thorsen, 2010: 204)

Sustaining such premises would require the ideal subject of neoliberalism to be always already making its "self" as a privileged corporate individual, coinciding as well with the upwardly mobile subjects articulated in the women-in-management literature.

Here we recall Gill's (2007) remarks connecting postfeminism and neoliberalism, noting that women to greater extent than men

> are required to work on and transform the self, to regulate every aspect of their conduct, and to present all their actions as freely chosen. Could

it be that neoliberalism is always already gendered, and that women are constructed as its ideal subjects?

(164)

In light of our observations, our response is yes, but with some qualifications: the ideal subject of neoliberalism may be found in the reductive arguments of the women-in-management literature, but finding the connections between neoliberalism and the contours of postfeminisms described by Gill may require a longer analytical path.

During the 1980s, the women-in-management narrative formulated classed subjects; that is, an affluent and privileged corporate woman (attempting to break the glass ceiling) constructed on the otherness of (often silenced) women's inequality (e.g., working mothers). The evolution of this narrative appears today in full global neoliberal garb in the likes of decision makers with agency and control: Davos woman (Elias, 2013)) and contemporary corporate feminism (Sandberg, 2013). Yet, in the wake of these subjects, another one necessarily appears: the women who cannot rise to the top in corporate arenas. In affluent settings, their impediments might be tied to their womanhood (e.g., motherhood in "the west"); in less affluent settings, their impediments have explicit economic ties (poverty in "the rest"). One way or another, solutions to these problems arrive from developing entrepreneurial capabilities, putting once again a market solution into the hands of individual women.

This logic shows up in the interpretive repertoires Gill et al. (2017) derived from their empirical examples. Here (evidently younger) working women (in the west) articulated contours of postfeminism by routinely allocating gender inequalities to the past or to other countries or contexts. As we see it, these recent examples capture the normalization and activation in today's terms of 1980s neoliberal/women-in-management narrative, now rearticulated as *corporate individualism* (Gershon, 2011). It would be unacceptable for these women to concede that they cannot make it to the top as equals because that would imply they are not trying hard enough as market entities (i.e., being morally depraved according to *individual rights moralism*). Reference to other countries or contexts is necessary to maintain the hierarchical privilege between their place/space and other places where less affluence (and more inequality) may be found. Nonetheless, from this perspective, market benefits may have not reached everyone *yet* but eventually will—as expected from the neoliberalization of feminism projects we described, with market benefits moving from "the west" to "the rest".

However, Gill et al. (2017) further noted that women often saw themselves as the advantaged sex and accepted the status quo as just how workplaces are. What explains this? Conditions of possibilities for these last two interpretive repertoires were enabled later in women-in-management discourses and *solidified* the gendering of neoliberalism.

Corporate Feminism Redux

Psychologically oriented literature emphasizing stereotypes and other cognitive processes disadvantaging women's careers continued at steady pace, but a significant reorientation happened in the 1990s. While earlier literature argued that women's assumed differences (from men) were a problem accounting for their difficulties in reaching leadership positions, a new literature was emerging arguing that such differences were a positive "female advantage"—in a nod to the increasingly ascendant rhetoric of "competitive advantage" (Porter, 1985).

As mentioned, in the 1980s liberal feminism had taken a turn to clarify that women did not need to claim equality with men on the basis of "sameness" (a biological or socialization argument) but on the basis of "gender justice" (a legal status) recognizing women's (gender/race/sexuality) differences (e.g., Friedan, 1981), but in the popular imagination this complicated rights-based liberal humanist argument was barely noticed. It was overshadowed by influences from Carol Gilligan's (1982) psycho-moral feminist research on developmental differences between males and females in their approaches to moral judgment—*not superior or inferior but different.*

The "female advantage" as it relates to management (Helgesen, 1990), was born in the aftermath of Gilligan's work, probably receiving some reflected legitimization as consequence of this important research. Yet the subtleties of Gilligan's argument were mostly lost in their managerial applications, often becoming unmoored from her actual research. Re-valuing formerly devalued women's female/feminine characteristics as of benefit for management and organizations transformed Gilligan's "ethics of care" into a new tool for women-in-management research and practice (e.g., Liedtka, 1999; Rosener, 1990). Women's "difference" became female traits enhancing the competitive advantage of corporations, and an essentialized "female advantage" became a secret weapon in the globalization competitive milieu (e.g., Jelinek and Adler, 1988; Rosener, 1995).

The instrumental use of these ideas did not go without critique even from within the management literature in the United States, in particular from feminist gender and organization scholarship developing at this time (Calás and Smircich, 1993; Fletcher, 1994; Fondas, 1997). Yet, critiques notwithstanding, women's "differences" as positive traits continues to appear in women-in-management academic research on leadership and other topics (e.g., Kark, Waismel-Manor and Shamir, 2012) and, under premises of "feminist perspectives", to explain for instance, women entrepreneurs' choices about the growth and profitability of their businesses (Buttner and Moore, 1997; Morris et al., 2006). Positive women's "differences" is also the assumption behind developing women's entrepreneurship in recent poverty alleviation projects in the Global South, as discussed (e.g., Prügl, 2015; Tornhill, 2016).

Further, and key to our arguments, the "female advantage" facilitated making the "business case" for women leaders under an *almost feminist* mantle (e.g., Shrader, Blackburn, and Iles, 1997), naturalizing market logic to the point that nothing but women's quantifiable market value could be taken into account (see also Waddock, 2016), That is, the "female advantage" became "priced", justifying "women at the top" in corporate positions not on the basis of rights but on the basis of benefits they would accrue to firms' financial performance. This thinking has extended to research on women entrepreneurs, identifying women with graduate education—not exactly lower-class women—as those capable to "break through to equity financing" (Carter et al., 2003), thus echoing those elite women entrepreneurs in the original "glass ceiling" article.

There is much to critique about this turn of events, starting from the notable absence of a parallel literature justifying "men at the top" based on firm financial performance (e.g., Hoobler et al., 2016). More notable, though, contemporary "corporate feminism", and the neoliberal logic behind it, was in fact ratified by the commoditization of women's "difference" under the aegis of a feminist sensibility. The appendix included in *Lean In* cited much women-in-management research emphasizing women's difference, making it possible for that book—and similar books and articles- to become best sellers. Yet, *Lean In* said nothing new, but said it when many would want to believe it, still looking for something to explain and remedy ongoing gender inequality without discarding meritocratic illusions. One could see, thus, the naked articulation of the subject of neoliberalism normalizing this logic: certain women becoming powerful agents of their own destiny—they themselves a business as per Gershon's (2011)—marketing their entrepreneurial subjectivities as *corporate individualism*.

Where does this leave Gill et al.'s (2017) interpretive repertoires, noting that women in their examples often saw themselves as the advantaged sex, and accepted the status quo as just how workplaces are? In light of our discussion, it would not be surprising if these women already had sufficient taken for granted "female advantage" cultural lexicon from which to draw. A more interesting twist in these examples, however, is the acceptance of the status quo in relational patterns between men and women "young professionals".

In the context of the early 1980s, Gordon noted that to enter the business world both women and men "must shed" their politics, emotions, ideals while also standardizing their attitudes, behaviors and skills, and "[w]omen must become company women because there is nothing left to be" (1983: 5). While we can see the heritage in this line of discourse, and the din of neoliberalism playing in the background, Gill et al.'s recent examples require considering *what has happened through the spread of neoliberalism between then and now*. The conformity highlighted by Gordon in the 1980s might have had then a hopeful element for a better future since neoliberalism's advent was just congealing. Meanwhile, the precariousness of employment and other negative market conditions impelled by neoliberalism *since then and manifested at present*—when things should have been better—clearly do not bode well for contemporary "young professionals", and, therefore, their conformity or indifference: "The status quo as just how workplaces are" (Gill et al., 2017: 1).

Humanist Postfeminism: (In)difference or Survival?

However, we think there is more than indifference or conformity to be read in these recent examples. Gill et al.'s discussions, and critical analyses of *postfeminism as cultural manifestation* more generally, tend to describe the subjects of the discourse as unable to recognize the predicaments in which they find themselves—i.e., having become the subjects of neoliberalism or almost having been duped into it. To counter this tendency we offer other possible interpretations:

What if these examples demonstrate more cynical responses to the workings of neoliberalism? Isn't it possible that both women and men are clear in that precarious labor markets require "conforming" as a reasonable response? What about the possibility that such conforming constitutes women's strategies for surviving inequalities precisely by activating stereotypical versions of femininity? Aren't they appropriating the tools of neoliberalism by activating the "market value" of "the female advantage" while embodying, as suggested by Kara (2016: 17), a minimal "ethic of vulnerability" when recognizing the uncertainty of things that they cannot control?

Further, something else may be happening now perhaps captured in critiques of the *Lean In* book: many others would no longer buy into the neoliberal "logic". Beyond her irony, Foster's (2013) outburst of exasperation may say it all:

> If you just try, if you aspire, you and your hardworking family can have that great job and home life that Sandberg and Yahoo's CEO Marissa Mayer sell to us. Focusing on individual success stories, rather than structural inequality, is politically helpful to the Conservative squeeze on living standards. So if you're languishing at the bottom of the corporate ladder rather than hammering on the glass ceiling, well, that's because you didn't want it enough.

Said differently, contemporary "corporate feminism" is *a* humanist postfeminism reiterating neoliberalism; it is also women-in-management discourse repeated once again. What has changed, however, is that some are noting this repetition and not taking it anymore. Importantly, Foster was pointing explicitly to *the farce* of individual rights moralism at the core of what makes the discourse of neoliberalism still possible (e.g., Massey, 2014).

Thus, are we possibly at a moment of discontent eroding neoliberalism, and routine observations miss new forms of agency this discontent is provoking (e.g., Hall, Massey, and Rustin, 2014)? Perhaps new social movements, postfeminist included, are emerging as the curtains obscuring the workings of neoliberalism become transparent to many more (e.g., Schlosberg and Coles, 2016). And so, maybe the humanist postfeminism we followed throughout the chapter is not a last (human) gasp keeping intact the world we have now but a parody of its old self—liberal feminism—needed for survival when extinction, metaphorically and materially, is the other alternative. Something else may be brewing at present beyond McRobbie's (2015) pessimistic assessment of contemporary (post)feminist movements as still under the weight of neoliberalism.

Whatever may be brewing, though, may pass us by if we continue to produce knowledge about the present as we have been doing so far (e.g., Ergene, Calás, and Smircich, 2017). Despite our introductory arguments, it seems all our observations and commentaries thus far have been little more than *an incessant repetition and critique* of "the world that we know" and from which we seem unable to escape; this includes observations on the co-productions of the women-in-management discourse and the contemporary neoliberal political economy. Simply "observing" and "commenting", we argue, may be untenable at this time—the Anthropocene—when *new positive figurations* in our research and theorizing are needed. Can we imagine more-than-human subjects (Gibson-Graham, 2011; Gibson-Graham and Roelvink, 2009; Whatmore, 2013) and more-than-capitalist economies (Gibson-Graham, 2014) as representations of "the real"? What kind of "subjects" would allow for doing so? And for what reasons? Consistent with our arguments, *what kind of postfeminism(s) might be thus emerging* (e.g., McNeil, 2010)?

A Future Unlike the Present?

Kara's (2016) analyses of anthropocenema opened a door for moving toward answering these questions. In the prior section, his arguments brought us to search for other interpretations of contemporary humanist postfeminism as subversive rather than stereotypical gender performance under neoliberal regimes; however, we still need to *imagine* what else may be happening.

As noted, from conventional viewers' perspective the female protagonists—the survivors—exhibited stereotypically feminine traits, but Kara's analyses show these as embodiments of an ethic of vulnerability and part of their *survive-ability*. Engaged *with* end-of-the-world scenarios, the protagonists accepted the uncertainty of things they couldn't control *and* recognized the agencies of nature and nonhumans as actors—a form of embodiment of humans intermeshed with a more-than-human world. The films also constituted a political engagement and a response to macho neoliberalism. The central positioning of female characters as vulnerable but also as those who survive *with nature and others* could be read as disavowing, "an aggressive environmental politics that responds to ecological threats with destructive technofixes (often associated with masculinity and colonial attitudes)" (2016: 17).

These scenarios thus open up a wider space for reading what is happening now. They exemplify *reading differently* to imagine the happenings of a different world, different from articulations of a "conventional viewer" and requiring different ontological understandings. Such understandings, deriving from what is now known as *new materialisms* and its corollary *ontological turn*, are recognizable in Kara's analyses, focusing on *matter* and *materialization* as ontologically real and co-emergent in constant relational processes including humans and everything else. Importantly, new materialisms' arguments are not primarily about differences in discourse (or interpretations), but about the necessity for paying attention to real manifestations of *"what is going on"* (processes) in contrast to *"what is"* (objectified) in "conventional views". Differences in vocabulary articulate the immanent complexity of what is happening around us and within/between us as part of everyday life: all of these *matter(s)*.

Conventional views, are of course what one would consider "normal interpretations", but these are only so because of their mooring in the ontological premises of liberal humanism, whether "conservative" or "critical". Thus, the emphasis on an ontological turn beyond humanism is also about possibilities for a more complicated understanding of what is going on in the world, taking notice of what our conventional views may be missing. Ironically, one could say that neoliberal humanism, in its (economic) reductionism, brought us *to imagining* (and acting upon) a world that never was (and that would never become), while "new materialisms", no matter how strange these may sound, are bringing us *back to reality*.

Thus, this last section articulates an explicit space where things are happening in the larger context of contemporary culture/society/economy; an eventful space, where many new entities are emerging, including ontological/epistemological tools to articulate the advent of such entities. These tools, *new materialist* writings, most of them feminist and several attending explicitly to the Anthropocene, make it possible to imagine new figurations.

A Few Notes on "New Materialisms"

These notes, a *simple* practical device, may help making sense of our final arguments. As such, our gesture here is contradictory to the complexities we are trying to imagine. But if you are not yet conversant with these ideas, the notes also serve as suggestions for further reading.[3] If you are already "in the know", it is ok to move on to the next subsection.

Explanations about the advent of "new materialisms" point to current advances in the natural sciences and technology (e.g., new physics and biology; digital and virtual technologies) requiring questioning prior underlying beliefs about oneself, and about relations to others and to everything else. Coole and Frost (2010) note the emergence of pressing ethical and political concerns accompanying these scientific and technological advances, predicated on "new scientific models of matter and, in particular, living matter" (5), and thus a "materialist turn". In this context, environmental issues loom large—e.g., the growing literature on the Anthropocene—but also everyday issues such as work practices, food, recreation, and procreation requiring new thinking "about the nature of matter and the matter of nature; about the elements of life, the resilience of the planet, and the distinctiveness of the human" (6). Human agency is also being rethought, as well as notions of causation employed by humans to support the reasons for their actions. And there are concerns that constructivist approaches to social analysis and poststructuralist cultural and discursive orientations are insufficient for engaging with "the real" in the contemporary global political economy.

Coole and Frost (2010) identify three interrelated themes in new materialist scholarship: a posthumanist orientation conceiving of matter itself as lively and agentic, a focus on bioethical and biopolitical issues regarding life beyond the human and a critical reengagement with political economy, exploring relationships between everyday life and geopolitical and socioeconomic structures. This scholarship, usually interdisciplinary and from very early including feminist contributions, cuts across the social and natural sciences, the humanities and technology (for reviews, see Alaimo and Hekman [2008]; Åsberg et al. [2016]; Coleman [2014]; Frost [2011]; and for some debates, see Irni [2013]; and Washick et al. [2015]). All three themes share an emphasis on *processes of materialization* as complex, pluralistic and relatively open, and insist that humans—and, very important for our arguments—"*including theorists themselves*, be recognized as thoroughly immersed within materiality's productive contingencies" (Coole and Frost, 2010: 7, our emphasis). The latter point focuses on productive contingencies of matter existing beyond human control and brings in notions of responsibility emphasizing humility as a check on human's (including scholarly) hubris: What kind of knowledge are we (humans) producing? What claims are we making with it? And on what (ontological) basis?

The ontological rethinking that new materialisms bring about is from the start inimical to the dualisms pervading humanist philosophies and modernity in general—much like poststructuralisms and anti-essentialist feminisms—but does so in a materialist realist mode. For instance, " 'new materialist' approaches in feminist and political theory share a commitment to troubling those binaries central to humanist inquiry, for example, sensuous/ideal, natural/artificial, subject/object" but also "compel a rethinking of the boundary between human and nonhuman" (Washick et al., 2015: 63). The world presupposed by these arguments is made up of generative flows of matter, intensities and speeds, as ongoing processes of materialization of ever changing forms that occasionally congeal before they change again. These processes are ontologically co-emergences through human and nonhuman activity in heterogenous formations of their more-than-human relationships—i.e., *human/nonhuman assemblages*. Spinoza's monist philosophy and the work of Deleuze and Guattari (1987) are often associated with these notions; also Latour's works since 1993, and Haraway's (e.g., 2003).

Assemblages blur boundaries between bodies, objects and contexts; they are multiple and complex systems in constant relational flux; and their components, human and nonhuman are not static but engaged in ongoing ontological processes immanent to their co-production—i.e., incessant processes of *becoming*. When referred to as *posthuman*, it means primarily that these notions are no longer attached to humanist philosophies privileging the human, and can be considered anti-anthropocentric. They decenter notions of humanity where human individuals embody independent agency and are capable of predicting and controlling the consequences of their actions, including control over other humans and over the nonhuman world—i.e., liberal humanism (see McNeil (2010)).

Producing Subjects With/out a Cause?

Thinking *of* assemblages as posthuman subject beckons ecological thinking—the ecologies of assemblages as such, rather than their *fleetingly independent* components. Bennett (2010) calls for an ecological sensibility, since all matter is vibrant and agency becomes distributed throughout human/nonhuman collectivities, while Coole (2013), suggests rejecting a reified notion of agency—abstract individualism in liberalism—and thinking *with* new materialisms's notion of *agentic capacities*. Here agency becomes diffused across different types of material entities—assemblages' *distributed agency*—decoupling "agency from humans while raising questions about the nature of life and of the place or status of the human within it" (458). Thinking agency this way does not absolve humans from the consequences of their actions. While "new materialist ontology emphasizes the lack of control humans exercise over the complex systems with which they are melded" for that same reason they should become materially more accountable "for the destructiveness they are wreaking on vulnerable ecosystems" (461–462).

Thinking *with* assemblages' distributed agency complicates notions of causation. Frost (2011) writes explicitly on implications for conventional linear models of explanation, such as effects of power or power relations, with only humans taken into account. If culture and biology have reciprocal effects, or matter and biology are active in their own right, then causation must be "conceived as complex, recursive, and multi-linear" (71). Thinking in these terms, where complexity, interdependence, and ecology is the norm, asks for acknowledging "a zone of necessary ignorance" as well as for "epistemological and political humility" acknowledging full and definitive knowledge as impossible, and abandoning teleological assumptions that eventually humans "will achieve full mastery over ourselves and the world around us" (2011: 79). Frost calls for a feminist response—such as Barad's (2003, 2007)—to conventional (and privileged) notions of causation, because of their reductionism and simplification. What is required is "the specification and elaboration of the complex, creative, and sometimes surprising interplay between biology and culture" (80).

Here methodology also matters. New materialist analyses require multimodal methodologies, capable of tracing the complex interplay between the materiality and materialization of everyday life and that of large socioeconomic processes such as global capitalism (Coole and Frost, 2010). Coole (2013) highlights Latour's approach to Actor-Network theory (e.g., 2005) as appropriate, maintaining the irreducibility of hybrid human-nonhuman assemblages constantly emerging and transforming, and promoting notions of transversal or flat ontologies as horizontal planes of action where no entity is privileged a priori over others (see Calás, Ergene, and Smircich [2018 forthcoming] for an organizational example).

Finally, the term "affect" appears often in new materialisms writings but it is not equivalent to humanist notions such as "feelings" and "emotions" in feminist literatures from the "affective turn" (e.g., Kennelly (2014) on young women's social movements).[4] Latimer and Miele's (2013) introduction to articles addressing relations between humans and nonhumans in the production of scientific knowledge, clarifies more generally *new materialisms' notions of affect*. Here, *affect* is not understood first as emotion or sentiment, but as "attachment" and being "moved". "Emotion" is individuated, while "affect" is embodied interdependently and relationally. Thus, in assemblages one is *being affected and moved* by attachments/detachments to/from other bodies (human and nonhuman) and, reciprocally, so are they.

Concepts of affect such as these have implications for rethinking economic notions and practices. Gibson-Graham (2011) and Gibson-Graham and Roelvink (2009) use the notion "learning to be affected" from Latour (2004) to rethink in new materialist terms their long-standing Community Economies projects,[5] re-imagining economic possibilities for the Anthropocene in a more-than-human and, later, in a more-than-capitalist world (Gibson-Graham, 2014). Foregrounding "learning to be affected" highlights that

> we are created as bodies/beings by the entirety of human and non-human conditions of the world that affect us and from which we learn—if we are open to doing so [. . .] this learning is a process of coconstitution (sic) that produces a new body-world.
>
> (2009: 322)

Important for our arguments, conditions of possibility for re-imagining and remaking these economic projects in new materialist terms emerge as activism in academic research, with hybrid research collectives (human-nonhuman) at the center of change. Here *academic* functions less as critique (or observation, or commentary) of *what has already happened*, adopting instead an experimental stance to *learn from what is already happening*, previously occluded by conventional habits of observation and explanation. Gibson-Graham and Roelvink (2009) assert, "We are being called to read the potentially positive futures barely visible in the present order of things and to imagine how to strengthen and move them along" (:342). Thus, hybrid research collectives make all (human-nonhuman) *subjects with a cause*. What other hybrid subjects with a cause might be out there if we care to learn (to be affected) *with* what is already happening? And, what about postfeminisms?

Posthumanist (Post)feminist Organizing: Environmentalism, New Generations, Imaginaries

A special section in *Feminist Theory* on new materialisms and feminisms (Fannin et al., 2014), noted from the start that notions of postfeminism, even as critique, misrecognize the vibrancy of contemporary feminist activism, including social movements and scholarship. Accordingly,

> [t]he recent resurgence of activism by young women in the UK and beyond demonstrates the limitations of this [postfeminist] narrative, and the dangers of moving too quickly [. . .] to classify and categorise the lively and creative energies of a movement that encompasses and seeks to transform all domains of life.
>
> (261–262)

Forwarding explicitly new materialist theorizations, the articles included empirical examples such as the Young Women's Group's allotment[6] project in the United Kingdom (Moore et al., 2014), following happenings in one allotment garden and the young women and others who cultivate it. The article's framing develops "privatepublic naturecultures" as neologisms (Haraway, 2003), and its writing style reiterates ontological emergings from human/nonhuman engagements in the allotment space: "a shadow world, temporarily recedes into the corner of one's eye, and for a while a different world, an everyday utopia of an almost unimaginable intimate privatepublic natureculture, comes into being" (340).

Similarly, Schlosberg and Coles (2016) highlight a range of social movements offering new modes of organizing and ways of democratic living, all of them based in re-formed relations between humans and between them and the natural world. Oriented with new materialisms premises, these movements represent an environmentalism of everyday life "a new politics of sustainable materialism" (161) flowing through human/nonhuman communities. These movements, now widespread and growing in developed economies but also appearing in developing ones, include, for instance, collective food systems enacting new models for the circulation of agriculture and food; and community energy cooperatives "linking new flows of energy, finance, technology and political communities to resist and create alternatives to the mega-circulations of the carbon industry" (164). Also, community movements proliferating around crafting and *making* include what is dubbed as "the new domesticity", often criticized as renouncing gains from feminism, (e.g., Matchar, 2013). However, Schlosberg and Coles further specify that crafting and "the new domesticity" are based on both postfeminist and postpunk do-it-yourself movements, and often complemented by technology making movements (e.g. open source), enabling empowering movements disarticulating corporate-promoted consumerism.

Further, fostering *making*, including crafts, Carr and Gibson (2016) reiterate that amidst increasingly volatile environmental futures, maker cultures cultivate community, networks and connections between producers and consumers, informing as well "localized responses to climate change framed around resource preservation and stewardship" (2016: 300), and enabling possibilities for resisting gender norms and neoliberal entrepreneurial subjectivities. In fact, Schlosberg and Coles emphasize that the movement groups they studied are noting that current practices of everyday life "weaken the capacities of selves, human communities, and human-ecological assemblages alike" thus these groups "begin to question the daily participation in social and material practices that have led us to our current predicament" (2016: 178). Altogether, these often younger and more inventive communities enable human-nonhuman entities by valuing knowing and doing, reclaiming processes of material life and disconnecting from the mega-circulation of global capitalism.

Catastrophe and Hope?

By bringing in these examples we are joining others already noting that people (across generations, but younger ones in particular) are yearning for ways to engage and contend against current circumstances, environmental problems explicitly included, as makings of neoliberal global regimes (complex and multiple) with their relentless prodding of production-consumption cycles at a global scale. Aspects of our examples sound very familiar, evoking perhaps bucolic narratives of a past era. Thinking that, however, is another intrusion by our conventional humanist past. These literatures produce hopeful ways to engage (thinking and doing) with where we are now, and to avoid repeating ourselves in grandiose masculinist technofixes that humans can hardly control; they are the narratives of those able to survive while exhibiting an ethic of vulnerability.

Thus, if we care and learn to be affected by present happenings, there will be assemblages in our future: groups and communities human-nonhuman, at first look as if they don't amount to much, but on second look, their transversal connections among and between entities are already inventing what perhaps ends up being the only livable futures after neoliberal global regimes implode. This future may not happen, though, unless our scholarship is able to represent and claim conditions of possibility already in the offing for new figurations to appear. In so doing, we are highlighting the ontological potential, already there, for the (be)coming of a posthuman postfeminism. Feminism always already becomes inventive (Coleman, 2014), and thus always already becomes *post*, at this moment posthuman, otherwise we couldn't be having this conversation. And, to circle back to where we started, this conversation is also a response to Grosz's request "to enable more action, more making and doing, more difference [. . .] to enable women to partake in the creation of a future unlike the present" (2010: 154). There is much more to write/do in this regard, but that will become another making.

Notes

1 The development of women-in-management research in the US business schools paralleled the development of voluminous literature on sex segregation in organizations mostly within US sociology departments (e.g. Bielby and Baron, 1984; Reskin and Hartmann, 1986) seldom crossing over to business schools.
2 Fisher's (2012) ethnography of the pioneering generation of Wall Street women uses 'market feminism' IN A DIFFERENT SENSE to describe these women's activities.
3 We suggest reading first Coole and Frost's (2010) collection—their introduction in particular—and then Bennett (2010) and Braidotti (2013).
4 Newer works in organization studies with new materialist inflections are attempting to escape these strictures (e.g. Ashcraft, 2017; Pullen et al., 2017).
5 Actual alternative economies, research and projects originally framed through feminist post-Marxist imaginaries (e.g. Gibson-Graham, 2006) www.communitye conomies.org/Home.
6 Tracts of land for city residents to cultivate, codified in modern UK law as public obligation responding to the enclosures of common land in eighteenth and nineteenth centuries.

References

Abramovitz, M., and Hopkins, T. (1983). Reaganomics and the Welfare State. *Journal of Sociology & Social Welfare*, 10(4): 563.
Acker J. (2004). Gender, capitalism and globalization. *Critical Sociology*, 30(1): 17–41.
Adamson, M. (2017). Postfeminism, neoliberalism and a :successfully" balanced femininity in celebrity CEO autobiographies. *Gender, Work & Organization*, 24(3): 314–327.
Ahlers, R., and Zwarteveen, M. (2009). The water question in feminism: water control and gender inequities in a neo-liberal era. *Gender, Place and Culture*, 16(4): 409–426.
Alaimo, S., and Hekman, S. (Eds.). (2008). *Material Feminisms*. Bloomington, IN: Indiana University Press.
Åsberg, C., Lorenz-Meyer, D., Fredengren, C., Sõrmus, M. and Treusch, P. (2016). Anthropocene ecologies: Biogeotechnical relationalities in late capitalism. *New Materialism Cost Action*, 1307.
Ashcraft, K.L. (2017). "Submission" to the rule of excellence: Ordinary affect and precarious resistance in the labor of organization and management studies. *Organization*, 24(1): 36–58.

Banks, J., and. Zimmerman, P.R. (1987). The Mary Kay way: The feminization of a corporate discourse. *Journal of Communication Inquiry*, 11(1): 85–99.

Barad, K. (2003). Posthumanist performativity: Toward an understanding of how matter comes to matter. *SIGNS: Journal of Women in Culture and Society*, 28(3): 801–831.

Barad, K. (2007). *Meeting the Universe Halfway: Quantum Physics and the Entanglement of Matter and Meaning*. Durham: Duke University Press.

Bartol, K.M. (1978). The sex structuring of organizations: A search for possible causes. *Academy of Management Review*, 3(4): 805–815.

Bem, S.L., and Lenney, E. (1976). Sex typing and the avoidance of cross-sex behavior. *Journal of Personality and Social Psychology*, 33(1): 48–54.

Bennett, J. (2010). *Vibrant Matter: A Political Ecology of Things*. Durham: Duke University Press.

Beutell, N.J., and Greenhaus, J.H. (1983). Integration of home and nonhome roles: Women's conflict and coping behavior. *Journal of Applied Psychology*, 68(1): 43.

Bielby, W.T., and Baron, J.N. (1984). A woman's place is with other women: Sex segregation within organizations. In B.F. Reskin (Ed.), *Sex Segregation in the Workplace: Trends, Explanations, Remedies* (pp. 27–55). Washington, DC: National Academies Press.

Blum, L., and Smith, V. (1988). Women's mobility in the corporation: A critique of the politics of optimism. *Signs*, 13(3): 528–545.

Braidotti, R. (2013). *The Posthuman*. Hoboken, NJ: Wiley.

Braje, T.J. (2015). Earth systems, human agency, and the Anthropocene: Planet Earth in the human age. *Journal of Archaeological Research*, 23(4): 369–396.

Butler, J. (1990). *Gender Trouble: Feminism and the Subversion of Identity*. London: Routledge.

Buttner, E.H., and Moore, D.P. (1997). Women's organizational exodus to entrepreneurship: self—reported motivations and correlates with success. *Journal of Small Business Management*, 35(1):34.

Calás, M.B., Ergene, S., and Smircich, L. (forthcoming 2018). Becoming possible in the Anthropocene? Becomingsocialentrepreneurship as more-than-capitalist practice. In P. Dey and C. Steyaert (Eds.), *Social Entrepreneurship: An Affirmative Critique* (Ch. 15). Cheltenham, UK: Edward Elgar.

Calás, M.B., Ou, H., and Smircich, L. (2013). "Woman" on the move: Mobile subjectivities after intersectionality. *Equality, Diversity and Inclusion*, 32(8): 708–731.

Calás, M.B., and Smircich, L. (1993). Dangerous liaisons: The "feminine-in-management" meets "globalization". *Business Horizons*, 36(2): 71–81.

Calás, M.B., and Smircich, L. (1996). From "the woman's' point of view": Feminist approaches to organization studies. In S.R. Clegg, C. Hardy, and W.R. Nord (Eds.), *The Handbook of Organization Studies* (pp. 218–257). London: Sage.

Calás, M.B., and Smircich, L. (2006). From the "woman's point of view" ten years later: Towards a feminist organization studies. In S. Clegg, C. Hardy, W. Nord, and T. Lawrence (Eds.), *Handbook of Organization Studies* (2nd edition, pp. 284–346). London: Sage.

Calás, M.B., and Smircich, L. (2014). Engendering the organizational: Organization studies and feminist theorizing. In P.S. Adler, P. du Gay, G. Morgan, and M. Reed (Eds.), *The Oxford Handbook of Sociology, Social Theory and Organization Studies: Contemporary Currents* (pp. 605–659). London: Oxford University Press.

Calás, M.B., Smircich, L., and Bourne, K. (2009). Extending the boundaries: Reframing entrepreneurship as social change from feminist perspectives. *Academy of Management Review*, 34(3): 552–569.

Calás, M.B., Smircich, L., and Holvino, E. (2014). Theorizing gender-and-organization: Changing times. . . . changing theories? In S. Kumra, R. Simpson, and R. Burke (Eds.), *The Oxford Handbook of Gender in Organizations* (pp. 17–52). London: Oxford University Press.

Calkin, S. (2015). Feminism, interrupted? Gender and development in the era of "smart economics". *Progress in Development Studies*, 15(4): 295–307.

Carr, C., and Gibson, C. (2016). Geographies of making: Rethinking materials and skills for volatile futures. *Progress in Human Geography*, 40(3): 297–315.

Carter, N., Brush, C., Greene, P., Gatewood, E., and Hart, M. (2003). Women entrepreneurs who break through to equity financing: the influence of human, social and financial capital. *Venture Capital: An International Journal of Entrepreneurial Finance*, 5(1): 1–28.

Centeno, M.A. and Cohen, J.N. (2012). The arc of neoliberalism. *Annual Review of Sociology*, 38: 317–340.

Chapman, J.B. (1975). Comparison of male and female leadership styles. *Academy of Management Journal*, 18: 645–650.

Clarke, S. (2005). The neoliberal theory of society. In A. Saad-Filho and D. Johnston (Eds.), *Neoliberalism-A Critical Reader* (pp. 50-59). London: Pluto Press.

Cockburn, C. (1991). *In the Way of Women: Men's Resistance to Sex Equality in Organizations*. Ithaca: Cornell University Press.

Coleman, R. (2014). Inventive feminist theory: Representation, materiality and intensive time. *Women: A Cultural Review*, 25(1): 27–45.

Coole, D. (2013). Agentic capacities and capacious historical materialism: Thinking with new materialisms in the political sciences. *Millennium: Journal of International Studies*, 41(3): 451–469.

Coole, D., and Frost, S. (2010). *New Materialisms: Ontology, Agency, and Politics*. Durham, NC: Duke University Press.

Deckha, M. (2016). Animal bodies, technobodies: New directions in cultural studies, feminism, and posthumanism. *Yale Journal of Law & Feminism*, 20(2): 7.

Deleuze, G., and Guattari, F. (1987). *A Thousand Plateaus: Capitalism and Schizophrenia*. Minneapolis: University of Minnesota Press.

Eisenstein, H. (2005). A dangerous liaison? Feminism and corporate globalization. *Science & Society*, 69(3): 487–518.

Eisenstein, H. (2009). *Feminism Seduced*. Boulder: Paradigm.

Elias, J. (2013). Davos woman to the rescue of global capitalism: Postfeminist politics and competitiveness promotion at the World Economic Forum. *International Political Sociology*, 7: 152–169.

Ergene, S., Calás, M.B., and Smircich, L. (2017, in press). Ecologies of sustainable concerns: Organization theorizing for the Anthropocene. *Gender, Work & Organization*. Special Issue "Gendering sustainability, the environment and organization".

Evans, J. (1995). *Feminist Theory Today*. London: Sage.

Fannin, M., MacLeavy, J., Larner, W., and Wang, W.W. (2014). Work, life, bodies: New materialisms and feminisms. *Feminist Theory*, 15(3): 261–268.

Fisher, M.S. (2012). *Wall Street Women*. Durham: Duke University Press.

Fletcher, J.K. (1994). Castrating the female advantage: Feminist standpoint research and management science. *Journal of Management Inquiry*, 3(1): 74–82.

Fondas, N. (1997). Feminization unveiled: Management qualities in contemporary writings. *Academy of Management Review*, 22(1): 257–282.

Foster, D. (2013). Why corporate feminism is convenient for capitalism. *TheGuardian.com* Wednesday 11 December.

Frank, A.G. (1981). After Reaganomics and Thatcherism, what? From Keynesian demand management via supply-side economics to corporate state planning and 1984. *Contemporary Marxism*, 4: 18–28.

Fraser, N. (2009). Feminism, capitalism and the cunning of history. *New Left Review*, 56: 97–117.

Fraser, N. (2013). *Fortunes of Feminism: From State-managed Capitalism to Neoliberal Crisis*. London: Verso Books.

Friedan, B. (1981). *The Second Stage*. New York: Summit Books.Frost, S. (2011) The implications of the new materialisms for feminist epistemology. In H.E. Grasswick (Ed.), *Feminist Epistemology and Philosophy of Science: Power in Knowledge* (pp. 69–83). Netherlands: Springer.

Frost, S. (2011). The implications of the new materialisms for feminist epistemology. In H.E. Grasswick (Ed.), *Feminist Epistemology and Philosophy of Science: Power in Knowledge* (pp. 69–83). Netherlands: Springer.

Gershon, I. (2011). Neoliberal agency. *Current Anthropology*, 52(4): 537–555.

Gibson-Graham, J.K. (2006). *A Postcapitalist Politics*. Minneapolis, MN: University of Minnesota Press.

Gibson-Graham, J.K. (2011). A feminist project of belonging for the Anthropocene. *Gender, Place & Culture*, 18(1): 1–21.

Gibson-Graham, J.K. (2014). Being the revolution, or, how to live in a "more-than-capitalist" world threatened with extinction. *Rethinking Marxism: A Journal of Economics, Culture & Society*, 26(1): 76–94.

Gibson-Graham, J.K., and Roelvink, G. (2009). An economic ethics for the Anthropocene. *Antipode*, 41(s1): 320–346.

Gill, R. (2007). Postfeminist media culture: Elements of a sensibility, *European Journal of Cultural Studies*, 10(2): 147–166.

Gill, R. (2016). Post-postfeminism? New feminist visibilities in postfeminist times. *Feminist Media Studies*, 16(4): 610–630.

Gill, R., Kelan, E.K., and Scharff, C.M. (2017). A postfeminist sensibility at work. *Gender, Work & Organization*, 24(3): 226–244.

Gilligan, C. (1982). *In a Different Voice: Psychological Theory and Women's Development*. Cambridge, MA: Harvard University Press.

Gordon, S. (1983). Dressed for success: The new corporate feminism. *The University News*, iii(ii) (6–12 April): 1, 5. Boise State University ScholarWorks Reprinted from The Nation, 1(5 February): 143.

Gray, J. (1995). *Liberalism*. Buckingham: Open University Press.

Grozs, E. (2010). Feminism, materialism, freedom. In B. Coole and S. Frost (Eds.), *New Materialisms: Ontology, Agency, and Politics* (pp. 139–157). Durham: Duke University Press.

Grusin, R. (2017). *Anthropocene Feminism*. Minneapolis: University of Minnesota Press.

Hall, S., Massey, D., and Rustin, M. (Eds.). (2014). After neoliberalism? The kilburn manifesto. *Soundings*. Open source, available at: www.lwbooks.co.uk/journals/soundings/manifesto.html/

Haraway, D. (2003). *The Companion Species Manifesto: Dogs, People, and Significant Otherness* (Vol. 1). Chicago: Prickly Paradigm Press.

Harvey, D. (2005). *A Brief History of Neoliberalism*. Oxford: Oxford University Press.

Heilman, M.E., and Martell, R.F. (1986). Exposure to successful women: Antidote to sex discrimination in applicant screening decisions? *Organizational Behavior and Human Decision Processes*, 37(3): 376–390.

Helgesen, S. (1990). *The Female Advantage: Women's Ways of Leading*. New York: Doubleday Currency.

Hennig, M., and Jardim, A. (1977). *The Managerial Woman*. Garden City, NY: Anchor Press/Doubleday.

Hird, M. (2013). Waste, landfills, and an environmental ethic of vulnerability. *Ethics and the Environment*, 18(1): 105–124.

Hisrich, R., and Brush, C. (1984). The woman entrepreneur: Management skills and business problems. *Journal of Small Business Management*, 22(1): 30–37.

Hoobler, J.M., Masterson, C.R., Nkomo, S.M., and Michel, E.J. (2016). The business case for women leaders: Meta-analysis, research critique and path forward. *Journal of Management*. DOI: 10.1177/0149206316628643.

Hymowitz, C., and Schellhardt, T.D. (1986). The glass ceiling: Why women can't seem to break the invisible barrier that blocks them from the top jobs. *The Wall Street Journal*, 24(March): 1.

Irni, S. (2013). The politics of materiality: Affective encounters in a transdisciplinary debate. *European Journal of Women's Studies*, 20(4): 347–360.

Jaggar, A. (1983). *Feminist Politics and Human Nature*. Lanham, MD: Rowman and Littlefield.

Jelinek, M., and Adler, N.J. (1988). Women: World class managers for global competition. *Academy of Management Executive*, 2(1): 11–19.

Kalleberg, A.L. (2009). Precarious work, insecure workers: Employment relations in transition. (2008 Presidential Address), *American Sociological Review*, 74: 1–22.

Kanter, R.M. (1977). *Men and Women of the Corporation*. New York: Basic.Kara, S. (2016) Antropocenema: Cinema in the age of mass extinctions. In S. Denson and J. Leyda (Eds.), *Post-Cinema: Theorizing 21st-Century Film*. University of Sussex: REFRAME Books.

Kark, R., Waismel-Manor, R., and Shamir, B. (2012). Does valuing androgyny and femininity lead to a female advantage? The relationship between gender-role, transformational leadership and identification. *The Leadership Quarterly*, 23(3): 620–640.

Kay, K., and Shipman, C. (2014). The confidence gap. *The Atlantic*, 14: 1–18.

Keating, C., Rasmussen, C., and Rishi, P. (2010). The rationality of empowerment: Microcredit, accumulation by dispossession, and the gendered economy. *Signs: Journal of Women in Culture and Society*, 36(1): 153–176.

Kennelly J. (2014). "It's this pain in my heart that won't let me stop": Gendered affect, webs of relations, and young women's activism. *Feminist Theory*, 15(3): 241–260.

Konrad, A.M., and Gutek, B.A. (1986). Impact of work experiences on attitudes toward sexual harassment. *Administrative Science Quarterly*, (September): 422–438.

Kotz, D.M. (2002). Globalization and neoliberalism. *Rethinking Marxism*, 12(2): 64–79.

Latimer, J., and Miele, M. (2013). Naturecultures? Science, affect, and the non-human. *Theory, Culture & Society*, 30(7-8): 5–31.

Latour, B. (2004). How to talk about the body? The normative dimension of science studies. *Body & Society*, 10(2–3): 205–229.

Latour, B. (2005). *Reassembling the Social: An Introduction to Actor-Network-Theory.* Oxford: Oxford University Press.

Lewis, P. (2014). Postfeminism, femininities and organization studies: Exploring a new agenda. *Organization Studies*, 35(12): 1845–1866.

Lewis, P., and Simpson, R. (2017). Hakim revisited: Preference, choice and the post-feminist gender regime. *Gender, Work and Organization*, 24(2): 115–133.

Liedtka, J. (1999). Linking competitive advantage with communities of practice. *Journal of Management Inquiry*, 8(1): 5–16.

Massey, D. (2014). Vocabularies of the economy. In S. Hall, D. Massey, and M. Rustin (Eds.), *After Neoliberalism? The Kilburn Manifesto: Soundings.* Open source, available at: www.lwbooks.co.uk/journals/soundings/manifesto.html.

Matchar, E. (2013). *Homeward Bound: Why Women Are Embracing the New Domesticity.* New York: Simon and Shuster.

McNeil, M. (2010). Post-millennial feminist theory: Encounters with humanism, materialism, critique, nature, biology and Darwin. *Journal for Cultural Research*, 14(4): 427–437.

McRobbie, A. (2015). Notes on the perfect: Competitive femininity in neoliberal times. *Australian Feminist Studies*, 30(83): 3–20.

Moore, N., Church, A., Gabb, J., Holmes, C., Lee, A., and Ravenscroft, N. (2014). Growing intimate privatepublics: Everyday utopia in the naturecultures of a young lesbian and bisexual women's allotment. *Feminist Theory*, 15(3): 327–343.

Morris, M.H., Miyasaki, N.N., Watters, C.E., and Coombes, S.M. (2006). The dilemma of growth: Understanding venture size choices of women entrepreneurs. *Journal of Small Business Management*, 44(2): 221–244.

Parvikko, T. (1990). Conceptions of gender equality: Similarity and difference. In M. Keranen (Ed.), *Finnish "Undemocracy": Essays on Gender and Politics* (pp. 89–111). Jyvaskyla: Finnish Political Science Association, Gummerus Printing.

Petr, J.L. (1982). Economic evolution and economic policy: Is Reaganomics a sustainable force? *Journal of Economic Issues*, 16(4): 1005–1012.

Porter, M.E. (1985). *Competitive Advantage: Creating and Sustaining Superior Performance.* New York: FreePress.

Powell, G.N., and Butterfield, D.A. (2015). The glass ceiling: What have we learned 20 years on? *Journal of Organizational Effectiveness: People and Performance*, 2(4): 306–326.

Prügl, E. (2015). Neoliberalising feminism. *New Political Economy*, 20(4): 614–631.

Pullen, A., Rhodes, C., and Thanem, T. (2017). Affective politics in gendered organizations: Affirmative notes on becoming-woman. *Organization*, 24(1): 105–123.

Rahman, A. (2001). *Women and Microcredit in Rural Bangladesh: Anthropological Study of Grameen Bank Lending.* Boulder: Westview Press.

Rankin, K. (2001). Governing development: Neoliberalism, microcredit, and rational economic woman. *Economy and Society*, 30: 18–37.

Reskin, B.F., and Hartmann, H.I. (Eds.). (1986). *Women's Work, Men's Work: Sex Segregation on the Job.* Washington, DC: National Academies Press.

Roberts, A. (2015). The political economy of "transnational business feminism". *International Feminist Journal of Politics*, 17(2): 209–231.

Rosener, J.B. (1990). Ways women lead. *Harvard Business Review*, 68(November-December): 119–125.

228   *Marta B. Calás et al.*

Rosener, J.B. (1995). *America's Competitive Secret: Utilizing Women as a Management Strategy.* New York: Oxford University Press.

Rottenberg, C. (2014). The rise of neoliberal feminism. *Cultural Studies,* 28(3): 418–437.

Saad-Filho, A., and Johnston, D. (Eds.). (2005). *Neoliberalism-A Critical Reader.* London: Pluto Press.

Sandberg, S. (2013). *Lean in: Women, Work, and the Will to Lead.* New York: Random House.

Sarkar, S. (2016). Durga, supermom, and the posthuman Mother India. In D. Banerji and M.R. Paranjape (Eds.), *Critical Posthumanism and Planetary Futures* (pp. 159–176). India: Springer.

Schein, V.E. (1973). The relationship between sex role stereotypes and requisite management characteristics. *Journal of Applied Psychology,* 57: 95–105.

Schein, V.E. (1975). Relationships between sex role stereotypes and requisite management characteristics among female managers. *Journal of Applied Psychology,* 60(3): 340–344.

Schlosberg, D., and Coles, R. (2016). The new environmentalism of everyday life: Sustainability, material flows and movements *Contemporary Political Theory,* 15(2): 160–181.

Shetty, S. (2010). Microcredit, poverty, and empowerment: Exploring the connections. *Perspectives on Global Development & Technology,* 9(3-4): 356–391.

Shrader, C.B., Blackburn, V.B. and Iles, P. (1997) Women in management and firm financial performance: An Exploratory Study. *Journal of Managerial Issues,* 9(3): 355–372.

Taylor, M.S., and Ilgen, D.R. (1981). Sex discrimination against women in initial placement decisions: A laboratory investigation. *Academy of Management Journal,* 24(4): 859–865.

Terborg, J.R. (1977). Women in management: A research review. *Journal of Applied Psychology,* 62(6): 647–664.

Thorsen, D.E. (2010). The neoliberal challenge: What is neoliberalism? *Contemporary Readings in Law and Social Justice,* 2(2): 188–214.

Tong, R.P. (1998). *Feminist Thought: A More Comprehensive Introduction.* Boulder, CO: Westview.

Tornhill, S. (2016). "A bulletin board of dreams": Corporate empowerment promotion and feminist implications. *International Feminist Journal of Politics,* 18(4): 528–543.

Waddock, S.A. (2016). Taking stock of SIM: Social issues in management division of the Academy of Management. *Business & Society,* 1–22. DOI: 10.1177/0007650316661306

Washick, B.,Wingrove, E., Ferguson, K., and Bennett, J. (2015). Politics that matter: Thinking about power and justice with the new materialists. *Contemporary Political Theory,* 14(1): 63–89.Whatmore, S. (2013) Earthly powers and affective environments: An ontological politics of flood risk. *Theory, Culture & Society,* 30(7/8): 33–50.

Yunus, M. (2011). Sacrificing microcredit for megaprofits. *Op-ed Contributor.* Available at: www.nytimes.com/2011/01/15/opinion/15yunus.html?_r=1, Published 14 January 2011.

Zalasiewicz, J., Williams, M., and Waters, C.N. (2014). Can an Anthropocene series be defined and recognized? *Geological Society, London, Special Publications,* 395: 39–53.

Index

For Product Safety Concerns and Information please contact our EU
representative GPSR@taylorandfrancis.com
Taylor & Francis Verlag GmbH, Kaufingerstraße 24, 80331 München, Germany

www.ingramcontent.com/pod-product-compliance
Ingram Content Group UK Ltd.
Pitfield, Milton Keynes, MK11 3LW, UK
UKHW020939180425
457613UK00019B/468